Christianity and Human Rights

Christianity
and
Human Rights

Influences and Issues

Edited by
Frances S. Adeney
and
Arvind Sharma

STATE UNIVERSITY OF NEW YORK PRESS

Published by
State University of New York Press, Albany

© 2007 State University of New York

For information, address State University of New York Press,
194 Washington Avenue, Suite 305, Albany, NY 12210-2384

Production by Ryan Hacker
Marketing by Fran Keneston

Library of Congress Cataloging in Publication Data

Christianity and human rights : influences and issues / edited by Frances S.
Adeney and Arvind Sharma.
    p. cm.
  Includes bibliographical references and index.
  ISBN-13: 978-0-7914-6951-4 (hardcover : alk. paper)
  ISBN-13: 978-0-7914-6952-1 (pbk. : alk. paper) 1. Human rights—
Religious aspects—Christianity. I. Adeney, Frances S. II. Sharma, Arvind.

BT38.15.C4755 2006
261.7—dc22

2006003061

10 9 8 7 6 5 4 3 2 1

Contents

Preface   vii

1. Introduction: Dialogue with Contributors
   Arvind Sharma   1

PART I.
Christian Influences on Human Rights

2. Human Rights and Responsibilities: Christian Perspectives
   Frances S. Adeney   19

3. The Sources of Human Rights Ideas: A Christian Perspective
   Max L. Stackhouse   41

4. Theology, Tolerance, and Two Declarations of Human Rights:
   An Interrogative Comparison
   Sumner B. Twiss   55

5. Religion and Human Rights: A Personal Testament
   David Little   77

6. Interreligious Dialogue and Human Rights
   Terry C. Muck   99

PART II.
Christian Perspectives on Human Rights Issues

7. The End of Man: Human Rights, Christian Theology, and the
   Rights of Human Persons
   Stephen G. Ray Jr.   117

8. Persons, Politics, and a Catholic Understanding
   of Human Rights
   Jean Bethke Elshtain — 139

9. Human Rights and Asian Values
   Kam Weng Ng — 151

10. Changing One's Religion: A Supported Right?
    Margaret O. Thomas — 167

11. Human Rights and Nonviolence: Testament of a
    Christian Peace Activist
    John Dear — 183

12. Christian Views in Dialogue with the UDHRWR
    Arvind Sharma and Frances S. Adeney — 197

    Appendix 1: UDHRWR: Universal Declaration of Human
    Rights by the World's Religions, McGill University 1999
    (Revised Edition, 2003) — 205

    Appendix 2: Christian Theological Sources for Human Rights
    in Relation to the UDHR and the UDHRWR
    Frances S. Adeney — 213

    Contributors — 217

    Index — 223

Preface

The relationship between Christianity and human rights has been ambiguous.

- Philosophically, some claim that the underlying value of human dignity in human rights discourse is a Christian value; others claim that human dignity has no need for religious underpinnings.
- Historically, some claim that the United Nation's Universal Declaration of Human Rights is a Western and Christian document, irrelevant to cultures in other parts of the world; others claim that this benchmark global document incorporates voices from cultures in every part of the globe.
- Theologically, some claim that the value of human rights appears in some form in every religion; others claim that human rights is not central to most religions, including Christianity.
- Sociologically, some claim that human rights have been supported by Christianity; others claim that Christianity has been a major violator of human rights.

In this book, voices of philosophers, theologians, and activists address some of those ambiguities. The language of human rights and who is included and excluded by that language becomes a topic of discussion in the U.S. context. Asian difficulties with human rights conceptions and applications are examined in their complexity. Both positive and negative views of human rights arising from Christian traditions are looked at and clarified. The relationship of religion to human rights principles and actions is studied from a number of perspectives. Ambiguities are confronted at the interface of Christianity and human rights discourse.

One significant reason for those ambiguities is the diversity of Christian theologies. Distinct Christian traditions have appropriated the moral sources of Christianity in differing ways. Some stress responsibilities over rights. Others emphasize community sustainability over individual self-determination. Contemporary debates within Christian circles suggest that divere views rather than unified views will continue to characterize discussions of Christianity and human rights. This volume presents views of authors from different Christian traditions without attempting to portray a universal or unified "Christian" view of human rights.

It is, rather, in the spirit of conversation with a goal of human understanding that these pieces are presented. In a similar spirit, other religions may dialogue among their diverse communities about implications of their religious faith for human rights. One of the reasons for the development of the Universal Declaration of Human Rights by the World's Religions, which is also a part of this project, is precisely to encourage that type of intermural discussion within religious traditions. Those discussions can unearth similarities and differences in religious views of human rights both within and among religions. Ambiguities will probably remain.

The human rights movement, however, moves within and beyond those ambiguities. The United Nations Universal Declaration on Human Rights was meant to spawn a movement and it has done that. The decades since 1948 have seen the development of international covenants, international human rights advocacy groups, and discussions of moral sources for human rights. Religious discourse becomes increasingly relevant to those developments as commonalities and distinctives among religions support human rights for all.

Authors in this volume show how Christian moral sources support the human rights movement and are supported by it. A Christian perspective on the sources of human rights ideas is outlined. Two major declarations of human rights are compared theologically. The grounding of human rights discourse in the language of the rights of man is challenged by an alternate Christian view of human rights sourced in the well-being of embodied persons. The right to choose one's religion as a human right is discussed in the context of contemporary forces that move nations to declare a specific religion as the only possible choice. A "personal testament" by a religious scholar argues for a direct link between Christian sources and the human rights movement. A Catholic perspective on the rights of women and children bring Christian moral sources to bear on current human rights abuses. A discussion of the importance of Christian nonviolent action in peace making as a necessary corollary to human rights activism is made. An assessment of Christian views of human rights shows that various applications can be made from biblical and traditional sources.

Since the UN Declaration was put forward, numerous declarations of human rights by specific organizations have been published. One of the recent important documents in this development is the Universal Declaration of Human Rights by the World's Religions, a document on human rights that brings together voices of religious scholars from around the world. An essay on the importance of interreligious dialogue in human rights discourse is augmented by interreligious dialogue in the volume itself through discussion of the Universal Declaraion of Human Rights by the World's Religions.

In this way, the book addresses the relationship of Christianity and human rights and also examines the significance of this relationship in the context of the religious perspectives of the Universal Declaration of Human Rights by the World's Religions.

That document is an attempt to formulate a successor to the Universal Declaration of Human Rights, which was adopted by the General Assembly of the United Nations on December 10, 1948. The occasion for drafting Universal Declaration of Human Rights by the World's Religions arose while plans were being finalized for a World Conference, held in Montreal, December 7 through 9, 1998, to celebrate the fiftieth anniversary of the Universal Declaration of Human Rights. The Faculty of Religious Studies at McGill University approached the coalition sponsoring the conference with a proposal to include a draft of a "Universal Declaration of Human Rights by the World's Religions" in the agenda.

Thereafter this draft also served as the basic document for an independent conference, "Human Rights and Responsibilities—The Contribution of World Religions," held at Chapman University in Orange, California, April 8 and 9, 1999. There it was decided that the draft should be circulated as widely as possible in the academic community so that responses to it might be incorporated in a revised text, and it was therefore published in the fall 1999 issue of the *Journal of Religious Ethics*.

The revised text was discussed at a panel in a plenary session of the International Conference on Ethics and Religion for a Global Twenty-first Century, held at Chapman University and Loyola Marymount University from March 25 and 26, 2000. The present text incorporates the suggestions made at that panel discussion.

The text has also been the subject of presentations at the 18th Quinquennial World Congress of the International Association for the History of Religions, when it met in Durban from August 5 through 12, 2000, and of the inaugural address at the Conference on Religion and Human Rights at the House of World Cultures, Berlin, December 7 through 9, 2001.

It was also presented for discussion at the UNESCO Conference on Mystical Traditions and Interreligious Dialogue at Barcelona, May 23 through 26, 2002, as well as at the International Roundtable on "The

Challenge of Globalisation: Towards a Shared Universal Spiritual and Moral Ethic," at Genting Highlands, Malaysia, November 25 through 27, 2002. Most recently the proposed declaration was part of the agenda of the Symposium on Religion and Human Rights, which was held during the Parliament of the World's Religions when it met July 7 through 13, 2004, in Barcelona.

The reasons for authors in this volume to dialogue with this important declaration are twofold. First, this book is one response to the quest for sources for the moral and political obligations undertaken by the movement toward universal human rights. Developed by Christian scholars and activists, the articles engage the more general Universal Declaration of Human Rights by the World's Religions in a conversation about moral sources, thus linking Christian perspectives to views of human rights put forward by scholars of world religions working together.

Second, the bridge built between the Universal Declaration of Human Rights and the Universal Declaration of Human Rights by the World's Religions links the United Nation's articulation of human rights to religiously inspired work on human rights. Each chapter in this volume places its topic in conversation with the Universal Declaration of Human Rights by the World's Religions. One chapter specifically stresses the importance of interreligious dialogue to the movement for human rights in our present context of religious pluralism. The first and last chapters of the book deepen this dialogue as the editors interact with each chapter and the work as a whole.

In today's fractious global climate, links between international, national, and religious perspectives on human rights are needed. This book represents one facet of that bridge-building process as specific Christian views are placed in dialogue with discussions of moral sources for human rights, contemporary issues facing the human rights movement, and the Universal Declaration of Human Rights by the World's Religions.

Each scholar who has contributed to this book worked not only from academic resources but from within specific contexts—geographical, social, economic, political, cultural, and religious. This book is a result of conversations within and among those lived realities.

We have many people to thank for the collaboration that grew from those conversations, resulting in this book. The contributors who gave freely of their scholarly expertise, their time, and their creative energy are the first to be applauded. Thanks also go to Joseph Runzo and Nancy M. Martin for their invitation to participate in the Symposium on Human Rights at the World Parliament of Religion in Barcelona, Spain, in July, 2004, where we announced the then-future publication of this volume.

We also want to thank Louisville Presbyterian Theological Seminary for their support of this project and Cristol Kleitz, Faculty Secretary, for the many hours she spent sending emails, organizing files, and preparing the manuscript. Nancy Ellegate's encouragement to work with State University of New York Press and Ryan Hacker's subsequent job of seeing the book through to publication is also much appreciated. Finally, we want to thank our readers, people of religious conviction and intellectual acumen who will dialogue with the ideas presented here, who will contribute to the Universal Declaration of Human Rights by the World's Religions and who will join forces on the issues presented with others of like mind, and by words and deeds will further the contribution of religions to the universal cause of human rights around the world.

CHAPTER 1

Introduction

Dialogue with Contributors

ARVIND SHARMA

The purpose of this chapter is to assess the contribution the various other chapters make in the context of the global movement for human rights and toward gaining a better understanding of the Universal Declaration of Human Rights by the World's Religions (henceforth UDHRWR). One way of accomplishing this task would be to present the main points of each chapter in the order in which they appear and analyze them in the light of this dual criteria. Once the various contributions have been discussed, the investigation could then be broadened toward the end to highlight the contribution of Christianity as a whole to human rights and to the UDHRWR. Such a procedure will be adopted in the present chapter.

FRANCES S. ADENEY

Frances S. Adeney identifies four Christian theological concepts which resonate positively with human rights: (1) the view that the human person is created in God's image (Gen. 1 & 2); (2) the belief that God established orders of authority and spheres of responsibility (Gen. 1); (3) the acknowledgment that evil in the world was brought about by human action (Gen. 2) and (4) the acceptance of a human family in general and the special community of believers in particular (Deut. 5).

The understanding of the human person, creation, sin and community thus provide the points of intersection between Christian theological

1

discourse and human rights discourse. These four items are of course understood in very different ways as they are filtered through the various sects which comprise Christianity, and as they are refracted through its long history. Nevertheless they do provide a basic frame of reference for viewing their multifarious dimensions. These four elements have been connected, in human rights discourse, with the emergence and articulation of that discourse in many ways, but it is striking how even in their stark statement above they converge with it.

For instance, human rights themselves involve a belief in the worth of the human person; they are sought to be implemented through a human rights regime; the need for human rights arises from human action which violates them and human rights discourse involves two kinds of communities: the human family at large and the special community of the advocates of human rights. One thus finds an interesting example of isomorphism between the four bedrock Christian theological ideas and the basic ideological framework of human rights discourse itself—a correspondence which becomes all the more intriguing if the appearance of human rights is primarily associated with secular movements such as the Enlightenment.

Of particular interest is Frances Adeney's suggestion that Christian sources for human rights can particularly augment the philosophical resources in this regard in the context of dialogue. That suggestion is much more powerful than might be apparent at first sight. From a certain perspective "dialogue" is looked upon as the watering down of "conversion"! That is to say, that it is a default position: ideally we would have liked to see our interlocutors become members of our fold but as that is not possible let us at least keep talking to them. Hence dialogue consists of being socially graceful in the face of failed mission. However, it becomes a morally assuasive position rather than a default position when we look at the way it is linked to human rights activism in this chapter. Here the Christian is not saying "as we can't convert you so let us at least chat"; the Christian is saying: "Here are our resources and now come and share your resources with us so that we can join forces." This has the potential of changing the very complexion of dialogue in interfaith situations.

The UDHRWR clearly involves dialogue in the double dimension of means as well as ends. The means by which it is being framed involves a conversation among the various religions on its numerous articles and its end is to promote continuing dialogue among religions through a creative juxtaposition of the world's religions with human rights. Part of the UDHRWR project also involves each religion producing its own declarations of human rights. One might venture the view that if a religious tradition articulates its moral vision while in a state of interaction with other religions, then it is bound to influence and be influenced by the moral visions of these other religions, and thus achieve in some measure that "authentic transformation" which sensitive practitioners of dialogue have upheld as its goal.

MAX L. STACKHOUSE

Max L. Stackhouse identifies the various challenges to human rights as understood in the West which have periodically surfaced. There is the early Marxist and socialist critique which questions the priority of civil and political rights over social and economic rights; there is the colonial critique of human rights discourse as being an exercise in imperialism by other means; there is the Asian values critique of the Eurocentric human rights, and now there is the manifold Islamic critique of human rights to be dealt with. Max Stackhouse points out with cautious optimism that despite these challenges "human rights ideas have, at the least, become a part of *ius gentium*, the cross-cultural operating consensus as to what constitutes proper behaviour by states and other formal institutions. That consensus also helps to evaluate what counts as compelling moral argument in contemporary ethical discourse," since as "even those who violate human rights plead special conditions, temporary delays, or hermeneutical differences; they seldom deny their validity as an ideal or goal."

The grave challenge to human rights discourse which Max Stackhouse identifies is not so much political or historical as philosophical, the fact that many doubt whether "we can have nonempirical principles to judge empirical life." This skepticism manifests itself in the view "that there is or could be no universalistic moral theology, master narrative, or *jus naturale* to support the idea." He is of course quick to note that such a claim in itself is one "that ironically presses towards a universal relativism." The more sophisticated exponents of this view would of course recognize the possibility of the relative nature of relativism itself and offer their position as a cultural preference. But for Stackhouse it lacks the starch to hold the collar in this age of globalization, the strength to support a global civil society, as no enduring society has historically existed without a religious core. The cultural relativists oppose human rights on grounds of its abstract universalism but in doing so they attack a straw figure, because human rights "require a synthetic judgement," one which combines a finding in law or in principle with a finding in fact, in the tradition of case studies.

Stackhouse makes a strong case for safeguarding the individualistic orientation of human rights, based on the theological principle of *imago dei*, on three grounds. The first is rooted in the argument of the previous paragraph, that "theologically based moral judgements themselves are pluralistic in their internal structure." Hence they should not be dismissed as excessively abstract. The second requires the individual person to be extracted from the social matrix so that "moral inviolability of each person" is preserved over "communitarian regard," which finds concrete expression in the idea that a human being, qua human being, must never be subjected to certain forms of degrading treatment irrespective of any circumstance. The third ground presents such an individualistic abstraction positively, that an individual must be allowed to act in defiance of the community, as when one wants to change one's religion.

Max Stackhouse's analysis is helpful in pointing to the complexity involved in the concepts of universality and individual autonomy any UDHRWR must take into account in order to be authentic.

SUMNER B. TWISS

Sumner B. Twiss's piece addresses the theme underlying the book most explicitly and concretely and therefore merits detailed comment. It is extremely helpful in providing historical depth to the discussion, just as other papers provided theological or moral depth to it. The importance of including the historical dimension is made clear by the light it sheds on an allied issue, namely, whether human rights are "Western." The charge is a common one and I think has substance but not in the way the charge is laid—implying either that non-Westerners were not present in influential numbers in the various committees or that non-Western points of view were only insufficiently debated or were not presented at all. It is clear from examining the record that such was simply not the case.

On the basis of such a historical investigation, Twiss concludes that the UDHRWR does not represent a measurable advance over the UDHR because the points it raises or incorporates were already raised and discussed and passed over in the debates around the formulation of the UDHR by the Third Committee. He draws pointed attention to three issues here: (1) that the UDHR discussed but discarded any reference to the divine in the preamble in the interest of religious tolerance, so that its incorporation in UDHRWR does not represent any improvement over the situation; (2) that concern with proselytizing excesses which might accompany the freedom to change one's religion were already aired in the debate on Article 18 so that the sensitivity displayed to the issue in UDHRWR hardly adds a new dimension; (3) that the mutual implication of rights and duties, which is emphasized in the UDHRWR is rather cumbersome, when such a relationship is already recognized more elegantly and perhaps equally comprehensively in Article 27 of UDHR.

These are solid points and I hope the responses will share that quality. The first point has to do with the preamble. It is true that religious or theological grounds are implicit in the "overlapping consensus" which is reflected in the preamble of the UDHR. But it is also true that thereby they are obscured. One has to add to this the consideration that the UDHR is viewed as a secular document in the sense that one important critique of religious fundamentalism is its proclivity to abridge these rights, so that UDHR takes on the semblance of a source that provides a secular critique of religious practices. This potentially negative positioning of religion vis-à-vis human rights may be prevented by explicitly associating religion as a source of human rights. Moreover, the preamble of the UDHRWR does not discard the purely humanistic orientation, it speaks of inspiration "both human and divine." In doing so it does not compromise the principle of tolerance embodied in Article 18 of the UDHR, a concern with which had originally led to the exclusion of such language from the preamble, perhaps because the formulations offered were couched too much in the idiom of a religion or ideology. A case could be made for altering the wording to "inspiration human or divine," but then the overlapping consensus referred to earlier may be as true of an individual person in the modern world as of a group of persons.

The second point relates to the question of proselytization and I think it is important here to recognize an ambiguity in the expression the right to "change" one's religion: the change can be (1) purely voluntary, (2) or brought about by someone else by force (3) or may be the outcome of someone else's influence exercised through teaching or persuasion. It seems likely that the framers intended only the first meaning and would accept the third sense as valid conversion brought about through manifesting one's religion in public and private. The second meaning involves coercion and so would have been rejected by the framers. It seems to me that the text is not always read as it was intended—if my reading of the intention is correct. The absence of a clear distinction among voluntary change, involuntary change and induced change and a further lack of clarity on how change might be induced, has led people to claim that the right to change one's religion includes the right to proselytize. The argument that "if it is an evil, it was essentially an evil from which all sides had to suffer" is not very helpful, because the "evil" can perhaps be remedied by rewording the right as attempted in the UDHRWR. As Tad Stahnke notes: "With the exception of the American Convention, which explicitly states in Article 12(1) that the right to freedom of religion includes the freedom 'to disseminate one's religion or beliefs' neither proselytism nor the freedom to disseminate a religion is mentioned in international instruments. The lack of any direct recognition of proselytism may be an indication of the sensitivity of states to the issues it raises and the difficulty of delineating agreeable standards."[1] The bullet cannot be dodged any more. The UDHRWR tries to face it, which is not to say that it has offered the best response. But it has tried to respond.

The question of how exactly the correlativity of rights and duties should be recognized is a contentious issue and brings us to the third point. That the UDHR was deadlined rather than deadlocked into presenting the relationship as it does is useful knowledge but the result may have been unfortunate. In the book to which Professor Twiss's own contribution is gratefully acknowledged (p. xii), Mary Ann Glendon notes about another set of articles: "With hindsight it is perhaps regrettable that the framers, in dealing with these provisions [Articles 23–26] did not adopt the obligation model. To couch the social security and welfarian principles in terms of a common responsibility might have resonated better than rights in most of the world's cultures and would still have left room for experiments with different mixes of private and public approaches."[2] Might a similar reflection not be in order with the benefit of hindsight in relation to Article 29 which, some have suggested, creates the impression of a bogey having been attached to the train as it was about to leave the platform. At least an earlier placement of it would have avoided the impression of UDHR being too light on duties. How important this point is in relation to the non-Western world was revealed to me during the course of a discussion with Professor S. H. Nasr on the proposed UDHRWR. His first question to me was whether it had taken due recognition of duties and in fact he wondered whether the proposed declaration should itself not be called A Universal Declaration of Human Rights and Duties by the World's Religions to take care of the "lacuna" (his word) in the UDHR.

DAVID LITTLE

David Little's powerful personal testament illustrates how commitment to a very specific tradition can generate a commitment of surprisingly universal reach. This focus on the personal also gives a new spin to the slogan "the personal is the political," by underscoring the role personal commitment plays in such discourse. Martin Luther King once famously asserted that what we are suffering from is not a deficit in human resources but a deficit in human will. David Little's piece forces us to focus on this will in relation to human rights.

He speaks of the four ways his own will has been strengthened by his reading of Calvin: (1) "According to Calvin, the theological conviction that moral knowledge is part of the structure of the universe undergirds and reaffirms the bindingness of primary moral reactions," (2) "religious conviction overcomes other sorts of doubt that can enfeeble moral commitment," (3) "religious knowledge for Calvin supplements moral insight in that it helps to illuminate the task of applying general principles to specific circumstances," and (4) "religious conviction provides motivation for living up to the demands of morality in the face of weakness of will." Most, if not all, of these principles would apply to the moral life led by people anchored in a particular faith. Therefore Little's personal testament becomes a testament which could be shared by many who champion human rights while remaining rooted in faith.

Little's testimony also sheds light on the nature of the UDHRWR as a document. Little is at pains to point out in his conclusion that while "the liberal Calvinist tradition provides a particularly strong historical and theological foundation for a belief in human rights. . . . It can by its very nature be nothing more than a recommendation" as human rights are "matters of 'conscience, religion or belief' and as such are subject to the conditions of 'the sovereignty of conscience' and the 'laws of spirit.'"

The UDHRWR as it stands is solely recommendatory in nature.

TERRY C. MUCK

Terry C. Muck focuses on the role of human rights. After noting that *sensu stricto* religions do not have to believe that human rights are religiously grounded in order to advocate them to ensure human flourishing, they might indeed take them to be so grounded. Taking the cue from Terry Muck's distinction between conversation and dialogue that—the former may not involve disagreements but the latter always does—one way of sharing his insights might be to indicate the disagreements within human rights discourse that call for dialogue and how religions may play a useful role in dealing with them.

Two such disagreements have been well documented by now: (1) between the Universality Principle, that the ideals represented by human rights are universally applicable and the Cultural Specificity Principle which "de-emphasizes the practice of applying universal principles of behaviour and understanding to all cultures everywhere" and indeed "insists that each culture be allowed to speak for itself and express its own ideals unencumbered by principles applied by outside observers"; and (2) between the two understandings of "human" as referring "to both individuals and to communities of human beings" or what might be called the Individual and Communal dimensions of being human. As a result of the way discourse on human rights has evolved over the past sixty years the "modern understanding of human rights . . . includes a careful balancing of the two spectrums of understanding, one a spectrum ranging from principles to specific cultural mores, the other ranging from an individual understanding of human rights to a communal understanding."

At one level, interreligious dialogue has developed a process of dialogue which may apply to all forms of dialogue, interreligious or otherwise. The three main principles identified here are those of Intentionality, Disagreement, and Respect. The point to note is that dialogue does not set out to end disagreements, it can even end in disagreements but the real question is whether it can provide the ground for agreement "wide enough on which to build common understandings and intercultural behaviors." This insight applies not only to dialogue in general but also to interreligious dialogue. The question may be asked, however, that if dialogue, in *any* of its forms, itself might adjudicate between the two spectrums mentioned earlier, why interreligious dialogue?

The answer Terry Muck provides is: "In order to have universal human rights, one must appeal to universal justification, and the only kind of universal justification that will work is the way the religions understand the transcendent" (as distinguished from the false secular universals of totalitarianism, fascism, and communism). By remaining rooted in an understanding of transcendence which is "truly transcendent," the religions can contribute to the human rights project by talking about universals in a way that "avoids the dangers of either totalitarianism or cultural relativism" and thus provide a forum that might make it possible to "arrive at both religious and cultural expressions of human rights at various places and at various times that will be acceptable to all the religions represented in that area."

This idea of interreligious dialogue operating within a well-defined area to establish human rights norms in order to implement them is a useful direction in which the UDHRWR project could move. It seems to represent a valuable application of the maxim of thinking globally but acting locally to human rights discourse.

STEPHEN G. RAY JR.

Stephen G. Ray Jr. begins by examining the conceptual basis of human rights and defends his approach by asserting that "ideas are the imaginative currency which give meaning to our world and our interactions in it," "lest it seem that I make too much of the power of an idea." The point is important because "the way ideas are rendered can have the power to motivate good people to challenge systems that work to destroy human persons or, conversely, the power to mystify persons into becoming silent bystanders."

Stephen Ray then takes note of the fact that "human rights" are the first casualty in any political or economic crisis. He attributes this to the "depravity of human beings," which involves "the inescapable entanglement of most human beings in some form of self-interest." This prevents a person from attaining the "situational self-transcendence" in the absence of which a person cannot relate to others truly in *agape*. According to him the "idea of depravity also serves to highlight the dual character of the problem," which is "by nature both universal and contextual. What is at stake in the concern for human rights is something universal—the guarantee of well-being to human persons simply because they are human persons. At the same time the guarantee must be achieved and mediated contextually (i.e., specific locations, eras, and cultures)."

Stephen Ray's specific context is the United States around the time of the Declaration of Independence and thereafter. His analysis proceeds by way of analyzing the lapidary utterance: "We hold these truths to be self-evident that all men are created equal and are endowed by their creator with certain inalienable rights, among them life, liberty and the pursuit of happiness." That statement is then treated as a "theopolitical" statement. Only in this light can one understand his claim that although the words of the declaration cited above had originally applied to "men of Anglo-Saxon" descent and have since been extended in a major way, Stephen Ray does not share the optimism that they are now serviceable in the context of human rights. Such optimism, he argues, "does not take seriously enough the matrices of meaning that attach to these words and, consequently, presumes a facility for the task that does not exist."

The crux of his argument is that the statement is riddled by an internal contradiction: "On the one hand, you have the assertion that the claims of the preamble are rooted in some quality which inheres to all men, while on the other you have the assertion that the claims of the preamble are explicitly not applicable to all people," for as Chief Justice Taney stated in the Dred Scott decision in 1847: "The framers of the Constitution believed that blacks had no rights which the white man was bound to respect."

Most scholars view the history of the United States as constituting a historical resolution of this contradiction, as more and more marginalized groups gain the status of full membership of the community. Stephen Ray's position is remarkable for taking a philosophical route as a result of which he is able to claim that while the expansion of rights in contemporary American society is undeniable, "these gains are ever and always tentative." His reason for arriving at this conclusion has to do with how the word "man" is understood in American culture.

American culture inherits its understanding of the term "man" from European culture, which espouses "a radical disjuncture between mind and body," and in which "the human person is primarily a creature of the intellect and only secondarily inhabits a physical body." This meant that women were not men because of their identification with the body and of the body with the womb. This also meant Meso-Americans and Africans were not men because they merely possessed human bodies and the same point was made with regard to men of Asian descent. Thus the differentiation of humanity by sex and race rendered them less than human, as the only sense in which they could be considered human was solely through possessing merely a human body, which was not enough.

Stephen Ray sees in Martin Luther King's concern with "material conditions of the body" the seeds of a new perspective, which is particularly promising in terms of redefining dignity in terms of the body. It is worth noting that Rosa Parks made history by refusing to remove her body from a seat.

This perspective allows a fresh Christian interpretation even in the context of the creation story as found in Genesis 1 and 2, wherein "three significant aspects . . . characterize the creation of human persons—the creation of the body, the imbuement of that body with the spirit of God, and a founding relationship between that soul and God." All three dimensions had to be cultivated for a complete life.

Stephen Ray's analysis is suggestive and may help explain how Hindu metaphysics, which sees both the Personal and Impersonal God as omnipresent, could reconcile itself to the practice of untouchability by perhaps cleaving to an excessively spiritual concept of "man." His analysis also strengthens the case for some of the provisions in the UDHRWR such as the right to food.

JEAN BETHKE ELSHTAIN

Jean Bethke Elshtain offers a stream of sustained reflection on the present state of human rights discourse from a Catholic perspective, which can be brought in relation first to the human rights discourse as anchored in the Universal Declaration of Human Rights and then to the UDHRWR. The framers of the Universal Declaration of Human Rights (1948) could probably not have foreseen the extension and differentiation human rights discourse has since undergone. In this respect Elshtain's warning—that the proliferation of human rights discourse might weaken it—is salutary.

Such a proliferation seems to have occurred on the basis of different groups of claimants pushing "claims they choose to couch in the language of particular rights that apply specifically, even exclusively, to that group of claimants" and thereby attenuate the concept of human rights, which all human beings possess without exception. Moreover, such "sectional" articulations of human rights tend to pit people against one another. They are often rooted in the secular conception of a human being, as one seeking power and freedom for oneself—"any rights culture derived from such premises becomes a way we confront and are protected from one other." Those conceptions lead to a plurality of organizations that view each other with antagonism.

If, however, one takes one's stand on a conception of human rights that celebrates human dignity and accepts the relationality of human beings, then the two parties, even in confronting each other, become agents of upholding human rights as in the case of the Mothers of the Plaza protesting the "disappeared." The plurality of such organizations becomes a limiting factor on the leviathenesque tendencies of the state on the one hand and helps human rights discourse steer clear of excessive individualism on the other. "Within this vision, commonality is at some level assumed and solidarity is an achievement."

This process of rearticulating human rights as based in human nature itself may also help to relieve, if not solve, the "late modern dilemma: we cannot do without rights, but the ways in which rights are generalized and universalized may not be capable of sustaining those rights at the most fundamental level because too much of the deep background and justification of rights has been jettisoned along the way."

The UDHRWR, it is worth noting, sets out to correct shortcomings of the prevailing human rights discourse noted by Elshtain: the disjunction between rights and duties within it and an inadequate recognition of a comprehensive human rights culture required to sustain human rights. Virtually every article in the UDHRWR correlates rights and duties, and the very idea of bringing religions together on the platform of human rights is meant to broaden and deepen their cultural roots.

KAM WENG NG

Kam Weng Ng addresses the emotive issue of human rights and Asian values with persuasive intellectual insights. It is true that the issue has receded somewhat into the background, with the West no longer in a position to project itself as the knight-in-shining-armor champion of human rights, given the kind of legislation it has had to introduce after September 11, 2001. At the same time, the governments of Southeast Asia are no longer in a position to trumpet Asian values the way it was possible to do before the financial crisis of 1997. Nevertheless the issue remains theoretically significant.

Kam Weng Ng identifies four main components of the Asian values argument: "1) that human rights are culture specific; 2) that community takes precedence over individuals; 3) that social-economic rights have priority over civil political rights; and 4) that the implementation of human rights should be respected as a matter of national sovereignty."

None of these arguments bear scrutiny, according to Kam Weng Ng. Human rights need not be considered culture specific because they are universalizable. Thus the "fact that the current concept of human rights originated in the West does not mean that it cannot and should not be applied to Asia. After all, Asians have no reservations applying Newtonian principles and quantum physics in their societies even though these physics originated from the West." As to the second argument, that the community take precedence over the individual, it is worth noting that "the debate/tension between communitarian and individualistic liberalism is not one divided geographically between Asia and the West." Even Western philosophers—Charles Taylor, Alasdair McIntyre, Michael Walzer, and Michael Sandel among them—have also argued for a communitarian social philosophy. Moreover Asian societies also contain elements that "affirmed tolerance and vigorous support for human freedom," which could and "should be retrieved in the development of a comprehensive framework for human rights in contemporary Asia." The third argument—that social-economic rights have priority over civil political rights—is challenged by the work of Amartya Sen who finds "no empirical verification for the idea that limiting civil and political rights supports economic growth." The view that "human rights form a seamless whole whether economic or civil-political," thus stands vindicated. The fourth argument—that implementation of human rights should be respected as a matter of national sovereignty—overlooks the fact that the concept of human rights itself arose out of a realization of the "need to limit the awesome power which a centralized state can wield."

Kam Wang Ng also makes the two additional points—that societies that appear closed may not be as impervious to new influences as it seems, and that the church can act as a witness for human rights. The first point is illustrated with the example of Malay/Muslim society, which may have appeared unchangeable but while the Sultan had "the trappings of absoluteness" the fact that he did not possess a state bureaucracy and had to rely on his feudal chiefs showed the cracks in the system. The emergence of an educated elite under colonialism further undermined such absoluteness. The second point can be exemplified with the help of the role the church has played in Korea, where the church "gained credibility when Christians were in the forefront in the fight for nationalism and fundamental rights of the Korean people."

The analysis may be supplemented by two points. The first is that while physics deals with objects, human rights deal with subjects. Objects do not possess an interior life but human beings or subjects do. This fact does not negate the universality of human rights but does complicate it. The second is that as colonialism was a way of coming between a people and their own government and supplanting it, human rights discourse, when it seems to be doing the same, revives fears of imperialism. These emotional realities need to be recognized even as the limitations of the Asian values arguments are exposed. The UDHRWR project, by encouraging the active participation of the cultures in framing of the declarations themselves, aims at overcoming these problems.

MARGARET O. THOMAS

Margaret O. Thomas focuses on the right to change one's religion and reports on the consultations on this point between the Christians and the Muslims at the initiative of the World Council of Churches (WCC). Although the number of people who change their religion is statistically small, it involves an important human rights issue. Moreover, while changing one's religion has limited social consequences in some societies, like the United States, it can have major consequences in other societies.

The importance of a consultation between Christians and Muslims on such a sensitive topic should not be underestimated. It requires considerable mutual trust to openly discuss the misuse of religion for political or other ends. Two key principles were articulated by the WCC to "open the space for constructive struggling with living human rights issues, including religious freedom. First, conflict should be de-globalized in order to avoid its spread and to allow a contextualized resolution. Second, in each community authentic witness should respect the integrity of others and abstain from competitive proselytizing methods." Sometimes the "diplomacy of reciprocity" was proposed in these dialogues, representing "a search for a kind of global symmetry between the Christian and Muslim communities whereby a privilege is demanded of a majority community in a specific place as a condition for giving what should be understood as a right in another place where the community's members are in a minority (e.g., a church building somewhere in the Middle East as a requirement for erecting a mosque in a European location)." This represents the antithesis of deglobalizing and also compromises the universality of the principle. Similarly, regarding the second point, "thoughtful Christians and Muslims are aware that neither can ask the other to abandon the witness of mission/evangelization/evangelism and da'wah in the name of avoiding mutual stress, since witness and invitation are integral to the faith of both. But WCC-convened dialoguers have also acknowledged the need for a mutually agreed, "tough ethic of witness."

Some specific and general points that emerge from this dialogue are not without interest. It was observed for instance that "entry into the Christian community, while welcomed, is usually a more complex process than in Islam. . . . Leaving the community, while undesirable, is more possible in theory than in practice." It was also observed that some of the difficulties arose from "the identification of Christianity with colonial, neo-colonial, and globalizing powers that are viewed by others as oppressors rather than promoters of the common good." Two issues of more general interest also came up: (1) the difference the use of the language of individual choice rather than that of individual change can make in the context of religious conversion in terms of human rights discourse and (2) that it is possible, "in practice, to adhere to a particular human right and also maintain other rights that have been articulated."

JOHN DEAR

John Dear focuses on two of the chief values that human rights discourse embodies—those of non-violence and peace. It is sometimes important to identify a value that is embodied in a discourse, for there is a tendency for the substance to get lost in style, or for the fruit to be obscured in the foliage of the tree. Furthermore, because the Universal Declaration of Human Rights was adopted by nation-states, it is sometimes tempting to look upon it as a political document with a moral inflection rather than as a moral document in a political idiom. By focusing on the values it enshrines, John Dear helps to maintain the goalposts where they are as against the temptation of shifting them.

The Universal Declaration of Human Rights does not say anything about disarmament although it does talk about peace. It is against genocide but does not speak of nuclear weapons. A declaration, of course, cannot contain everything, but Dear's point cuts deeper. One may not mention these items but one cannot fail to mention the attitudes, if not always the means, which will take one to the goal. And that attitude has to be one of nonviolence.

Gandhi developed his views outside of human rights discourse but that does not mean that they are not relevant to it. For Gandhi the very fact that the human race continues to exist is proof that, on the whole, so far, nonviolence has remained a step ahead of violence. John Dear warns us that the scale of destruction involved in modern warfare has shortened the distance by which nonviolence has managed to stay ahead of violence, a danger of which Martin Luther King was even more acutely aware, living as he did after Gandhi in a world frozen in place in a cold war through the doctrine of

MAD (mutual assured destruction). His rhetoric reflects this reality when he says: "The choice is no longer between violence or nonviolence. It's nonviolence or nonexistence."

War, it seems, violates human rights in a sense so fundamental that it cannot be captured in a declaration. It is striking that human rights discourse, so vigorous when the violence of a state is directed against its own citizens, becomes so platitudinous in the face of the violence of one state directed against another. There is an important lesson here for human rights discourse to learn. John Dear alertly notes how the UDHRWR does recognize the importance of nonviolence. His chapter encourages us to ask whether peace and disarmament should figure more prominently in it.

NOTES

1. Tad Stahnke, "Proselytism and the Freedom to Change Religion in International Human Rights Law," *Brigham Young University Law Review* (1999): 275–76.

2. Mary Ann Glendon, *A World Made New: Eleanor Roosevelt and the Universal Declaration of Human Rights* (New York: Random House, 2001), p. 189.

PART I

Christian Influences on Human Rights

CHAPTER 2

Human Rights and Responsibilities

Christian Perspectives

FRANCES S. ADENEY

Christian traditions have influenced and continue to influence the discourse and practice of human rights in both secular and religious contexts. While most contemporary Christians recognize the veracity and importance of human rights, different traditions understand human rights and the necessity of balancing human rights with human responsibilities in various ways. Understanding those diverse viewpoints and their moral sources can further an assessment of Christian influences on human rights discourse and practice. Comparison of Christian theologies of human rights with views of human rights held by other religions highlights similarities and differences and fosters dialogue about human rights from religious perspectives.

THEOLOGICAL CONCEPTS FOR HUMAN RIGHTS

Christian perspectives on human rights revolve around four theological concepts that are reflected in Christian traditions.

Image of God

A belief in the dignity and worth of persons as a source for the idea of human rights springs from a Judeo-Christian understanding that persons are created in God's image. The creation narratives in the Bible tell of an all-powerful yet good God who creates humans in God's own image (Genesis 1 and 2). Consequently, God's image defines humanity. That image is reflected in human intellect and abilities, language and sociality, morality, and a yearning to be in communication with God (Ps. 139). This theology asserts that because God created humans in God's image, human dignity and worth are axiomatic, nonnegotiable, and bestowed on all people (John 1, Heb. 1). Because persons are created in God's image, Christians through the ages have assigned a transcendent worth to human beings. Augustine (354–430) taught that God's image in humanity is reflected in the power of reason and understanding that sets humans over all irrational creatures.[1] Martin Luther insisted that forgiveness of sins and righteousness are imputed to all who have faith in Christ.[2] For many contemporary Christians, the value given by God to humans implies that no person is reducible to a societal role, no person is exactly like any other, and each individual is of incalculable worth by virtue of being human.

From this view twin tenants of human rights can be drawn: the freedom to choose and the freedom from harm. An emphasis on justice for individuals, equality, care for the poor, protection of life, and freedom of religion are human rights emphases that spring from this view. Image of God arguments can emphasize the inviolability of humans and the centrality of the individual. Civil and political rights can be derived from this theological point of view, especially religious liberty. Alternatively, image of God arguments can stress the relational nature of persons as created in the Trinitarian image of God. With this emphasis, communal rights and the well-being of the entire human family come to the fore.

For example, the Roman Catholic Church, in using this moral source, stresses the right to "everything necessary for leading a life truly human, such as food, clothing and shelter; the rights to choose a state of life freely and to found a family, the right to education, to employment, to a good reputation, to appropriate information, to activity in accord with the upright norm of one's own conscience, to protection of privacy and to rightful freedom in matters religious too."[3]

As early as 1891, Pope Leo XIII in the encyclical *Rerum Novarum* stressed the necessity of caring first for the poor and needy and preserving the economic rights of the labor class.[4] Religious liberty has been another strong theme in Catholic teaching, particularly during the early twentieth century when Catholics were immigrating to the United States in great numbers. In 1965 Vatican II put out *Dignitatis Humanae*, which stressed the right to search for truth in religious matters and worship according to one's conscience.[5]

Christian feminists provide another example of a human rights stance that grows out of a Christian theology of the image of God. Gender equality, both of status and opportunity, is a central tenet of Christian feminism.

Catholic theologians Rosemary Radford Reuther and Elizabeth Schüssler Fiorenza, and Protestant Beverly Harrison are representative of feminists that stress gender equality and the necessity of working toward equal rights for women.[6]

The image of God as a theological construct also informs Protestant Christian feminists in Indonesia who work for the rights of women to choice and leadership in the church. Using the story of creation in Genesis 1, in which God creates man and woman and sets them in the garden as stewards of the earth, Indonesian women support, yet go beyond, a gender partnership model of church leadership. While Indonesian women have worked toward gender equality in the church with a partnership model, some leaders question customs that appear to affirm women in partnership with men but do not result in women leaders. These women use a religion-identified resistance to move beyond partnership models to gender equality.[7] The rights of Christian women to pursue leadership in the church is balanced, in this view, by their responsibility to be good stewards of their own talents and of church resources.[8]

Order of Creation

A related theological position used to support human rights is the idea that the Sovereign God created and ordered domains and spheres of influence in the world. God is God of all, and creation, as God's work, is good (Gen. 1). God's sovereignty and will governs the world. Yet God established orders of authority and care and delegates authority and spheres of responsibility to human institutions and individuals (Gen. 1).

The task of humans is to love and glorify God.[9] In this view, God's will is obeyed when authority is properly delegated and utilized. Caring for those under one's charge is a way of glorifying God. Seeking one's own rights is not a priority in this view. Rather, properly fulfilling one's duty, which includes protecting the rights of others, is stressed. Since God created all, God is source of the rights of all. Human institutions, including governments, should properly order and fulfill their authority by respecting human rights, which are based on the higher authority of God. Government's protective role is given by God and is therefore subject to God's sovereign rule.[10]

Understanding human institutions as ordained by God leads to a stress on fairness and a separation of spheres of authority and rights belonging to each (Rom. 12). Political and social institutions thereby become God's agents in the world, ideally agents for justice. Order of creation arguments can emphasize the importance of humans as the crown of creation, leading to an individual rights emphasis or they can stress the interrelatedness of all creation and thus emphasize care for the environment and orders of creation in their own right. This theology does not separate public life from the private sphere or from religious convictions. A balance of duties is sometimes stressed so that each person and institution can glorify God by operating unhindered in their sphere of authority, thus fulfilling God's will.[11]

The Protestant Reformed tradition follows John Calvin in developing and applying this theology to the governance of the world and to the care of the earth. The Presbyterian Church (U.S.A.) builds these concerns into their denominational structure and activities.[12] The proportional rights of others, including future generations, and the care and protection of nature are important considerations that grow out of the order of creation understanding. Social and economic rights and ecological justice for animals and creation can each find a place in the order of creation theology as rights are ordered in their proper domains.

Catholic social teachings use an order of creation theology at many points. While government has a role in establishing and keeping order, for example, freedom of conscience should govern the individual in their worship and ethical behavior.[13] Therefore, governments should allow freedom of religion where more than one religion exists.[14] In other words, the state must respect the order of creation, allowing the individual to properly order their own domain when it comes to worshiping God.

An example of order of creation theology resulting in a conviction regarding human rights is illustrated by the Puritan free church movement for religious liberty in England in 1645.[15] This early movement for human rights influenced the enlightenment in Europe as individual freedoms became more central to societal mores.[16]

The German Protestant theology of Jüergen Moltmann stresses that not only did God create the world in an ordered fashion, the future kingdom of God will include a redressing of the problems that abound in the creation as we know it. Therefore justice and peace must be present and active in the lives of Christians. The church lives in the expectation of the coming of God's kingdom—a kingdom that embraces peace, righteousness, and the freedom and dignity of humans. For Moltmann, this eschatological vision becomes both a source of hope and an obligation to work for the transformation of society in the present.[17] The essence of the church itself is its engagement in the work of justice.[18]

Human Frailty and Sin

The other side of Christian attention to human rights on the basis of God's image and the good ordering of creation arises from a theology that recognizes human sin. A belief in the inability of individuals and communities to act rightly makes Christian traditions attentive to both individual wrongs and structural evil in the area of human rights. According to this theology, although God created the world and pronounced the creation good, human action brought evil into that good world (Gen. 2). Because of this fallenness, humans cannot do the good that they aspire to (Rom. 7 and 15). Instead, even with the best intentions, humans do wrong and mistake evil for good (Rom. 3).

That confusion results in a frail humanity that lacks both the wisdom to reasonably order the world and the will to do good.[19] Humans' inability to care for themselves and creation according to God's will leads to an emphasis in some traditions on dependence on God to enable people to do right.[20] Other traditions stress human responsibility, developing a constant vigilance that stresses duties over rights.[21] A third theology that develops from the concept of a fallen humanity is a belief in structural evil and a distrust of human institutions.[22]

Various responses arise from these understandings of sin in Christian traditions. Movements of resistance and liberation can result from evaluating human rights from the point of view of the presence of sin in the world. The anti-slavery movements of England and the U.S. worked against slavery on the basis of the sinfulness of the subjugation of other human beings. John Wilberforce and John Newton in England and Quakers Lucretia Mott and Angelina and Sarah Grimke in the U.S. were Christians who opposed the African slave trade.[23] Slaves' leader Harriet Tubman and free African-American Frederick Douglass are examples of African-American Christians who worked against slavery and for the extension of human rights and citizenship to African-Americans.[24]

New movements of liberation developed in the twentieth century. Christian women involved in the antislavery movement turned their attention to women's rights, achieving full citizenship rights for women in the United States in 1920.[25] In mid-century, many American Catholic theologians and religious orders joined forces with Protestants to work for self-determination for the colonized peoples of El Salvador, Nicaragua, and other Latin American countries.[26] In 1963, African-American churches in Birmingham, Alabama, gathered and Martin Luther King Jr. gave voice to their dream of equality igniting the civil rights movement.[27]

Critiquing society's activities and governmental policies on human rights and responsibilities and calling the public to accountability is another response to human frailty and sin.[28] Christians have formed coalitions with other religious groups and nongovernment associations to accomplish this. Martin Luther King Jr. called the nation to accountability and argued that the Constitution itself is both a reflection of Christian values and the basis for civil rights. Antinuclear protesters Daniel Berrigan and the Plowshares group in Washington D.C. protested U.S. nuclear proliferation by damaging nuclear warheads. Other antinuclear groups such as Witness for Peace and the Fellowship of Reconciliation stress the importance of nonviolence in resisting the structural evils of war and nuclear proliferation.[29]

In its long tradition of social teachings, the Catholic church makes qualifications on human rights due to the danger of self-interest that, according to this tradition, destroys justice. Obedience to truth and respect for rights of others become important considerations that limit human rights for individuals and institutions. For instance, a preferential option for the poor limits the right of the rich to amass as much wealth as they like.[30] Even the church itself must bow to the rights of others to choose their leaders in liberal democratic societies.[31]

Another response to human rights that develops from a theology of sin is vigilance in protecting human rights. When the United States was founded, Christians who had fled persecution in Europe demanded that freedom of religion be an operative principle in the new federation of states.[32] Because of their theology of sin, these Christians did not trust human institutions to insure citizens' tranquility and freedom to practice their religion.

This emphasis on the necessity of examining institutional policies and protecting individuals and churches from government intrusion fosters the human rights of minority groups today. Limits on government intervention in health care and education are two examples. Jehovah's Witnesses can refuse blood transfusions. Christians can choose home schooling for their children. Christian groups have insisted on limiting government's intrusion on an individual's right to practice their religion.

Conciliar Protestantism takes up this theme from a stance of inclusion rather than separation from society. Having lived through the horrors of World War II, German theologian Jüergen Moltmann understands dialogue about human rights as a requirement in a sinful world. The World Council of Churches sees human rights as part of the struggle against disorder and evil. During this "Decade against Violence" declared by the World Council, criticisms of state-perpetuated violence and injunctions to the church to struggle against such violence are emphasized by the World Council.[33]

A growing emphasis on the concrete historical situation and the role of churches in working for the protection of human rights around the world is evident in the work of the World Council of Churches, the Presbyterian Church (U.S.A.), and other Christian groups. Working against human rights violations takes different forms as cultures and situations demand a human rights response that fits, as much as possible, with cultural norms and values.

Freedom of religion as a basic liberty is also contextually determined according to John Courtney Murray's Catholic analysis, which became part of Vatican II teachings. Here the Roman Catholic church readjusts its classic teaching on the primacy of the church in world affairs to an emphasis on "articles of peace" and freedom of conscience that insure religious liberty in pluralistic contexts such as the United States.[34]

Another way to present human rights from a theology of human sinfulness is to highlight its counterpart—human responsibilities. The Reformed tradition generally follows Calvin in stressing human responsibility over human rights. Nineteenth-century Reformed theologian Abraham Kuyper understood sin to be a greater threat to human freedom than state power.[35] If persons are responsible, rights are protected. But without discipline, an emphasis on rights can lead to excess and sinful behavior. In this view it is better to emphasize duties to balance those possible excesses.

Despite this emphasis, the Presbyterian Church (U.S.A.) and other reformed groups (e.g., World Reformed Alliance), have been strong supporters of the Universal Declaration of Human Rights and actively work against human rights abuses around the world.[36] The Orthodox churches also make qualifications to human rights because of the dangers presented by self-interest that can destroy justice. Surrender to God and obedience to the church, while not relying on human attempts to do right or protect one's rights, can mitigate against human abuses due to sin. In this view, church tradition and authority plays a role in readjusting people's understanding and action regarding human rights and responsibilities.[37]

Dependence on God and the authority of the church is a response that can lead, not only to vigilance in protection of human rights, but alternatively to a separation from societal life and emphasis on a community set apart from a "sinful world." This view can lead to a withdrawal from working with public institutions or ideas that are purported in "secular" contexts—for example, human rights. Some Anabaptist traditions—for example, Amish and Plymouth Brethren—consider their communities to be special enclaves of Christians who should not adopt the practices of the surrounding outsiders. While order is maintained within the community, human rights for all are not a priority. The Amish communities in Indiana and Kentucky reject connection with wrong ideas by not using electricity or modern conveyances such as cars. The Plymouth Brethren show their separation from public life by not celebrating holidays or participating in political elections.[38]

The presence of sin in the world also leads some Christians to a critique of the very idea of human rights. Some Christians, suspicious of human rights, develop anti-human rights perspectives. An emphasis on the fall of humanity can result in a focus on negative qualities and possibilities, resulting in a fear of state authority or other races. Contemporary survival-ist Christian movements such as the Christian Identity Movement focus on the negative power of government and the need to protect their group against destruction by others.[39]

Not only antiauthoritarian responses but authoritarian responses can be developed on anti-human rights agendas. An exaggerated emphasis on human inability to do good can be a deterrent to fostering human agency and insuring human rights.[40] In the 1970s, Protestant Bill Gothard spawned a movement in the United States based in a theology of hierarchical author-ity that limited human freedom. Gothard influenced thousands of Christians to believe that only direct authority could curtail the strong sinful inclina-tions of persons. He stressed obedience to civil authorities and, with appeals to the Bible and analogies to the animal kingdom, developed strict lines of authority in church and family settings.[41]

A severe view of human sin can also result in a theology that teaches that humans can do nothing good. In this view, good can only come through God. Therefore, complete surrender to God and dependence on God's grace is required of Christ's followers. Human rights disappear from this view as persons are seen as totally sinful and without value without the presence of Christ in their lives. Some Christian leaders use this theology to keep per-sons from struggling for their rights or the rights of others. The only rights that are valid are the rights to practice and propogate the Christian reli-gion.[42] In this view, Christians are encouraged to remain childlike and dependent on strong leaders for instruction in living.

Understanding anti-human rights views of some Christians is crucial for any attempt to understand various viewpoints and attitudes toward human rights and responsibilities by Christian traditions.

Christian ideas of dependence on God, God's will, and God's grace need not result in anti-human rights positions. More often those theologies are used to balance understandings of human rights and serve as constructs in Christian evaluations of human rights and responsibilities.[43]

Christians sometimes use ethical standards of Biblical law rather than the language of human rights to support the values of human rights. Fuller Seminary President Richard Mouw tells a story from his school days that illustrates this. His punishment for making a racial slur to a classmate was to write out the Ten Commandments over one hundred times. The rationale for this discipline was that he was bearing false witness against his neighbor. Mouw implies that the truth, seen clearly by his teacher, was that his fellow student was a human being whose civil rights were violated by this uncivil behavior.[44]

Community and the Human Family

That the people of God are a part of the human family is a fourth theological construct that is central to an understanding of human rights for Christians. Two circles of community are important here: the unity of the whole human family and the special community of the church. Christian traditions have articulated those ideas in many ways, but the concepts of brotherhood/sisterhood and covenant stand out as two of the major constructs that describe the relationships of love among humans that define Christianity.

Israel, believing that they were the chosen people of God, separated themselves from surrounding communities in many ways. They operated out of the idea that they had a special relationship with God—a covenant that required obedience to God and assured God's protection over them (Deut. 5). A tradition of care for widows and orphans was part of this covenant (Old Testament Book of Ruth). This agreement predisposed those communities to protect the human rights of weaker members. Welcoming strangers into their community, protecting slaves, and limiting the authority of political leaders, including kings, were also part of the laws of the covenant of Israel. Those expectations point to a universality of human rights hinted at in the tradition, a universality that was sometimes blurred by the subjugation of the Jews by other tribes and the separation of the Jews from surrounding communities.[45]

When the covenantal tradition of the Jews was adopted by Christianity, the basis of belonging to the covenanted people shifted from ethnicity to belief. The writings of the Apostle Paul insisted on the unity of believers and articulated the hope of unity of all creation under Christ (Gal. 3:28, Eph. 1:9, Col. 1:16–17). In this way the covenant of the family of God became linked to unity and the brotherhood/sisterhood of all humankind.

The resulting views of human rights emphasize care for the covenanted people of God, the church, and care for the whole human family. The church has a special responsibility to love as Christ loved, to bring the love of God into the world to all people. Evangelicals often speak of the Christian mandate to love others rather than speaking of human rights. Loving others, in this view, requires going beyond a notion of rights to sacrificial love—loving others as Christ loved us[46] (Phil. 2:5–9, James 2:8).

The African-American church illustrates the combination of a strong covenanted people with a stress on the brotherhood/sisterhood of all. Founded in slave religion, an African American culture of survival emphasized the liberation of God's people from oppression and the spiritual power inherent in the African notion of the sacredness of all of life.[47] The "brotherhood of man," therefore, requires equality for all. Securing human rights through community action became a central theme of the African-American church. Both liberation from slavery and the active struggle against human rights abuses during the civil rights era utilized the covenanted people of God working together for the universal rights of all.[48] This ideal of brotherhood continues to be demonstrated in the willingness of African American Christians to include others in their associations, despite continued discrimination against them.

The Reformed tradition uses the idea of covenant in a proactive way to underscore the orders of creation theology that God has given Christians special responsibilities as part of the human family. As the people of God, brought into a special relationship with God through Christ, Christians bear a responsibility to act in love to others, to participate in God's liberating actions in history, and to care for the world.[49] Christians are duty bound to protect not only their own rights but the rights of others.

This theology is active in conciliar Protestantism as shown in the work of the World Council of Churches as well as the World Reformed Alliance of Churches. Protection of human rights in areas where abuses of human rights abound becomes a focus of attention in groups working out of this community construct. For example, the Presbyterian Church (U.S.A.)'s *Human Rights Update* gives information on human rights abuses and shows how Presbyterians can add their voices to alleviating those abuses. The World Council of Churches focuses on a different area of human rights each decade: the decade for women, the decade for children, and currently, the decade against violence.

When the United States was founded, Baptists were an important force in protecting the religious liberties of all people. They vigorously opposed a state church to protect the freedom to worship that had caused them to flee from Europe. Their survival as a community of Christians was at the heart of this movement. At the same time, they helped to secure the same rights for all people. This movement and similar efforts have resulted in the pluralism in the United States that has continued to expand. Today the rights of all to religious freedom is central to our national identity.

The Quakers also strongly supported the freedom of all to worship as their conscience dictated. The community of the whole family of God, universal brotherhood, was strongly upheld by Quaker founder George Fox and his followers. Pennsylvania, founded by William Penn, was the first state to support freedom of religion for all, thus avoiding the religious persecutions that characterized Massachusetts and other areas of the fledgling nation. Today the unprogrammed Friends, the liberal wing of Quakerism, take a strong stand for universal human rights and the ending of violence through political oppression and wars.

The peace movement centered in the Catholic church also works against war and violence on the basis of a theology of the human family. Catholics have joined with persons of all faiths to protest the proliferation of nuclear weapons.[50] Their work is part of a broader effort by the Roman Catholic Church to interpret morality to society. The church understands the state to have a limited role in protecting human rights. The voice of the church also needs to be heard, a voice that emphasizes the rights of family and communities and is committed to the flourishing of the whole human family.

CONTRIBUTIONS OF CHRISTIAN TRADITIONS TO HUMAN RIGHTS

The beliefs about human rights described above display a diversity of theologies and approaches. Those perspectives find their sources in understandings of the image of God, creation, sin, and community. The diversity of those approaches offers a variety of emphases that can be used to further understandings and actions to support human rights in today's world.

The four theological sources for Christian views of human rights are assertions that are based in an ontological understanding of humans, God, and the world. While specific organizations and delineations of those views differ according to the history and societal settings in which they arose, the belief in a cosmology that exists beyond the material world and the social constructions of reality—a metaphysical sourcing—is operative in them all.

In the transition between modern and postmodern understandings of human rights, the faith-based sources of human rights in Christian and other religious traditions can add strength and bring harmony to other sources.

The *universality of human rights* becomes difficult to argue now that postmodern understandings of the situatedness of all knowledge and the cultural-conditionedness of expressions of knowledge are evident.[51] John Rawls argued for a rational justification for human rights in *A Theory of Justice* (1971). More recently he moved from an "original condition" to a situated one that calls for human rights in societies striving for a democratic form of governance. Arguments for an autonomous moral discourse presuppose the search for universals that marks the modern period. If the discourse becomes situated, as Rawls attempts to locate the "original condition" in liberal democracies, the universality of the discourse evaporates.

Another universal argument sources human rights in the sacredness of persons. Ronald Dworkin argues for a sacredness of human beings *without* sourcing that belief in religious convictions.[52] But the notion of sacredness itself is linked to the idea of transcendence.

Some who have more fully embraced a postmodern situated and interpreted view of a socially constructed reality find themselves arguing for incommensurable differences among cultures. The Asian values debate exemplifies this point of view.[53] Viewing human rights as distinctly Western and modern leads to a relativistic view of human rights that prevents the possibility of human rights from being used as a starting point for international discourse.

Kenneth Morris finds a way through this dilemma by arguing for a communitarian synthesis that sees the possibility of human rights values in what he describes as a common experience among cultures. As cultures come into conflict, reciprocity and equality arise as values to arbitrate difference. As such, Morris claims those values are universally available and lead to a human rights ethic.[54]

The weakness of Morris's position is that, as a theoretical argument, he cites no empirical evidence that such common values arise in situations of conflict. Sourcing human rights in humanitarian "sacredness" or human dignity, autonomous moral discourse, or common human experience of shared values are arguments that are each thin in themselves in supporting a universal value of human rights.

However, religious traditions, Christianity in this case, can bring those arguments together in a faith-based ontological framework that strengthens each of them. Human rationality and the notion of the moral impulses of persons and communities find support in Christian tradition. Moral discourse need not be "autonomous" but can be sourced in the religious tradition. The sacredness of persons also finds a stronger base in the Judeo-Christian notion of humans created in the image of God than in a humanitarian intuition that persons are of inestimable worth. The Christian idea that God redeems the world through Christ further strengthens the value of persons in the Christian view. The common experience of shared values of reciprocity and human equality as sources for human rights need not remain theoretical. Those experiences, documented in the Hebrew and Christian scriptures, can be interpreted as precursors to the rise of human rights.

As the Christian tradition is used to source human rights as a universal value, the support for human rights from arguments of autonomous moral discourse, human sacredness or dignity, and common experience of the values that support human rights can be harmonized. Taken together those arguments present a stronger case for human rights than each does as it stands alone. Religious sensibilities and faith are then included in the dialogue which allows for a critical standard to be invoked that can critique cultural perceptions and arbitrate cultural differences.

CHRISTIAN VIEWS IN DIALOGUE

The above argument is one example of the way Christian sources for human rights can augment philosophical views when placed in dialogue. Theologies and values of other religions also present an arena for meaningful discourse about human rights.

Arvind Sharma's work on the Declaration of Human Rights by the World's Religions has brought the discussion of religious values that support human rights to the fore. The Declaration of Human Rights by the World's Religions demonstrates that religions carry common convictions that can be interpreted in the human rights framework developed by the UN Declaration on Human Rights. Ecumenical and interreligious dialogue can also be fostered by a clear identification of Christian themes in the Declaration of Human Rights by the World's Religions.

This dialogical project leads to further questions. What kinds of human rights emphases are most important in our world today—a justice or care emphasis, an individual or a communal emphasis, a protective or a liberative focus? How can Christian theologies be used to support the views of human rights articulated in both the UN Declaration and the Declaration of Human Rights by the World's Religions? What kinds of actions might arise as Christian groups dialogue and cooperate with others in the struggle for human rights in today's world?

As Christians and people of all religions struggle with those questions, working to articulate and practice their convictions about human rights, they can join together to support human rights arguments from philosophies and cultures around the globe. In this way, commitments to respecting all people and working to see the value of each person upheld within and between communities will be strengthened.

NOTES

1. Augustine of Hippo, *The Confessions of St. Augustine*, trans. E. B. Pusey, D.D. New York: Dutton, 1907; reprinted, 1949, p. 345. (First published 397 CE.)

2. Martin Luther, "Commentary on St. Paul's Epistle to the Galations," in *Martin Luther: Selections from His Writings*, ed. John Dillenberger. New York: Doubleday, Anchor Books, 1961, p. 111.

3. "Pastoral Constitution on the Church in the modern World," in *Documents of Vatican II*, Walter M. Abbott, S.J., general ed., New York:

Herder and Herder, Crossroads Publishing, 1966, op. cit., p. 680f. (See also pp. 210–11.)

4. "Rerum Novarum," AAS 23 (1890–1891), p. 651. Cited in *The Documents of Vatican II*, op. cit., p. 278, note 222.

5. "Declaration on Religious Freedom," *The Documents of Vatican II*, p. 225.

6. Rosemary Radford Reuther, "The Liberation of Christology from Patriarchy," in *Feminist Theology: A Reader*, ed. Ann Loades (Louisville, KY: Westminster/John Knox, 1990), p. 139; Elizabeth Schüssler Fiorenza, "For Women in Men's World: A Critical Feminist Theology of Liberation," in *The Power of Naming: A Concilium Reader in Feminist Liberation Theology* (Maryknoll, NY: Orbis, 1996), p. 5; Beverly Wildung Harrison, "The Power of Anger in the Work of Love," *Making the Connections: Essays in Feminist Social Ethics*, ed. Carol Robb. Boston: Beacon, 1985, ch. 1.

7. Frances S. Adeney, *Christian Women in Indonesia: A Narrative Study of Gender and Religion*. Syracuse, NY: Syracuse University Press, 2003, pp. 96–97.

8. Magdalena H. Tangkudung. *Mitos dan Kodrat: Suatu Kajian Mengenai Kedudukan dan Peranan Wanita Kristen di Minahasa*. Master's Thesis, Graduate Program in Religion and Society, Satya Wacana Christian University, Salatiga, Indonesia, 1994, p. 2.

9. Westminster Larger Catechism, *Book of Confessions* (Office of the General Assembly, Presbyterian Church U.S.: 1996), p. 201.

10. John Calvin, *Calvin's Institutes*, Mac Dill AFB, Florida: MacDonald, book 4, chapter 20, "Civil Government," section 4, p. 787.

11. See Calvin on the authority of Christian princes and magistrates in *Calvin's Institutes*, book 4, chapter 20, section 9, op. cit. p. 790.

12. The Advisory Committee on Social Witness Policy publishes research and advises the General Assembly on issues of economic justice, human rights, and environmental concerns.

13. See Vatican II, "Gaudium et Spes and Dignitatis Humanae" in *The Documents of Vatican II*, op. cit., pp. 229 and 679.

14. See Vatican II, "Dignitatis Humanae," in *The Documents of Vatican II*, op. cit. p. 685.

15. See Glen Stassen's forward to Christopher D. Marshall, *Crowned with Glory and Honor: Human Rights in the Biblical Tradition*. Telford, PA: Pandora, 2001, pp. 11–14.

16. See David Little's chapter in this volume.

17. Juergen Moltmann, *A Theology of Hope: On the Ground and the Implications of a Christian Eschatology*. New York: Harper & Row, 1967, p. 327.

18. Ibid., p. 328.

19. Augustine of Hippo, *The Confessions of St. Augustine*, op. cit., p. 166.

20. See, for example, John Wesley's sermon "The Way to the Kingdom," in *The Works of John Wesley*, vol. 5, ed. Gerald R. Cragg, London: Oxford University Press, 1975, p. 78, in which he declares that a person could be orthodox in every point and yet have no religion at all. In the pietistic stream of Christianity, the Bruderhof Community in Europe also stands out as an example of dependence on God. Emmy Arnold, cofounder of the community stated: "Efforts to organize community in a human way can only result in ugly, lifeless caricatures. Only when we are empty and open to the Living One—to the Spirit—can he bring about the same life among us as he did among the early Christians." *A Joyful Pilgrimage: My Life in Community*. Farmington, PA: Plough, 1999, pp. 168–69.

21. In Roman Catholic social teachings, according to "Mater et Magistra," a community of persons active in the ordering of their lives must be formed, one in which all members are . . . conscious of their own duties and rights, working on a basis of equality for bringing about the universal common good., "Mater et Magistra," ET as appendix to E. Guerry, *The Social Teaching of the Church*, 1961, pp. 185, 190, and 208. (Quoted in Moltmann, op. cit. p. 318.) In the Reformed tradition, the duties of Christians to act toward reconciliation in society includes action for political, economic, and social rights of all persons. *The Book of Confessions*, op. cit., Confession of 1967, section 4, "Reconciliation in Society" 9:43–9:47, pp. 267–69.

22. An example can be found in Carl F.H. Henry's discussion of international law in *God, Revelation and Authority: God Who Stands and Stays*, vol. 6, part 2, Waco, TX: Word Books, 1983, p. 422. Here he argues that because modern rulers do not depend on transcendent law but only protect their own interests, a might-makes-right philosophy takes over. "In fallen human history," he concludes, "no political document can be presumed to fully elucidate what divine justice implies."

23. The Philadelphia Female Anti-Slavery Society, formed in 1833, became the strongest and longest lasting antislavery organization. It included black and white, Quaker and non-Quaker participants. Sarah Grimke went on to make the clarion call for women's suffrage, basing her argument "not on Quaker testimony but on the grounds of human rights." Margaret Hope Bacon, *Mothers of Feminism: The Story of Quaker Women in America*. San Francisco: Harper and Row, 1986, pp. 104–105.

24. Frederick Douglass worked for universal sufferage on the basis of human rights and was dubbed by a white supremasist the father of the nineteenth amendment. "The only true basis of rights was the capacity of

individuals, and as for himself, he dared not claim a right which he would not concede to women," said Douglass. *Frederick Douglass on Women's Rights*, ed. Philip S. Foner, New York: DaCapo, 1992, pp. ix and 51.

25. See *Mothers of Feminism*, op. cit., chapter 8, "Quaker Women and the Early Sufferage Movement," pp. 120–36.

26. See articles by Gustavo Gutierrez, Juan Luis Segundo, and a letter from Third World Bishops entitled "A Letter to the Peoples of the Third World," in *Liberation Theology: A Documentary History*, ed. Alfred T. Hennelly, S.J., Maryknoll, NY: Orbis, 1990, pp. 29–38; 48–57; 62–76.

27. *Birmingham Revolutionaries: The Reverend Fred Shuttlesworth and the Alabama Christian Movement for Human Rights*, ed. Marjorie L. White and Andrew M. Manis, Macon, GA: Mercer University Press, 2000, p. vii.

28. Evangelical Christian Gretchen G. Hull quotes A. W. Tozer on the necessity of a higher authority to provide values and theological understandings that enable Christians to critique society. She points to Dietrich Bonhoeffer's warning against following a human understanding of what Christian action is. "The Complementarity of God's Love and God's Righteousness," in *The Global God: Multi-Cultural Evangelical Views of God,* ed. Aida Bescancon Spencer and William David Spencer, Grand Rapids, MI: Baker, 1998, pp. 71 and 75.

29. See chapter in this volume by John Dear.

30. Vatican II traces the obligation to the poor back through the history of the church, emphasizing that in extreme necessity all goods are to be shared, and concluding that "If a person is in extreme necessity, he has the right to take from the riches of others what he himself needs." "The Church Today," in *The Documents of Vatican II*, op. cit., p. 278.

31. In the American situation of plurality, John Courtney Murray outlines two distinct orders, civil and religious. Articles of peace are the civil laws that, while not deduced from divine law, are rational and meant to insure peace. In this situation the church defers to the temporal order, not imposing a higher spiritual law on society. See chapter 2, "Civil Unity and Religious Integrity: the Articles of Peace," in *We Hold These Truths*, John Courtney Murray, S.J. New York: Sheed and Ward, 1960, pp. 45, 49, and 78.

32. In a special address at the American Academy of Religion, San Francisco, Nov. 22, 1997, Robert N. Bellah stated that the dominant religious tradition of American beginnings was sectarian religion. It was the radical sects of the Protestant reformation, groups like the Baptists, that gave rise to the movement for freedom of conscience and the right of religious freedom. It was not the influence of the dominant religion of John Winthrop and the Puritans but the work of Baptists like Roger Williams, founder of Rhode Island, that insured a society now hospitable to multiculturalism.

33. See http:/www.wcc-coe.org World Council of Churches Home Page for information about projects on the Decade against Violence.

34. "We, as a people, are agreed that government should not undertake responsibility for the care of the sacred order of religious life; governmental responsibility is limited to a care for the freedom of religion." *We Hold These Truths*, op. cit., p. 153.

35. "*Sin* threatens freedom within each sphere just as strongly as *State power* does at the boundary. . . . At the heart of every sphere there smolders and smokes the flame of passion, whence the sparks of sin fly upward. That unholy blaze undermines the moral vitality of life, weakens resiliency, and finally bends the strongest stave. In any successful attack on freedom the state can only be an accomplice. The *chief* culprit is the citizen who forgets his duty, wastes his strength in the sleep of sin and sensual pleasure, and so loses the power of *his own initiative*." "Sphere Sovereignty" (1880), Inaugural address at the Free University, in *Abraham Kuyper: A Centennial Reader*, ed. James D. Bratt, Grand Rapids, MI: Eerdmans, 1998, p. 473.

36. See "Human Rights and the Fullness of Life: Fiftieth Anniversary of the Universal Declaration of Human Rights Issue," *Church and Society*. Presbyterian Church (U.S.A.) 88, 4 (March–April, 1998).

37. See *Orthodox Women Speak: Discerning the Signs of the Times*, ed. Kyriaki Karidoyanes Fitzgerald, pp. 1–2 for a statement on the authority of bishops and formal statements of the church in regards to women's ministries.

38. The Grant-Kelly exclusive Plymouth Brethren (Group Number 8) do not celebrate any holidays or participate in elections. Many also conscientiously object to military service.

39. For a history and profile of this movement, see http://religious-movements.lib.virginia.edu/nrms/identity.html.

40. Carl Henry states that "A naturalistic exposition of law makes inevitable a positivistic relativizing of law, since naturalism provides no safeguard against totalitarian rulers who authoritatively arbitrate the nature and limits of human liberty; it actually puts in doubt the very character and validity of human rights." *God, Revelation, and Authority*, vol. 6, part 2, op. cit., p. 422.

41. See Bill Gothard's "Umbrella Policy" at his Home Page http://www.billgothard.com/news/basicseminar.php. Key topics: Protection under Authority.

42. See Joyce Meyer's article "Your Voice Can Return Our Religious Freedom," at http:capwiz.com/joycemeyer/issues/alert/?alerted=5245916&type=ml.

43. See, for example Christopher D. Marshall's discussion on rights and responsibilities in *Crowned with Glory and Honor: Human Rights in the Biblical*

Tradition, op. cit., pp. 104–105, and Ismael Garcia's remarks on personal responsibility in "On Human Dignity," in *Insights: The Faculty Journal of Austin Seminary* 114, 1 (Fall, 1998), p. 11.

44. Richard J. Mouw, *Uncommon Decency: Christian Civility in an Uncivil World,* Downers Grove, IL: InterVarsity, 1992, pp. 47–48.

45. Christopher D. Marshall argues that despite the ambiguity of the biblical witness ("the bible appears to mandate such human rights abuses as slavery, war, conquest, genocide, the subjugation of women, bridal sale, racial separation, the denial of religious freedom to idolaters, and the execution of wrongdoers") yet "The overarching narrative structure of Creation-Fall-Redemption-Consummation, fleshed out in teaching on God's righteousness and the covenantal nature of community, (that) has sweeping implications of a human rights kind," *Crowned with Glory and Honor: Human Rights in the Biblical Tradition,* op. cit., p. 51.

46. In a chapter on Christian mission and the future, the authors of *Introducing World Missions: A Biblical, Historical and Practical Survey.* (Grand Rapids, MI: Baker, 2004,) make the challenge to love sacrificially, "Missionaries may very well find themselves at the epicenter of devastation on a global scale unheard of in human history. Will they be prepared to minister *in love* in the midst of such tragedy? By God's grace they will, though the price may be higher than today's church can ever imagine," p. 313.

47. Gayraud S. Wilmore, *Black Religion and Black Radicalism: An Interpretation of the Religious History of the Afro-American People,* 2nd ed., Maryknoll, NY: Orbis, 1983, pp. 219 and 222.

48. Dwight Perry, *Breaking Down Barriers: A Black Evangelical Explains the Black Church,* Grand Rapids, MI: Baker, 1998, pp. 106–107.

49. *Selected Theological Statements of the Presbyterian Church (U.S.A.) General Assemblies (1956–1998),* Presbyterian Church (U.S.A.), 1998, pp. 65–66.

50. E.g., Witness for Peace brings together people of all faiths to work against nuclear arms proliferation and political injustices perpetuated by governmental policies.

51. See chapter 3 "Are Human Rights Universal? The Relativist Challenge and Related Matters," in *The Idea of Human Rights: Four Inquiries,* by Michael J. Perry, New York: Oxford University Press, 1998, pp. 57ff.

52. "Some readers will take particular exception to the term 'sacred' because it will suggest to them that the conviction I have in mind is necessarily a theistic one. I shall try to explain why it is not, and how it may be, and commonly is, interpreted in a secular way." *Life's Dominion: An Argument about Abortion, Euthanasia, and Individual Freedom (1993),* p. 25, quoted in Michael Perry, op. cit., p. 108, note 13.

53. See Kam Weng Ng's chapter in this volume.

54. "Western Defensiveness and the Defense of Rights: A Communitarian Alternative," in *Negotiating Culture and Human Rights*, ed. Lynda S. Bell, Andrew J. Nathan, and Ilan Peleg, New York: Columbia University Press, 2001, pp. 68–95.

BIBLIOGRAPHY

Abbott, S.J., Walter M., general ed. *The Documents of Vatican II*. New York: Crossroad Publishing, Herder and Herder, 1966.

Adeney, Frances S. *Christian Women in Indonesia: A Narrative Study of Gender and Religion*. Syracuse, NY: Syracuse University Press, 2003.

An'Naim, Abdullahi A., Jerald D. Gort, Henry Jansen, and Hendrick M. Vroom, eds. *Human Rights and Religious Values: An Uneasy Relationship?* Grand Rapids, MI: Eerdmans, 1995.

Arnold, Emmy. *A Joyful Pilgrimage: My Life in Community*. Farmington, PA: Plough, 1999.

Augustine of Hippo, *The Confessions of St. Augustine*. Trans. E. B. Pusey, D.D. New York: Dutton, 1907, reprinted, 1949. (First published 397 CE.)

Bacon, Margaret Hope. *Mothers of Feminism: The Story of Quaker Women in America*. San Francisco: Harper and Row, 1986.

Bell, Lynda S., Andrew J. Nathan, and Ilan Peleg, eds. *Negotiating Culture and Human Rights*. New York: Columbia University Press, 2001.

Bratt, James D., ed. *Abraham Kuyper: A Centennial Reader*. Grand Rapids, MI: Eerdmans, 1998.

Calvin, John. *Calvin's Institutes*. Mac Dill, AFB, Florida: MacDonald, n.d.

Fabella, Virginia M.M., and Sun Ai Lee Park. *We Dare To Dream: Doing Theology as Asian Women*. Hong Kong: Asian Women's Resource Centre for Culture and Theology and EATWOT Women's Commission in Asia, 1989.

Fiorenza, Elizabeth Schüssler. "For Women in Men's World: A Critical Feminist Theology of Liberation," in *The Power of Naming: A Concilium Reader in Feminist Liberation Theology*. Maryknoll, NY: Orbis, 1996, pp. 3–13.

Fitzgerald, Kyriaki Karidoyanes, ed. *Orthodox Women Speak: Discerning the Signs of the Times*. Geneva, Switzerland: WCC Publications, 1999.

Foner, Philip S., ed. *Frederick Douglass on Women's Rights*. New York: Da Capo, 1992.

General Assembly of the Presbyterian Church (U.S.A.). *Book of Confessions*. Westminster/John Knox, 1996.

———. *Human Rights Update: 1999–2000*.

Harrison, Beverly Wildung. *Making the Connections: Essays in Feminist Social Ethics*, ed. Carol Robb. Boston: Beacon, 1985.

Heideman, Eugene. "The Missiological Significance of the Universal Declaration of Human Rights," in *Missiology: An International Review* 27, 2 (April, 2000): 163–76.

Hennelly, Alfred T., S.J., ed. *Liberation Theology: A Documentary History*. Maryknoll, NY: Orbis, 1990.

Henry, Carl F. H. *God, Revelation and Authority: God Who Stands and Stays*, 6: part 2. Waco, TX: Word Books, 1983.

Institute for Ecumenical and Cultural Research. *Confessing Christian Faith in a Pluralistic Society*. (Cooperative statement by National Council of Churches and National Conference of Catholic Bishops.) Collegeville, MN: Institute for Ecumenical and Cultural Research, 1995.

Lancaster, Kathy, ed. "Human Rights and the Fullness of Life." *Church and Society* 88, 4 (March/April, 1998). National Ministries Division, Presbyterian Church (U.S.A.).

Lauren, Paul Gordon. *The Evolution of International Human Rights: Visions Seen*. Philadelphia: University of Pennsylvania Press, 1998.

Luther, Martin. "Commentary on St. Paul's Epistle to the Galations," in *Martin Luther: Selections from His Writings*, ed. John Dillenberger. New York: Doubleday, Anchor Books, 1961.

Marshall, Christopher D. *Crowned with Glory and Honor: Human Rights in the Biblical Tradition*. Telford, PA: Pandora, 2001.

Moltmann, Juergen. *A Theology of Hope: On the Ground and the Implications of a Christian Eschatology*. New York: Harper and Row, 1967.

Morris, Kenneth. "Western Defensiveness and the Defense of Rights: A Communitarian Alternative," in *Negotiating Culture and Human Rights*, ed. Lynda S. Bell, Andrew J. Nathan, and Ilan Peleg. New York: Columbia University Press, 2001, pp. 68–95.

Mouw, Richard J. *Uncommon Decency: Christian Civility in an Uncivil World*. Downer's Grove, IL: InterVarsity, 1992.

Muck, Terry C., ed. "Human Dignity." Issue of *Insights: The Faculty Journal of Austin Seminary*, 114, 1 (Fall, 1998).

Murray, John Courtney, S.J. *We Hold These Truths: Catholic Reflections on the American Proposition*. New York: Sheed and Ward, 1960.

Perry, Dwight. *Breaking Down Barriers: A Black Evangelical Explains the Black Church*. Grand Rapids, MI: Baker, 1998.

Perry, Michael J. *The Idea of Human Rights: Four Inquiries*. New York: Oxford University Press, 1998.

Pittman, Don A., and Terry C. Muck, eds. *Ministry and Theology in Global Perspective: Contemporary Challenges for the Church*. Grand Rapids, MI: Eerdmans, 1996.

Rawls, John. *A Theory of Justice*. Cambridge, MA: Belknap, 1999.

Renteln, Alison Dundes. "Human Rights," in *Encyclopedia of Violence, Peace, and Conflict*. New York: Academic Press, 1999, pp. 167–78.

Reuther, Rosemary Radford. "The Liberation of Christology from Patriarchy," in *Feminist Theology: A Reader*, ed. Ann Loades. Louisville, KY: Westminster/John Knox, 1990, pp. 138–48.

Scott, A. Moreau, Gary R. Corwin, and Gary B. McGee, eds. *Introducing World Missions: A Biblical, Historical and Practical Survey*. Grand Rapids, MI: Baker, 2004.

Spencer, Aida Bescancon, and William David Spencer, eds. *The Global God: Multi-Cultural Evangelical Views of God*. Grand Rapids, MI: Baker, 1998.

Tangkudung, Magdalena H. *Mitos dan Kodrat: Suatu Kajian Mengenai Kedudukan dan Peranan Wanita Kristen di Minahasa* (Myth and Fate: An Analysis of the Position and Role of Christian Women in Minahasa). Master's Thesis, Graduate Program in Religion and Society, Satya Wacana Christian University, Salatiga, Indonesia, 1994.

Wesley, John. "The Way to the Kingdom, " in *The Works of John Wesley*, vol. 5, ed. Gerald R. Cragg. London: Oxford University Press, 1975.

White, Marjorie L., and Andrew M. Manis, eds. *Birmingham Revolutionaries: The Reverend Fred Shuttlesworth and the Alabama Christian Movement for Human Rights*. Macon, GA: Mercer University Press, 2000.

Wilmore, Gayraud S. *Black Religion and Black Radicalism: An Interpretation of the Religious History of Afro-American People*, 2nd ed. Maryknoll, NY: Orbis, 1983, second printing, 1984.

CHAPTER 3

The Sources of Human Rights Ideas

A Christian Perspective

MAX L. STACKHOUSE

M ore than a quarter century ago, shortly after the Helsinki Accords of 1975 with their "third basket" dealing with human rights were signed, I was invited by the Board of Global Ministries of my church (The United Church of Christ) to participate in ecumenical discussions and to serve as a visiting lecturer in the theological academies of sister churches in the former German Democratic Republic (Evangelische Kirche der Union) and in South India (United Church of South India). I became fascinated with the way in which different ideational and social traditions treated human rights, including the United Nations Declaration of 1948 and its subsequent "Covenants." The resistance to "Western" definitions of human rights were intense in the Marxist parties of Eastern Europe and, it turned out, in both the leadership of the Congress Party under Indira Gandhi in India, when she declared her "Emergency" in 1976, and in the emerging "Hindutva" parties that issued in the current Hindu nationalist government. On the basis of these extended exposures to non-Western interpretations of human rights at

---

*This essay is related to a series of papers and articles on the same topic. See my "Sources and Prospects for Human Rights Ideas: A Christian Perspective," *The Idea of Human Rights: Traditions and Presence*, ed. Jindrich Halama (Prague: Charles University Protestant Theological Faculty, 2003), pp. 183–200; "The Sources of Human Rights Ideas," in *Religion and Human Rights: Conflict or Convergence*, ed. Adam Seligman (Boston: Inter-religious Center on Public Life, 2005), pp. 69–84; and "Why Human Rights Need God: A Christian Perspective," *Does Human Rights Need God?*, ed. Elizabeth M. Bucar and Barbra Barnett (Grand Rapids, MI: Eerdmans Publishers, 2005), pp. 25–40.

that time, I engaged in a comparative study of the roots and conceptual framework that made modern human rights discourse possible.[1] The invitation to contribute to this forum is timely, given current new conditions, and I will try to restate and refine some of my findings and convictions on these matters and to refine my views in view of subsequent developments.

The new conditions are probably obvious. The great struggles facing issues of human rights and pluralism of the last third of the previous century had to do with racial justice, the rising parallel movements for the equal rights of women, and the worldwide movements for decolonialization. All these took place in the context of a life-and-death confrontation of the "free nations" with "world communism." The questions were whether human rights are in any sense universal and, if so, whether civil and political rights had any priority over social and economic rights, or whether the latter had to be actualized before the former could be realized. In some ways the consensus has grown that they are universal, at least with regard to the issues of race and sex—especially in South Africa and North America even if acute problems remain in both, and in the Balkans, South Asia,[2] and the Mid-East. Still, the suspicion that human rights are an invention of the bourgeois West designed to preserve the West's capitalist interests remains in many quarters in spite of the fact that the Soviet world has collapsed and, with it, the chief advocates of that view.

In some ways, their place has been taken by the rise of Islamist militance, and with it a theocratic rather than a humanistic vision of hope for a revolutionary change that will overthrow the influence of the world's largest religion, the culture based largely on it, and particularly the one remaining superpower. This has taken place in the context of the massive globalization of those forms of technology, science, democracy, professional standards, ecological consciousness, media influence, and corporate capitalism that carry with them human rights ideals. To be sure, many people think about globalization only in economic terms. But this narrow understanding of our present situation—as if the current economic transformations were not themselves largely a function of educational, legal, technological, communication, and, indeed, moral and spiritual developments—blinds us to one of the most difficult problems of contemporary reflection in this area, the encounter of religions and the apparent conflict of values held by them. In spite of the fact that there are "many globalizations"—both many conceptions of it, and many processes in many places by which it is being adopted and adapted, bringing new conflicts—globalization is on the whole the forming of a new and wider human interdependence that raises the prospect of a new world civilization. It forms a new context in which every people, nation, and state must find its place and in which the renewed encounter of the world's cultures, societies, and religions requires us to think again about universalistic ethical principles and values, whether they are possible and real, what difference they make and whether they inhibit or enhance the prospects of a genuine and principled pluralism.

On this point, those who defend human rights as global principles have reason to be cautiously optimistic. We can be optimistic, for human rights ideas have, at the least, become a part of the *ius gentium*, the cross-cultural operating consensus as to what constitutes proper behavior by states and other formal institutions, and what counts as compelling moral argument in contemporary ethical discourse. Although it seemed in the middle years of the mid-twentieth century that the barbarism of neopagan nationalism and the militant antiliberalism of socialist secularism, both legitimated by radically existentialist philosophies that denied any kind of "essentialist" normative order, could not be contained by theological, ethical, or social wisdom and would bring only Holocausts and Gulags to the future, it was to the often-obscured Judeo-Christian ethical principles, frequently in their religiously neutered Enlightenment formulations, that the nations turned to frame both the UN Declaration of Human Rights[3] and its subsequent "Covenants." These are what leaders from most of the world's great cultures and religions have now endorsed, and what today, oppressed peoples from minority cultures and religions appeal to for justice, functionally recognizing principles of universality in the legacy of these quite particularist traditions.[4] Moreover, more people are presently living under democratically ordered constitutions that seek to protect human rights, and a broader public constituency is interested in defending them than at any point in human history, and there is little evidence of their fading from normative use soon.[5] Indeed, even those who violate human rights plead special conditions, temporary delays, or hermeneutical differences; they seldom deny their validity as an ideal or goal.

Yet if these facts give us reason to be optimistic, it must be a cautious optimism, not only because the rights of so many people continue to be savagely violated in so many places, and the exigencies of earlier battles against domination by colonialized peoples and now against threats of terrorism in many countries seem to justify the use of means that themselves now threaten the rights of groups and persons in ways that are more than "collateral damage." For those who seek to defend civil rights and liberties and see them as a way to love their neighbors near and far, the erosion of universalistic normative ideas of human rights (since civil rights are granted by a state and thus can be withdrawn by it), is a matter of immediate and pressing practical concern.

Yet, this is not the deepest threat, for the world has known that murder is wrong for many centuries, and every people has laws against it. People know they occur, with few "justifiable homicides," but the empirical fact that things happen does not negate the normative principles by which we judge them. No, the threat is deeper; it is fundamentally intellectual and spiritual, for many have come to doubt that we can have nonempirical principles to judge empirical life. And since the roots of human rights ideas are historically derived from those branches of the biblically based traditions, especially Jewish and Christian, that were willing to recognize, learn from, and selectively embrace philosophical and ethical insights from several cultures if they recognized that humanity lives under universal principles of right and wrong that they did not construct and could not deconstruct.[6] We cannot say that these traditions have been faithful to the implications of their own heritage at all times, and the horror stories of our pasts also have to be told to mitigate any temptation to arrogant triumphalism. Still, intellectual honesty demands the full recognition of the fact that what passes as "secular, Western, humanist" principles of basic rights developed nowhere else than out of minority strands of the biblically rooted religions.[7] And while many scholars and leaders from many other traditions have endorsed them, and found resources in their own traditions that point to similar principles, today these views are under suspicion both by some Asian leaders who appeal to "Asian Values" and by some communitarian and postmodern philosophers in the West who have challenged the very idea of human rights. The deepest threat comes from those intellectual leaders who have adopted antiuniversalist, antiprincipial perspectives, or who hold that it is impossible for a universalistic set of principles to derive from a particular religious tradition, because they hold that religions are by definition and must remain particularistic whereas philosophy is or can be universalistic.

Those who doubt human rights do so either on the ground that there is or could be no universalistic moral theology, master narrative, or *jus naturale* to support the idea.[8] That, of course, is a universalistic claim in itself, one that ironically presses toward a universal relativism. Thus, they see "the West's" pressure to affirm human rights as rooted in a positive *jus civile* of a particular civilization or (in some versions) in the philosophical or religious "values" of distinct traditions or historical periods of thought, and doubt that either humanwide "first principles" or universalistic ends can be found in the face of religious variety and cultural multiplicity. The fact of the diversity of religions and cultures is taken as an argument for a relativism in normative morality. Thus, human rights are a matter of sociohistorical context. While some lament that more universal principles cannot be found, many celebrate the fact, making diversity, multiculturalism, and religious distinctives themselves universally positive moral values, although on their own grounds it is difficult to see how they could defend the view, except as a cultural preference. In this situation, to insist that all people be judged according to principles of human rights is seen as an act of cultural imperialism.[9] In addition, some argue that the "Western," actually Christian, especially Protestant and Enlightenment "values" are altogether too individualistic, and that since abstract individuals do not exist, only concrete persons-in-relationship do, we need an ethic based essentially in the particularities of specific community-embedded practices and duties.[10]

Politically, such arguments can be seen to feed the interests of those states that are the least democratic and the most likely to violate the rights of their own citizens, as clearly seen by the interfaith Project on Religion and Human Rights. Nearly a decade ago they recognized that:

> To date, governmental claims that culture justifies deviating from human rights standards have been made exclusively by states that have demonstrably bad human rights records. State invocations of "culture" and "cultural relativism" seem to be little more than cynical pretexts for rationalizing human rights abuses that particular states would in any case commit. (Some) . . . emulate China in appealing to...national sovereignty. . . . (Others) . . . such as Saudi Arabia, . . . maintain that they are following Islamic human rights norms, while failing to adhere to the norms that they officially deem Islamic.[11]

Yet these critics have one valid point that fuels their argument. They are partially correct insofar as they know that abstract principles and abstracted autonomous conceptions of human nature do not and cannot supply a full ethic for humanity or provide the general theory to guide a just and peaceful civil society in a global era. They also know that particular kinds of ethical obligations, rooted in specific traditions of duty, are authentic aspects of morality and identity and that the most significant of these are rooted in commitments that have become joined to religious loyalties, and that something precious would be lost or betrayed if these were denied.

But these critics are only partly correct. They are also partly wrong when they view the matter as a situation where we must turn *either* to first principles of an abstract universalistic kind *or* to concrete, networks of culturally, historically, and biographically gained commitments, loyalties, and expectations that shape our senses of responsibility, especially if that is how they view the highest level of religious or theological truth. In fact, most ethical issues, including those of human rights, require a synthetic judgment, one in which we must join normative first principles to the concrete matrices of experience by which we know events and read the existing ethos of our lives—that concrete network of events, traditions, relationships, commitments, and specific blends of connectedness and alienation which shape the "values" of daily experience and our senses of obligation. The classic traditions of case study, codified in casuistry as in Judaic "Responsa" or Christian "Penitential" literature, as well as in the modern strictures of court procedure, exemplify this joining. They require both a finding of law, which involves the critical reflection on first principles behind the law, *and* a finding of "fact," which requires reliance on the experience-gained common sense or wisdom, often of a jury of peers. Even more, they require an anticipatory assessment of the various consequences of various courses of action implied by a judgment about the interaction of principle and fact.

Indeed, it is theologically paradigmatic that following accounts of the Decalogue in both Exodus and Deuteronomy, surely prime examples of universalistic abstract principles, the next several chapters are repositories of the casuistic results of the blending of the implications of those principles with the situations that people experienced concretely in their ethos. That joining binds rendered judgments that are held to contribute to the protection of innocent persons, to the well-being of the common life and to the development of a morally righteous people. Similarly, much in the prophetic tradition makes the case against the infidelities of the people or the people in power by identifying the enduring principles in the covenants of old, the experience of social history in the present, and the prospects for a bleak, or a redeemed, future according to human deserts and divine mercy. And, for Christians specifically, to deny that such absolute universals can be connected to the realities of concrete historical experience in ways that lead to a redeemed future, is in fact a denial of the deepest insight of our faith: that Christ was both fully God and fully human, and that his life both fulfilled the commands of God, was concretely lived in the midst of a specific ethos, and nevertheless pointed to an ultimate future that we could not otherwise obtain.

This should be our first lesson in understanding the bases of human rights and all that it entails: theologically based moral judgments themselves are pluralistic in their internal structure. They demand critical reflection on the first principles of right and wrong, continued analysis of the actual events and experiences of life in a particular context, and a vision of the ultimate future—one that will more nearly approximate what is right, judge what is wrong, and fulfill what is already potentially good as we live toward the future.[12] The philosophies and politics of "either/or" are inevitably lopsided. And the implications of this brief excursus about "abstractions" for our question are these: do not trust theologians, philosophers, or social critics who repudiate first principles or advocate positions or policies that encourage humanity to ignore them in favor of the concreteness of historical experience; and do not trust those who do not take into account the complex matrices of experience that people have in the contexts of life. Moreover, we should place both under scrutiny on the question of whether what they propose regarding the prospects for the ultimate future can reach beyond the limits of the present and point to a horizon able to recognize all our synthetic judgments as proximate.

Not only do I want to argue that the affirmation of such "universal absolutes" as those stated in the Ten Commandments and less perfectly embodied in human rights provisions of our constitutions and such documents as the United Nations Declaration are compatible with and in fact derivative from the deeper theological heritage, there are two other ways in which "abstraction" is required by the best of Christian views. At the practical level, persons are sometimes abstracted from their concrete historical contexts and need the protection of abstract laws and rules and procedures of enforcement that say: "This person is already alienated from his or her matrix of ordinary moral relationships and the dismantling of this person's integrity must not proceed beyond specifiable limits—it is 'indivisible/undividable'." To put it another way: "Thou shalt not wantonly torture, abuse, violate, exploit, or execute even the most miserable and guilty specimen of a human being!" We can see this in one way when we are dealing with someone accused of a crime, imprisoned, subjected to slavery or forced labor, victimized by rape or torture, forced to submit to arranged marriages or liaisons, or denied the ability to participate by voice or vote in familial, political, or economic institutions that decide their fate. In these imposed situations, persons are functionally alone as they face a power they cannot control and to which they do not consent. Without knowing what the race, gender, nationality, cultural background, social location, political preferences, character, network of friends, or faith of a person may be, "some things ought never to be done to them." And if persons, to live and sustain some shred of dignity in the midst of some one or other of such situations need help, "some things ought to be done for them," as Michael Perry has put it.[13] This implies that other people and institutions have duties to limit their powers with regard to persons, and not to define the whole of the meaning of a person by the communities, traditions, and habits in which they are embedded. This means also that, in some ways, a profound individualism, in the sense of the moral inviolability of each person, in contrast to communitarian regard, is ethically required of all in regard to every other.

At other points, people abstract themselves from the matrices of life in which they dwell ordinarily, when they choose to leave home, get married (especially if the partner is one of whom the parents do not approve for reasons, say, of ethnicity), seek access to a profession other than that of the "station in life" into which they were born, decide to have or not to have a child by the use of pregnancy technology, and, most critical in many locales today, decide whether to follow the faith in which they were born and raised with dedication and devotion, or turn to another by overt rejection of the faith community in which they were raised or positive conversion to a faith that is new to them—that is, by joining the inchoate company of atheists or agnostics or joining another community of believers of a different sort. Here, in quite a different way than in some humanly imposed violation of person-hood, one stands as an individual before the deepest levels of his or her own soul and before God. People may be informed by other persons' advice, pleas, or arguments, and a person's community of origin may have rules and regulations about such things, but in the final analysis the individual person stands sociologically quite alone in such moments. All the current debates about "proselytism" and hence of the freedom of religion at the personal level are at stake here.[14] Moreover, this personal freedom implies the necessity of the right of people of like "chosen" faith to associate and form "voluntary associations" on religious grounds and to engage in free speech and press to seek to persuade others to join their faith.[15]

In these two areas of life, when people are under coercion that alienates them from their communities of life, or when they choose to leave their community of origin to join an alternative association of conscientious, committed orientation, they must have the right to do so. These two areas illustrate a certain "soul sovereignty" with regard to individual human rights that, if denied, leads to the dehumanization of humanity. From a Christian point of view, as it developed (all too slowly in consciousness and practice), each person must be free from the miseries of oppression and the threat of arbitrary destruction, and must have, at least, the basic rights also to form families, to find a calling, and to form associations, parties, unions, and advocacy groups to shape their political, economic, and cultural environments according to a personal understanding that is consistent with their convictions about what is the "best light." Christians hold that these matters ought not be matters of coercion, and that the use of it in these areas to force or restrict a person's decisions in such issues leads to a lie in the soul and the corruption of society. In this regard, a pluralism in civil society is fundamentally affirmed as a corollary of the faith. This makes the social embodiment of human rights more likely.

At the deeper, presuppositional level, Christians hold this view because we believe that each person is made in the "image of God," and that while every area of our life is at least imperfect, often distorted by sin and false desires or corrupted by exterior influences in sinful circumstances, the dignity conferred on us by the gift of the *"imago"* demands both a personal regard for each and social political arrangements to protect the relative capacities to reason, to choose, to work that are given with this gift. Moreover, Christians hold that each person is called into particular networks of relationships in which they may exercise these capacities and to order these networks by justice and with love, as God has loved us. We believe that in

Christ, we have seen how to reorder the institutions of life (some say sacra-mentally, others say covenantally) made under conditions of sin to preserve us, that we might make them more nearly approximate the redemptive pur-poses God has for the world. Those Christians who know the history of the development of the social and ethical implications of their faith, believe that the historical and normative defense of human rights derives from precisely these roots and that this particular tradition has, in principle, in spite of many betrayals of it by Christians, disclosed to humanity something univer-sally valid with regard to human nature and the necessities of just social exis-tence.[16] These principles were adopted into international law in the Helsinki Final Act of 1974, and have been accepted by many European churches which were established by the states and had not previously affirmed them.

Still a third implication for pluralism is signalled by the direct mention of the term "churches." I have elsewhere argued at some length that the for-mation of the Christian church, anticipated in certain sociological ways, of course, in the older traditions of the synagogues and, to a degree, in the ancient Mediterranean mystery cults and Asian monastic traditions, was a decisive influence in the formation of pluralistic democracy and in the gen-eration of civil society with legal protection of the rights of free associa-tion.[17] I shall not speak extensively about these matters here. Still, I think it fair to claim that the formation of the church as an institution was a revolu-tionary moment. It was differentiated from both familial-ethnic identity and from imperial political authority in early Christianity by slowly making the claim stick that the church as the Body of Christ had a sovereignty of its own. This was reinforced later in those now obscure ancient struggles between pope and emperor, bishop and king, and preacher and prince, and again more fully in the modern Protestant, especially Puritan and Pietist, demanding of the right to form congregations outside of state authorization in struggles for tolerance. This development has, in a long history, generated a social fabric where multiple independent institutions can flourish.[18] This has not only led to a civil society in which colleges and universities, multi-ple political parties, a variety of economic corporations, and a mass of self-governing charitable and advocacy groups are formed, it has established the legitimacy of their claims to rights as associations with their own purposes. Indeed, it has made for a kind of pluralism in those parts of the world where these influences are most pronounced that provides the safest havens for non-Christian religions to flourish without political control. The empirical consequence is that the Christian faith and its concrete social embodiment in the church, for all the ambiguities, foibles, and outright betrayals of Chris-tianity's own best principles (this faith did not abolish original sin, after all, not even among its adherents), has opened the door to the development of dynamic pluralistic democratic polities that are both protected *by* human rights ideals and laws and provide the organizational infrastructure for the protection *of* human rights of both persons and of groups.

Two related problems in this area face us as we face a global future. One is the basic question as to whether we can form a global civil society that does not have a theologically based inner moral architecture at its core. Historically, no society has ever existed without a religion at its center and no complex civilization capable of including many peoples and subcultures within it has endured without a profound and subtle religiously oriented philosophy or theology at its core.

Indeed, if the current trend toward globalization does continue, it will have to develop some kind of political order beyond the present arrangement of relative anarchy by sovereign nations with provisional agreements around limited shared interests—such as the IMF or WTO. After all, some civilizations have seemed to have been repeatedly renewed by the development of doctrines and innovative social institutions based in its deepest heritage while others seem incapable of perpetual self-reformation. The present worldwide rhetoric and legal agenda of human rights, with its several "generations" of rights is, I believe, most deeply grounded in a highly refined critical appropriation of the biblical traditions, one that can be of great help. However, many of the current activists on behalf of human rights have little place for religion or theology in their conception of what they advocate. Can human rights principles become more effective without attention to their roots and justifying ultimate legitimations? I seriously doubt it.

However, if human rights are universal in principle and the biblical and theological traditions here identified provide a very strong, possibly the best, grounds for recognizing and enacting them in social history, as I have suggested, we still have to ask what this means for those religions, philosophies, and cultures not shaped by this legacy. I am personally convinced of the fact that the theological motifs I have identified as biblical and theological are, in this area of thought and action, scripted into the deepest levels of the human soul, even if they are overlaid by obscuring other doctrines, dogmas, practices, and habitual ways of thinking in many of the traditions of the world's religions—including some branches of Judaism and Christianity. Thus our task is to identify where, in the depths of these traditions, that residual capacity to recognize and further refine the truth and justice of human rights insights lies, for this is necessary in order to overcome what, otherwise, is likely to be a perilous "clash of civilizations." And even if, God willing, we are able to survive such a clash, it is these motifs that could, more than any other option, provide a model for a just reconstruction of a global civil society.

NOTES

1. Although deeply engaged in the movement for civil rights in the 1960s, as led by Martin Luther King Jr., my experiences in India and the old East Germany in the 1970s forced the question to the level of human rights. The results of my explorations led to "Some Intellectual and Social Roots of Modern Human Rights Ideas," *Journal for Scientific Study of Religion* 20, 4 (Dec., 1981): 301–309, then to *Creeds, Society, and Human Rights* (Grand Rapids, MI: Eerdmans, 1984), and several related subsequent efforts.

2. ENI (Ecumenical News Information) reported that Dalits in India rejoiced when a UN Committee voted in September, 2002, to classify "casteism" as "racism." Caste has been recognized as evil cross-culturally.

3. A fascinating recent account is Mary Ann Glendon, *The World Made New: Eleanor Roosevelt and the Universal Declaration of Human Rights* (New York: Random House, 2001). The British scholar, Canon John Nurser presently has researched also the Protestant influence on the historic idea of human rights used in drafting the UN Declaration, a theme not fully developed in Glendon's work, but already present in A.S.P. Woodhouse, *Puritanism and Liberty* (London: Dent, 1938); and James Hastings Nichols, *Democracy and the Churches* (Philadelphia: Westminster, 1943).

4. Hans Küng, ed., "Parliament of World Religions' Global Ethic," *National Catholic Reporter* (Sept. 24, 1993), pp. 1lf. See also his *Global Responsibility: In Search of a New World Ethic* (New York: Crossroad, 1991); *A Global Ethic for Global Politics and Economics* (New York: Oxford, 1997). These are deeply related to his earlier works, one with Josef van Ess et al., *Christianity and the World Religions: Paths to Dialogue with Islam, Hinduism, and Buddhism* (New York: Doubleday, 1986); and another with Julia Ching, *Christianity and Chinese Religions* (New York: Doubleday, 1989). Similarly, the Millennium World Peace Summit of Religious and Spiritual Leaders, meeting in Moscow in November of 2001, declared that "Believers have a right to make their lives conform with their beliefs. But no one has a right to use their beliefs to take the lives or violate the rights of others. No religion allows for that." [peacesummit@ruderfinn.com]

5. See, e.g., John Witte Jr., "A Dickensian Era of Religious Rights: An Update on *Religious Human Rights in Global Perspective*," *William and Mary Law Review* 42, 3 (March, 2001): 707–70; and his "God's Joust, God's Justice: The Revelations of Legal History," *Princeton Seminary Bulletin* 20, 3 (1999): 295–313, which have informed the views contained in this chapter at several points.

6. Most Christians hold that this adoption or "baptism" of nonbiblical ideas that are compatible with the universalist moral and spiritual insights of

the Gospel is quite possible, and sometimes able to refine what the tradition held reflexively, that is themes that are anticipated in earlier portions of the Bible itself, perhaps especially in the Wisdom literature. It was extended in the traditions that developed after the fuller formation of Judaism and Christianity in the selective embrace of Greek philosophy, Roman Law, and, later, certain social theories from northern European cultures. (See note 3, above.) This tendency to recognize and honor universalistic norms is being further extended today as converts from many cultures bring other philosophical, moral, social, and even religious insights with them into contemporary theological understanding. See my *God and Globalization*, vol. 3, *Christ and the Dominions of Civilization*, ed. with Diane Obenchain (Harrisburg, PA: Trinity Press International, 2002). The famous passage in Acts 2, where all the gathered people are inspired to understand the preaching "in their own language," is being reenacted in many places outside the West.

7. In this regard, the great Jewish jurist of the nineteenth century, Georg Jellinek, was surely correct in his *Die Erklärung der Menschen- und Bürgerrechte: Ein Beitrag zur modernen Verfassungsgeschichte* (Leipzig, 1895), that the roots of modern views of human rights are utterly dependent on Jewish roots and Christian developments.

8. The idea of "natural law" and its relationship to theology has been debated for centuries and is subject to many interpretations—complicated by the rise of modern scientific views of the "laws of nature" that have no ethical content. I intend the use most common in jurisprudence, an appeal to universal principles of justice discernable by reason, a usage that leaves open the question of whether or not they, and the capacity to discern them, are given by God. The ethical traditions of natural law that have given rise to modern concepts of human rights are essentially theological in nature, as we can see in the Roman Catholic and the Calvinist heritage. The instability in the concept often derives from the ignoring or denial of this historical fact. See the cluster of books that came out to celebrate the fiftieth anniversary of the United Nations Declaration of Human Rights, e.g., Brian Tierney, *The Idea of Natural Rights* (Atlanta: Scholars, 1997), Guenther Haas, *The Concept of Equity in Calvin's Ethic* (Waterloo, Ontario: Wilfred Laurier University Press, 1997), Knud Haakonssen, *Natural Law and Moral Philosophy* (Melbourne: Cambridge University Press of Australia, 1996); and the increasing conversation between these traditions, Michael Cromartie, ed., A *Preserving Grace: Protestants, Catholics, and Natural Law* (Grand Rapids, MI: Eerdmans, 1997).

9. Some of these objections to human rights are catalogued and critiqued in "Religion and Human Rights: A Discussion," with Louis Henkin, Vigen Guroian, John Langan, S.J. et al., *Journal of Religious Ethics* 26, 2 (Fall, 1998): 229–71. I attempted to address with some of the key objections in my

response, "The Intellectual Crisis of a Good Idea," ibid., as well as in "Religion and Human Rights: A Theological Apologetic" with S. Healey, *Religious Human Rights In Global Perspective*, ed. J. Witte and J. van der Vyver. (The Hague: Martinus Nijhoff, 1996), 485–516; and, "Human Rights and Public Theology: The Basic Validation of Human Rights," *Religion and Human Rights: Competing Claims?* ed. Carrie Gustafson and Peter Juviler (New York: Sharp, 1999), pp. 12–30.

10. This view is argued by Alasdair MacIntyre, *After Virtue* (Notre Dame, IN: University of Notre Dame Press, 1981), who after years advocating Hegel, Marx, and Nietzsche, attacks both Protestantism and the Enlightenment, especially as represented by Kant, which he says generated the Modernity that led to the terrors of the twentieth century (ignoring the fact that the statism of imperial Germany, which Hegel approved, the socialism of Marx, and the nihilism of Nietzsche all sought to dismantle the Christian and Enlightenment defenses of human rights against these forces of terror). Other noted critics of the rights traditions are Michael Sandel (vs. John Rawls), Selya ben Habib (vs. Jürgen Habermas), and Stanley Hauerwas (vs. Reinhold Niebuhr). Certain parallel discussions appear in Asian philosophy: see, e.g., Wm. T. de Bary and Tu Wei Ming, eds., *Confucianism and Human Rights* (New York: Columbia University Press, 1998), and Gustafson and Juviler, op. cit.

11. John Kelsey and Sumner Twiss, eds., *Religion and Human Rights* (New York: Project on Religion and Human Rights, 1994), p. 38.

12. This "ethical trinity" of moral judgment is one of the basic themes of my teaching and writing, and is most recently presented in *God and Globalization*, 3 vol. (Harrisburg, PA: Trinity Press International, 2000, 2001, 2002).

13. The masterful treatment of the ethical implications of policies and judgments based on human rights and their religious foundations are summarized as "Some things ought not to be done to anyone, and some things should be done for everyone" (which implies "anyone"), in Michael Perry, *Religion and Human Rights: Four Inquiries* (New York: Oxford University Press, 1999). See also the forum on this work, *Journal of Law and Religion* 14, 1 (1999–2000): 1–120.

14. John Witte Jr. and R. C. Martin, eds., have collected a remarkable series of essays on this issue from Jewish, Christian, and Islamic perspectives: *Sharing the Book: Religious Perspectives on the Rights and Wrongs of Proselytism* (Maryknoll, NY: Orbis, 1999).

15. A useful collection of essays debating these points, their origins and implications for the present, can be found in R. C. White and A. G. Zimmerman, eds., *An Unsettled Arena: Religion and the Bill of Rights* (Grand Rapids, MI: Eerdmans, 1989). I think the evidence is convincing that the

entire First Amendment to the United States Constitution—which has been the model for United Nations agreements and hosts of new constitutions in emerging democracies around the world—and not only the so called establishment and free exercise clauses—derive from this theological view of human rights with these implications.

16. The antichurch policies of the French Revolution with its "Declaration of the Rights of Man," asserted on antitheological, positive law grounds, in contrast to some dominant theocratic views of Christianity of the time, prompted the established churches in Europe to resist human rights arguments for several centuries, with disastrous results. But the longer and deeper legacy of the tradition has reasserted itself, as mentioned above. However, the major Christian traditions, led in large measure by the work of Catholic Jacques Maritain and Protestant Charles Malik, have recovered and recast the legacy of their deeper insights in a series of teachings and authoritative statements: Walter Abbot and Joseph Gallagher, *"Dignitatis Humanae"* (Vatican Declaration on Human Freedom, 1965); see also George Weigel & Robert Royal, *A Century of Catholic Social Thought* (Washington: Ethics and Public Policy Center, 1991); David Hollenbach, *Claims in Conflict: Retrieving and Renewing the Catholic Human Rights Tradition* (New York: Paulist Press, 1991); World Council of Churches, *Human Rights and Christian Responsibility* (Geneva: World Council of Churches, 1976); Allen O. Miller, ed., *A Christian Declaration of Human Rights: Theological Studies of the World Alliance of Reformed Churches* (Grand Rapids, MI: Eerdmans, 1977); Lutheran World Federation, *Theological Studies of Human Rights* (Minneapolis: Fortress, 1978).

17. Note 1, supra; also, e.g., "Piety, Polity, and Policy," in *Religious Beliefs, Human Rights, and the Moral Foundations of Western Democracy*, ed. C. Esbeck (Columbia, MO: University of Missouri Press, 1987), pp. 13–26; and "Christianity, Civil Society, and the State: A Christian Perspective," *Civil Society and Government; The Ethikon Series*, vol 5, ed. Nancy Rosenblum and Robert Post (Princteon and Oxford: Princeton University Press, 2002), 255–65.

18. For key historic documents of this development see A. S. P. Woodhouse, op. cit. See also Michael Walzer, *The Revolution of the Saints* (New York: Athenium, 1968); and Robert N. Bellah, David Hollenbach, et al., *Christianity and Civil Society: Boston Theological Institute Series, Vol. 4*, ed. R. L. Peterson (Maryknoll, NY: Orbis, 1995).

CHAPTER 4

Theology, Tolerance, and
Two Declarations of Human Rights

An Interrogative Comparison

SUMNER B. TWISS

INTRODUCTION

The Universal Declaration of Human Rights by the World's Religions (hereinafter UDHRWR) is in explicit conversation with the 1948 Universal Declaration of Human Rights (hereinafter UDHR).[1] Not only was the UDHRWR promulgated on the fiftieth anniversary of the UDHR, but also its preamble specifically cites the UDHR, taking apparent issue with the UDHR's approach and attempting to supplement its shortcomings. In this chapter I want to elucidate certain theological and quasi-theological interventions in the debate surrounding the adoption of the UDHR in an effort to comprehend and assess the value of selected emendations to the UDHR proposed by the UDHRWR.

The principal emendations are threefold, two of which are stated quite clearly in the preamble to the UDHRWR: (1) human rights are properly inspired by and grounded in sources both human and divine, and (2) human rights are integrally related to human duties in conception and execution.[2] The third type of emendation involves certain substantive articles of the UDHRWR which address, for example, the nondenigration of religion and the activities of religious proselytization. Given the apparent complaints that the UDHR offensively excludes the world's religions as positive resources for human rights, myopically separates rights and duties, and fails to address adequately what are sometimes called "religious"

55

human rights, it might come as a surprise that these matters were carefully and repeatedly considered by the Third Committee, which brought the UDHR to the floor of the UN General Assembly after lengthy debate, and further, that much of the relevant debate had theological overtones.[3] Revisiting this discussion will, I believe, put us in a better position to evaluate the accuracy of the aforementioned complaints and thus of the wisdom of the proposed changes or additions. In my reconstruction and analysis of the Third Committee's discussion, the presence of theological claims will be clear. It does seem important to note, however, that the participants were not, by and large, professional theologians or philosophers; they spoke as "lay" persons interested in reflecting what they and others took broadly as characteristic of the wisdom housed in their respective religious and cultural traditions. Furthermore, some of the theological overtones can only be identified by inference from the theological heritage of certain delegations and their principal constituencies.

PRELIMINARY DEBATE

The debate of the Third Committee began with a rather free-ranging discussion of the role and nature of the proposed UDHR. Nonetheless, for our purposes, it is crucial to note that various delegations constantly returned to three major themes: (1) a proposed theological grounding of human rights; (2) a concern to identify "social duties" in addition to human rights; and (3) a perceived need for the declaration to be crafted in such a manner as to accommodate and be acceptable to diverse ideologies and philosophies. On the first point, the Pakistani representative, for example, declared: "Whenever liberty, equality, and fraternity were threatened, the divine element in men manifested itself. Such a crisis [Nazi atrocities] had arisen, but man, created in God's image, would save the world from bondage and ensure the birth of a new and better civilization." The Brazilian delegate later took this claim even further by proposing "in order to safeguard the rights it proclaimed" that the UDHR "should include, in the preamble, a reference to God as the absolute origin of the rights of man and of all rights. That would be an acknowledgment of the importance of the great spiritual trends toward the maintenance and development of international cooperation among nations."[4]

With respect to the second point, some delegations, particularly from Latin America, proposed listing social duties in addition to human rights within the declaration. The Argentinean representative, for example, said that "the declaration should contain an enumeration of social rights . . . and should also, possibly in a separate chapter, list the social duties which men must assume if the corresponding rights were to be guaranteed." The Cuban representative concurred, saying that "the text of the declaration [should] indicate precisely what the duties were." So too, the representative of the Dominican Republic said: "equal rights naturally entailed equal obligations and her delegation would accept any amendment intended to make that fact clear." She was subsequently joined by the Paraguayan representative who asserted that "the declaration of human rights should be accompanied by a similar declaration on the duties of man."[5] In large part, these proposals were likely inspired by the 1948 American Declaration of the Rights and Duties of Man (also known as the Bogota declaration), which had separate chapters listing rights and then duties.[6] Although this latter declaration is said to owe much to the influence of socialism in Latin America,[7] I cannot help but reflect on the fact that many of the delegations in both Bogota and the UN represented countries having large Roman Catholic constituencies and thus for that reason were interested in giving equal weight to human rights and duties. The Roman Catholic social tradition (like many other religious traditions) is communitarian in outlook with a special concern for duties to community and the common good. As if to highlight this possible connection in the Third Committee discussion, the representative from Belgium (another Catholic country) observed that "while Article [29] mentioned man's duties to the community, no mention was made of his duties towards his neighbor, his family, or himself. In dealing with that subject, mankind had as yet been unable to improve upon the precept underlying the Ten Commandments: 'Thou shalt love thy neighbor as thyself.'"[8]

With regard to the third theme—acceptability of the declaration to diverse peoples and ideologies—Santa Cruz (Chile) was perhaps the most pointed and eloquent: "In preparing a declaration of human rights . . . it had been necessary to reconcile the different ideologies of the Soviet Union and other Eastern European countries and of other Members of the UN; the difference between the economic and social rights recognized by Christian Western civilization and those recognized by the Oriental civilization."[9] Other delegates, including those from China, Belgium, and Guatemala, offered similar observations about the importance of crafting a declaration that would be acceptable to diverse cultures, ideologies, and traditions.

These three issues—theological grounding, duties corresponding to rights, and a concern to accommodate ideological diversity—subsequently reappear in the committee's debates over Article 1 (grounds for human rights), Article 18 (religious freedom and tolerance), and Article 29 (duties and communities). It is important to be aware of the tenor of these later debates and how they were resolved, in order to assess properly their reemergence in the UDHRWR. As we will see, the delegates of the Third Committee greatly sharpened their thinking about the three themes at issue.

ARTICLE 1

The text of Article 1 as finally adopted by the Third Committee and General Assembly reads as follows: "All human beings are born free and equal in dignity and rights. They are endowed with reason and conscience and should act toward one another in a spirit of brotherhood."

Serious controversy over this article was initiated by a Brazilian proposal to add the language that "all human beings are created in the image and likeness of God," which in that delegation's view expressed not only the religious sentiments of the Brazilian people but also those shared by all peoples.[10] The Argentinean, Columbian, and Bolivian delegations joined in support of Brazil's proposal, with some sympathy but not formal support expressed by the Lebanese delegate. Taken collectively the reasons for advancing this theological intervention were threefold, involving, respectively, (1) a factual claim, (2) a moral-psychological claim, and (3) a justificatory claim. In laying out the nature of these claims, I will cite, without specific attribution, some of the actual language used by supporters of the amendment.

The factual claim was this: "the amendment refers to a belief shared by all the peoples of the world, a belief which all hold in common," with the clear implication that this consensus therefore constitutes a sound starting point for thinking about issues of our humanity and equality before God. The moral-psychological claim was that "religion gives man the inspiration he needs to follow in paths of peace" and provides "proper guidance by evangelical principles . . . not unlike the Ten Commandments." The point here is that religious beliefs of the sort invoked have historically provided a psychological impetus and guide to right moral conduct, which in turn establishes the basis for peace. And the third more justificatory consideration was this: "Article 1 would be given additional strength by reference to God, for then the whole declaration would rise above mere politics . . . and convey an element of universality, a breath of the divine," thereby "rooting human equality at a deep level." That is, reference to religious belief of this sort would provide an absolute grounding for the declaration beyond the level of mere contingent politics or secular ethics because it locates human rights and equality in the deepest possible source—"the positive reality of God."[11]

Remarkably, at the same time that these reasons were being advanced, the very same delegations were at pains to emphasize that "there is no need to fear the results of such a reference to God, since freedom of religion is guaranteed in a subsequent article [18] and all groups can still profess whatever faith or philosophy they choose."[12] I say "remarkably" because much time would elapse before the Third Committee actually took up and debated the article on freedom of religion. That article's force, then, was being invoked at the outset of the Third Committee's deliberations even before its consideration and adoption. The intention of the theologically inclined delegations was not at first blush to commit an act of religious intolerance, but rather to provide what they regarded as the most stable basis—pragmatically, psychologically, and religiously—for the human rights recognized by the UDHR. As we will see, other delegations did not see the issue in the same way.

The counterresponse to this theological intervention was led by a veritable coalition of delegations, involving Belgium, Cuba, China, Ecuador, Uruguay, the USSR, the UK, the United States, India, and France, which were joined by yet others in a less robust manner—for example, Chile, Mexico, and Saudi Arabia. Before I detail the counterresponse, I believe we should take note of the East-West, North-South array of countries and traditions involved—Christianity, Confucianism, Marxist socialism, Hinduism, Buddhism, and Islam—a fact which belies the common perception (and criticism) that the UDHR is an exclusively Western product and document. As might be anticipated from such a diverse coalition, the counterresponse took a variety of forms, chief among which were: a factual counterclaim to a religious *consensus gentium*, a charge of religious intolerance and coercion, a pragmatic moral vision about the universality of human rights, and a theological criticism. Let me take each of these in turn.

On the matter of a supposed universal religious-theological consensus, the coalition delegates rebutted this claim by pointing to the manifest fact of diversity about religion throughout the world, which, if the amendment were pressed, "would undermine the declaration's universal acceptance by the world's peoples" for the simple reason that "they have different [foundational] beliefs about man's origins as well as the origins of human rights." Moreover, invoking the themes of religious intolerance and freedom of religion, as well as the yet undebated Article 18, the coalition members charged the promoters of the theological amendment with not "showing equal consideration for other traditions" and with taking a course of action that bordered on religious intolerance and coercion—"an attempt to try to force one's own faith on others, reverting to concepts current at the time of the crusades." The third counterresponse imbedded a pragmatic moral vision of the UDHR that was shared by delegations both East and West; namely, "although it might be possible to reach agreement on fundamental practical principles [or "ideals of social justice and freedom"] that could be endorsed by believers and non-believers alike, it would be useless to try to reach agreement on their origins," because there are so many different philosophies, religions, and ideologies in the world. In making this point, the Chinese delegate cited his own Confucian tradition, the Indian delegate cited the multiple traditions she represented, and the French delegate even invoked the moral authority of "that great Catholic thinker Jacques Maritain," who had taken a similar position at a concurrent UNESCO symposium on the philosophical and religious bases of human rights. Finally, there was an interesting theological response put forward by the Ecuadorian delegate that "the Committee should distinguish between divine and human and should refrain from placing the divine on a political plane by introducing it into the declaration," with the clear implication that divine nature or authority would be denigrated by subjecting it to a political vote.[13]

The debate ended with myriad calls for acting "in the spirit of tolerance" and with the Brazilian delegation, in that spirit, withdrawing its proposed amendment, even before it could be voted on. The amendment's other supporters concurred in that withdrawal in the same spirit of tolerance and cooperation. In light of what I have recounted here, I think it is not too much of a stretch to say that in debating Article 1 the Third Committee's delegates on both sides of the issue not only acted in the spirit of religious tolerance but also were guided in their thinking by the UDHR's article on religious freedom and tolerance, which they had surely read but not yet formally considered. Article 18 was a background force in the debate, which is a likely indication of its importance in mitigating interreligious conflict.

Before we turn to consider the Third Committee's discussion of Article 18, it seems pertinent to report that the substance of the preceding debate recurred at the very end of the committee's deliberations, when it took up the question of what should and should not be included in the UDHR preamble. In this instance, the delegate from the Netherlands proposed amending the preamble by including a clause affirming "the relation existing between the Creator and man," for in a declaration of human rights "the whole nature of man should be described, and that could only be done by giving that nature a comprehensive definition," thereby recognizing "the fundamental relations existing between man and his Creator." In this case the intent for including such a reference was mainly justificatory, for the Netherlands delegate went on to argue that "it would be illusion to think it possible to draft a declaration of human rights, without referring to metaphysical data," and since human dignity and equal human rights "derived from the nature of man and since that dignity was inherent in man, by his very nature, one could not but ask what that nature was." Furthermore, "in order to fulfill his destiny, man must comply with many obligations towards his Creator, his fellow human beings, society . . . and the community of nations. . . . It was precisely in order to enable him to fulfill his obligations that man possessed inherent and inalienable rights." This argument was supplemented by the Brazilian delegate in the following manner: "From time immemorial, man had been attempting to set out his thoughts [about rights and freedoms and the dignity and worth of the human person], and that effort would not have been made had he not been of divine origin. . . . The Netherlands amendment would have the effect of relating the declaration to the human conscience and because that was the element which bound people together the declaration would thus become more understandable to [those] for whom it was intended."[14]

There is a complex set of claims and arguments being advanced here, and if only for clarity it would be useful to sort them out. First, one claim is that since human rights inhere in human nature, and since that nature is of divine origin, so too are human rights of divine origin (an ontological argument). Second, since human destiny involves fulfilling moral obligations to the Creator and the human community, and since obligation fulfillment involves the freedom, security, and integrity necessary to do so, human rights are justified by that destiny—they are requisite for fulfilling human destiny as established by the creator (a teleological argument). Third, human rights are the manifestation of a God-given human conscience, and recognizing this is what binds people together in the common effort of building a truly humane world (an epistemic argument). Here I would observe that these theological justifications proffered for human rights appear considerably more sophisticated than in the earlier debate over Article 1—more sophisticated but still not convincing enough to other Third Committee members.

Although a considerable number of other delegates expressed personal sympathy for the Netherlands proposed amendment, because, in the words of the Belgian delegate, "it provided the idea of the equality of man with perhaps the only possible ultimate argument," even the sympathizers acknowledged that "the proposal raised a very delicate philosophical problem . . . that it would be inconceivable . . . to try to solve . . . by a vote." And once again a veritable coalition of delegates resisted the amendment on the grounds of toleration for religious (and nonreligious) diversity in the world. The Indian delegate, for example, declared that "India was a secular state, in which numerous creeds, ranging from animism to atheism, were practiced. The declaration, which was to be universally applicable, could not make a dogmatic statement on that point." The French delegate concurred, arguing that "It was necessary for the declaration to be acceptable to as many governments as possible so that there might be the most favorable circumstances for its implementation." The Ukrainian delegate charged that the amendment "violated the right to freedom of conscience." The UK delegate argued that "to include the concept of God in the declaration might rouse the opposition of delegations representing more than half of the world's population" and that "if the declaration was to have a universal character the views of those delegations should be respected." And, for a final example, the Chilean delegate "recalled that Chile, where the bulk of the nation was sincerely Catholic, had no mention of Providence in its constitution, out of

respect for the convictions of an important minority," and "for similar reasons, Chile would not support the Netherlands amendment."[15]

The upshot of the debate was similar to that surrounding Article 1:
the Netherlands withdrew its proposed amendment. Implicit in the
counterresponses to the proposed theological interventions is the position
that while theological grounds for human rights can be entertained and
accepted by delegations so inclined, these delegations have no right to
force their views—by insisting on their inclusion within a declaration
intended for a diverse world—on other delegations which might entertain
and accept different grounds. Thus, in the spirit of tolerance based on
mutual respect for freedom of religion and conscience, the Third Committee eschewed building into the declaration any explicit type of philosophical or religious justification.

ARTICLE 18

It seems clear, then, from the preceding discussions about the role and limits
of theological appeals in Article 1 and the preamble, that the delegates were
very concerned to protect freedom of religion and conscience and to foster a
robust notion of religious (and nonreligious) tolerance. Indeed, as we have
seen, Article 18 was invoked—whether explicitly or implicitly—in both of
the debates. Thus, it seems relevant to consider the debate over Article 18
itself, however briefly, in order to appreciate fully its role in the Third Committee's discussions. I will begin by briefly sketching that debate and its resolution—carrying over even to the floor of the General Assembly—and
then return to focus certain points that may be relevant to later understanding and evaluating certain aspects of the UDHRWR.

Article 18 as both first introduced and finally adopted reads as follows:
"Everyone has the right to freedom of thought, conscience, and religion; this
right includes freedom to change one's religion or belief, and freedom, either
alone or in community with others and in public or private, to manifest his
religion or belief in teaching, practice, worship, and observance." It is clear
from the historical record that the vast majority of delegations regarded this
article as one of the most important in the UDHR because, to cite representative comments, it "ensured the inviolability of that profound part of
thought and conscience" and "the integrity of individual beliefs making it
possible for each to determine his or her destiny."[16] The Third Committee
members were fully cognizant of the fact that past violations of such a principle had often been bound up with warfare and imperialist oppression. It is
unnecessary to cite here the many historical cases of abuse and conflict men-

tioned by the various delegations. Amid, however, these sorts of concerns, the Saudi Arabian delegate proposed a change to the article involving initially the deletion of everything after the opening clause and then modified to deleting only the phrase "freedom to change one's religion or belief."

The purported reason for this proposal was that explicitly protecting "the freedom to change one's religion" opened the door to "missionary abuses" and provided "an easy pretext for inciting hatred and encouraging dangerous difference of opinion." Subsequently, however, as debate over this amendment progressed, it became clear that the Saudi delegate regarded the provision protecting the freedom to change one's religion as "offending the religious beliefs of Moslems" the world over, because, according to him, the right to change one's religion was not recognized in Islamic law.[17] The Saudi proposal was supported by Iraq and Syria, with some sympathy (but not formal support) expressed by Greece and Cuba. The rest of the delegations roundly challenged the proposed deletion on the grounds that it essentially eviscerated the meaning of religious freedom, violated the inviolable (i.e., freedom of conscience), and if adopted could (ironically) lead to religious conflict in the future by so weakly defining and protecting freedom of conscience and religion. Interestingly, in this debate no alternative Islamic position was offered, and it was the Chinese delegate, invoking the thought of Confucius on "pluralistic tolerance" (implicitly referring to *Analects* 6:22), who developed the most robust critique of the Saudi proposal.[18] The amendment was defeated by an overwhelming vote amid many claims that the spirit of religious tolerance justified such action.

In this case the debate over Article 18 did not end with the Third Committee's deliberations, but carried over into the General Assembly's discussion of the UDHR on December 10, 1948. There on the floor of the General Assembly, and explicitly referring to the Third Committee debate, the Pakistani delegate not only made it clear that Pakistan (an Islamic country) accepted the entire article as proposed but also wished to "defend the honor of Islam regarding the question of freedom to change one's religion or belief." In this regard, he explicitly argued that "neither faith nor conscience could have an obligatory character, for the Koran expressly said, 'Let he who chooses to believe, believe, and he who chooses to disbelieve, disbelieve,' and furthermore formally condemned not lack of faith but hypocrisy. . . . His delegation wanted to repeat that for its part the Moslem religion had unequivocally proclaimed the right to freedom of conscience and had declared itself against any kind of compulsion in matters of faith or religious practices."[19]

This subsequent intervention in the General Assembly, then, constituted a powerful Islamic response to the earlier Saudi amendment, calling into serious question whether the views of the Saudi delegate represented those of the entire Muslim world (as had been claimed) and effectively bringing Islam into the defense of the notion of religious tolerance.[20]

Having the contours of the Article 18 debate before us, I now want to focus on two of its features in a bit more detail. First, a subtext of the debate involved a rather consistent concern on the part of some delegates about the issues of religious proselytization and missionary activity. Much of this had to do with historical instances of religion wielding power in alliance with Western imperialism in less developed parts of the world: for example, "throughout history missionaries had often abused their rights by becoming the forerunners of a political intervention . . . [leading to] murderous conflict."[21] These sorts of claims were made in criticism of religious intolerance combined with imperialist oppression. Occasionally, however, the concern was more contemporary and less political, focusing on actual or potential interreligious competition. For example, the Greek delegate "wondered whether the phrase 'freedom . . . to manifest one's religion or belief' might not lead to unfair practices of proselytizing . . . he had occasion to observe religious competition in a country where all religions were represented . . . [where] free lodgings, material assistance and . . . other advantages were offered to persons who agreed to belong to one religion or another . . . he felt that the danger of such unfair practices was a threat, not only to minority groups . . . but also the religious majority."[22] Thus was posed the question as to whether or not to prohibit or otherwise limit in some manner religious proselytization. The Third Committee demurred from revising Article 18 to explicitly address this sort of concern largely because it felt first that, in the words of the Belgian delegate, "In professing or propagating a faith one could, to a certain extent, interfere with the freedom of others by seeking to impose an unfamiliar idea upon them. But proselytism was not limited to any one faith or religious group. If it was an evil, it was essentially an evil from which all sides had to suffer"; and second that, in the words of the Philippine delegate, referring to Article 29, "so long as attempts at religious proselytism remained within the limits of public order, freedom of thought was not threatened."[23]

The context for the latter remark is the second clause of Article 29, which expressly stipulates that "in the exercise of his rights and freedoms, everyone shall be subject only to such limitations as are determined by law solely for the purpose of securing due recognition and respect for the rights and freedoms of others and of meeting the just requirements of morality, public order, and the general welfare in a democratic society." This clause permits state regulation of religious activity when it manifestly interferes with the rights and freedoms of others in such a manner as to aversely affect the public order and the general welfare, subject to requirements of legal and democratic processes in developing such regulation. We will consider Article 29 in more detail shortly.

In adopting this position—and this is the second feature of the debate on which I want to focus—the delegates were led to make some surprisingly strong claims about humankind's spiritual capacities and development. For example, the Lebanese delegate asserted that "Even if the list of social, economic, political, and juridical rights of man were complete . . . it would count for nothing if men were denied freedom of thought and belief. Those were essential freedoms which made life richer and constituted the supreme goal of all aspirations . . . the freedom of thought and of conscience ensured the integrity of inward beliefs and the possibility for each individual to determine his own destiny . . . the freedom to change his belief . . . might be at the root of a new spiritual impulse." The Cuban delegate observed that "as a believer he wished to speak in the name of all men—for all, whether they knew it or not, had some kind of faith, even those who had no religious belief—and all could attain the same moral elevation. He therefore considered that no distinction should be made between the different faiths, which were all worthy of respect."[24] Such claims can be interpreted in two ways, which are not mutually exclusive. First, they may well represent theological claims, or at least theologically inspired claims, that are advanced to support equal respect for all fundamental beliefs, religious or otherwise. Second, whether or not they were theologically inspired, the fact that they were made and went unchallenged tends to show the immense (and equal) respect that all the delegates had for the development and expression of humanity's spiritual impulses.

ARTICLE 29

Article 29 of the UDHR as adopted reads as follows: "1. Everyone has duties to the community in which alone the free and full development of his personality is possible. 2. In the exercise of his rights and freedoms, everyone shall be subject only to such limitations as are determined by law solely for the purpose of securing due recognition and respect for the rights and freedoms of others and of meeting the just requirements of morality, public order and the general welfare in a democratic society. 3. These rights and freedoms may in no case be exercised contrary to the purposes and principles of the United Nations." The first clause stipulates that all people have duties to their communities, and it acknowledges in a communitarian manner that people can only develop and flourish as persons within community—an explicit rejection of atomistic individualism. The second clause sets limits on the exercise of individual human rights as defined by reciprocal respect for the rights of others as well as the just requirements of the commonweal as determined by law and a democratic process. The third clause sets the further limit that human rights cannot be exercised in a manner contrary to the purposes of the UN, which include international peace and security, promotion of equal human rights, establishing conditions of justice and respect, and promoting social progress, better standards of human life, and freedom.[25]

We have seen that at the outset of the Third Committee's deliberations many delegates were concerned that the UDHR enumerate in some way duties corresponding to rights. The motivations for such concern were various, ranging from a desire to avoid the appearance of excessive individualism, a desire to accommodate aspects of socialist thinking, a desire to build into the declaration a communitarianism possibly associated with religious worldviews. This concern was even expressed in debates over other UDHR articles. For example, in the debate over Article 1, the Chinese representative, who was much influenced by Confucian communitarianism, stated that "a happy balance was struck [in that article] by the broad statement of rights in the first sentence and the implication of duties in the second . . . the various rights would appear more selfish if they were not preceded by a reference to 'a spirit of brotherhood.'" He went on to say that "similar reasoning applied to Article [29], which contained a statement of duties."[26] The whole issue of duties and rights naturally resurfaced in the debate over Article 29 itself.

Before we revisit aspects of that debate, I should make it clear that by the time Article 29 was discussed, close to the conclusion of the Third Committee's work, it was pragmatically impossible for the committee to draft *de novo* a whole set of duties coordinate with the preceding articles and hope to meet the deadline imposed on it by the General Assembly. Thus much of the discussion devolved on insuring that the article had a communitarian dimension and that limitations on human rights did not leave a large loophole for government abuses of human rights. In so doing, the Third Committee paid considerable attention to semantic nuances of terms. In what follows I want to focus particular attention on the committee's discussion of two terms the inclusion of which had various advocates as well as critics: the term "alone" in the article's first clause (whose inclusion was adopted) and the term "solidarity" in the second clause (the proposal of which was not adopted). I will begin with the second proposal, since it came up first in the debate.

The Cuban, Brazilian, and Chilean delegates led the way in forcefully reraising the issue of citing precise human duties in addition to human rights. I interpret their collective interventions as reflecting the strong communitarian spirit of the Latin American delegations, which, as I suggested earlier, is significantly shaped by their Roman Catholic heritages and constituencies. So it is possible that theology may be at work here, albeit in a very subterranean manner, since theological discourse is nowhere used in this particular debate. At the outset of the debate, the Cuban delegate opined that the draft Article 29 "tended to give too much importance to the individualistic side of man's character" and then subsequently elaborated as follows: "the individual should also be reminded that he is a member of society and that he must affirm his right to be deemed a human being by clearly recognizing the duties which are corollaries of his rights." Supporting this view, the Brazilian delegate affirmed that "it is impossible to draw up a declaration of rights without proclaiming the duties implicit in the concept of freedom which made it possible to set up a peaceful and democratic society."[27] As I have already indicated, there was no time left for the Third Committee to develop a full list of such duties, and it may in part be for this reason—the historical record is unclear on this point—that the Chilean delegate proposed explicitly incorporating the language of "solidarity" in the second clause of the article, suggesting "the principle of solidarity" as an additional limitation on exercising one's rights and freedoms. Unfortunately, the record is also unclear on what precise meaning the Chilean delegate assigned to this term that is not covered by the notions of reciprocal respect and general welfare already in the clause. The proposed amendment was strongly supported by the Cuban delegate, who claimed that "solemn declaration of social solidarity would be a safeguard against the exaggerated individualism which had done so much ill."[28] Thus, I am inclined to interpret "solidarity" (or "the principle of solidarity") to mean the union of individual interests and responsibilities within a social group, wherein these are in reciprocal balance and fostered by a sense of group cohesion.

The response of many other delegations to this proposed language betrayed a similar degree of uncertainty as to its meaning, role, and implications. This response is well represented by the delegates from the United States, the UK, and the Philippines, respectively (I select these three for their clarity). Eleanor Roosevelt, who was certainly a friend to Latin America, asserted that "the word 'solidarity' was not generally used . . . except in the Western hemisphere" and that its inclusion might, when combined with notions of national sovereignty, "be used to justify arbitrary acts [of a government against its own people]." The UK delegate concurred in part, saying that "The word 'solidarity' had no meaning for a number of delegates; the concept, as explained by the Chilean representative, was covered by the basic text." And the Philippine delegate added that while the concept "would be most useful as part of the political vocabulary of the UN and of democratic society . . . it did not fit into the general structure of the declaration."[29] The inclusion of such language was rejected by majority vote.

This rejection should not be taken to mean that the Third Committee was somehow averse to communitarian thought, and it endeavored to make this clear by adopting another amendment originally proposed by Australia and later revived by the USSR. This amendment proposed inserting the phrase "in which alone the free and full development of his personality is possible" in the first clause of Article 29. As I suggested at the outset of this section of the chapter, this part of the first clause clearly acknowledges that people can only develop and flourish within the communities to which they have significant duties. The USSR delegate was particularly eloquent on capturing this meaning and implication: "The word 'alone' . . . seemed to him excellent. It rightly stressed the fact that the individual could not fully develop his personality outside society. The example of Robinson Crusoe [previously invoked by another delegate to challenge the sensibility of the clause] . . . had, on the contrary, shown that man could not live and develop his personality without the aid of society. Robinson had, in fact, had at his disposal the products of human industry and culture [from] . . . the wreck of his ship."[30] This proposed language of communitarian implication was strongly supported by many delegates, including the UK, France, and Lebanon, and was adopted by majority vote.

UDHRWR DECLARATION

The time has now come to see whether the preceding historical account and analysis of the UDHR can help in illuminating and assessing certain aspects of the more recent UDHRWR.[31] Any reasonable reading of the latter will reveal the following distinctive features: (1) an effort to ground human rights in the divinely inspired sources of the world's religions, combined with an implicit critique of the UDHR in failing to do this; (2) an attempt to coordinate systematically human rights with human duties—virtually article by article—combined with an implicit critique of the UDHR in failing to do this; and (3) an attempt to identify certain human rights and duties as distinctively informed by religious sources, notably including (but not restricted to) the nondenigration of one's religion and a limitation on proselytization, combined with an implicit critique of the UDHR in failing to explicitly address such matters.[32] Two systemic issues are raised by these features: Are the critiques of the UDHR warranted? Does the UDHRWR's method of redress make it somehow more adequate than the UDHR's approach to such matters?

The supposed failure of the UDHR to ground human rights in the world's religions betrays a significant misunderstanding of the Third Committee's intentions. While it is obviously true that the delegates resisted grounding these rights in any one philosophy or religious tradition—especially Christian theology—it did so for the purpose of allowing diverse cultures, religions, and philosophies to construe and justify their acceptance of human rights in their own unique ways. In effect, to use more contemporary terms, the committee achieved an overlapping consensus on human rights norms that specifically accommodates diverse comprehensive worldviews and justifications.[33] Far from offensively excluding the world's religions as positive resources for human rights, the committee advanced a vision of ideological tolerance precisely to be inclusive of various resources, including diverse religious traditions, for justifying and developing human rights norms and practices. That vision is compatible with—indeed encouraging of—a development such as that represented by the UDHRWR itself. The UDHRWR is redressing a nonexistent problem presumably posed by the UDHR. Furthermore, the supposed redress of appealing to inspiration both human and divine is itself problematic inasmuch as "divine" connotes a restriction to—or preference for—theistic traditions, whether of Abrahamic origin or otherwise (e.g., Hinduism), since it implicitly favors a notion of transcendent source or inspiration alien to some religious traditions, ranging across, for example, Confucianism, Buddhism, Taoism, and animism of varying types. In this regard—the avoidance of religious intolerance or preferential treatment—the UDHR appears more successful than the UDHRWR.

With respect to the coordination of human rights and duties, we encounter a different line of criticism of the UDHR. We have seen that this issue was of considerable concern to some Third Committee delegations, which were especially worried about avoiding the advocacy of an excessive individualism. But we have also seen that the latter worry was explicitly addressed by the Third Committee's building into Article 29 a communitarian understanding of the person and his or her rights and duties. Inasmuch as the UDHRWR seems to overlook or discount this fact, its implicit criticism of the UDHR in this regard misfires. Moreover, the criticism also appears to overlook or discount the fact that the UDHR was expressly designed to impose duties on *states* regarding the protection and advancement of human rights, in the belief that states and state agents were the primary violators of people's human rights and that the former ought to be the principal guarantors of such rights. The question remains as to whether the UDHRWR's explicit correlation of rights and duties—article by article—is somehow more adequate than the UDHR approach of attempting to bind state actors and of reserving the identification of individuals' duties to only one article. About this matter, two things must be noted. First, the UDHRWR nowhere explicitly singles out state actors as the primary and most powerful agents regarding the protection and advancement of human rights: this, I think, is a significant shortcoming, since the quality of achievement in human rights standards is largely dependent on state action (or inaction). Second, while I have no objection to coordinating individual human rights and duties article by article, it seems to me to be an unnecessarily cumbersome and redundant way to bring out the reciprocal and communitarian dimensions of rights and duties.

With regard to substantive articles of the UDHRWR, it must be conceded that some of these deal with matters not explicitly addressed by the UDHR, such as the duty to promote a constitutional global order (Article 15), the right to seek restitution for colonial and neocolonial wrongs (Article 8), the right to a just socioeconomic and political order at all levels of political organization (Article 28), and the right of the earth to rest (Article 24).[34] Some of these I regard as contestable—for example, it is not obvious, without considerable argument, that a single constitutional global order is either feasible or desirable (e.g., think about the effects of a world government gone awry); for another, it is not obvious what it means for the earth to have a right, nor whether if such a right exists, it is proper to call it a human right. The other rights mentioned above (restitution; just order) are matters which, while not in the UDHR explicitly, have been addressed by declarations and conventions subsequent to the UDHR.[35] The UDHR itself was only intended to get the ball rolling, so to speak, for a progressively developing and expanding human rights movement. As an integral part of that movement, it would be incorrect to view the UDHR as simply a static document unrelated to its progressive interpretation, refinement, and expansion in other conventions and treaties to which it was parent.

One additional substantive area in the UDHRWR—nondenigration of one's religion and placing limits on proselytization—was, as have seen, discussed by the Third Committee. I interpret this dimension of the UDHRWR as another implicit criticism of the UDHR's approach to such matters. I believe that the criticism is largely misguided, and it is not clear to me that the UDHRWR does any better in this substantive area. The criticism is misguided if it is predicated on the view that the UDHR fails to foster a robust position on the importance of respect and tolerance for all religious traditions—all the evidence cited in the historical analysis above points to the contrary. So I believe that the right not to have one's religion denigrated in the media or academia (Article 12) is quite compatible with the UDHR's notion of respect and tolerance, although it is not clear to me what advantage is gained by singling out such nondenigration. Nor is it clear to me what would be the threshold for the right's violation and how this would be balanced with freedom of thought and expression (Article

19).[36] I suspect that a violation would occur at the level of hate speech inciting to violence, in which case it seems to me that the UDHR's Article 29 takes care of that sort of violation through the limitations of its second clause. Similarly, while the UDHRWR stipulates that the attempt to prose-lytize against the will of another person amounts to arbitrary detention (Article 9), it seems to me that nothing is gained by singling out this viola-tion, rather than having a generic set of limitations on the exercise of rights such as the UDHR's Article 29.[37] I would also add that the UDHR is parent to a number of declarations and conventions dealing with specific issues of religious intolerance and discrimination against religious minorities in a more capacious manner.[38]

CONCLUSION

In summary, I believe that the preceding historical analysis of the Third Committee debates over the preamble and selected articles of the UDHR does much to illuminate the preamble and certain articles of the UDHRWR—that is, why the latter declaration emphasizes certain themes and why certain of its articles are cast in the way that they are. Moreover, knowledge of the details of the UDHR debates provides a useful perspective from which to evaluate the UDHRWR's own claims, explicit and implicit, and trajectories of protecting and promoting human rights. It is my hope that by comparing and contrasting the two declarations as I have done, I have offered something useful for further reflection on and refinement of the UDHRWR.[39]

NOTES

1. There are multiple sources for the texts of these two declarations. The ones used for this chapter were as follows: the UDHR as printed in Ian Brownlie and Guy S. Goodwin-Gill (eds.), *Basic Documents on Human Rights*, 4th ed. (Clarendon: Oxford University Press, 2002), pp. 18–23; the UDHRWR as printed in Joseph Runzo, Nancy M. Martin, and Arvind Sharma (eds.), *Human Rights and Responsibilities in the World Religions* (Oxford: Oneworld, 2003), pp. 141–47. All subsequent references to and quotations from these declarations are from these editions; as their pream-bles and articles are clearly identified, I will not give further citations.

2. The UDHRWR preamble in part reads as follows:

> "*Whereas* human beings are led to affirm that there is more to life than life itself by inspiration both human and divine;
>
> *Whereas* the Universal Declaration of Human Rights, as adopted by the General Assembly of the United Nations on December 10, 1948 bases itself on the former;
>
> *Whereas* any exclusion of the world's religions as positive resources for human rights is obnoxious to the evidence of daily life; . . .
>
> *Whereas* rights are independent of duties in their protection but integrally related to them in conception and execution; . . .

3. The "Third Committee" is shorthand for the Third Social and Humanitarian Committee of the General Assembly, which met and debated the UDHR draft from September to December 1948. The record of its deliberations was published in *Official Records of the Third Session of the General Assembly, Part I, Social, Humanitarian and Cultural Questions, THIRD COMMITTEE, Summary Records of Meetings 21 September–8 December, 1948, with Annexes* (Lake Success, NY: United Nations, 1948). It should be noted that these records represent a historical summary of proceedings, not necessarily a precise word-for-word transcription of quotations from speakers. Hereinafter I will cite this work as simply, *Third Committee*, followed by page references.

4. Preceding quotations from *Third Committee*, pp. 37 and 55.

5. Preceding quotations from *Third Committee*, pp. 38, 40, and 41.

6. The text of the 1948 Bogota declaration can be found in Brownlie and Goodwin-Gill, *Basic Documents*, pp. 665–70.

7. See, for example, Johannes Morsink, *The Universal Declaration of Human Rights: Origins, Drafting, and Intent* (Philadelphia: University of Pennsylvania Press, 1999), ch. 7.

8. *Third Committee*, p. 49.

9. *Third Committee*, p. 49.

10. *Third Committee*, p. 91.

11. Preceding quotations from *Third Committee*, pp. 109, 112, and 113.

12. *Third Committee*, p. 109.

13. Preceding quotations from *Third Committee*, pp. 96, 98, 100, 111, 116, and 117. Jacques Maritain's position was that a universal declaration of human rights should represent "a practical goal, agreement between minds can be reached spontaneously, not on the basis of common speculative ideas, but on common practical ideas, not on the affirmation of one and the same

conception of the world, of man and of knowledge, but upon the affirmation of a single body of beliefs for guidance in action"; for this quotation and Maritain's fuller position, see his Introduction to UNESCO (ed.), *Human Rights: Comments and Interpretations*, originally published in typescript by UNESCO (Paris, 1948), then by Columbia University Press (New York, 1949), and reprinted more recently by Greenwood Press (Westport, CT, 1973).

14. Preceding quotations from *Third Committee*, pp. 755–56 and 766.

15. Preceding quotations from *Third Committee*, pp. 760–61, 764, 767–68, 772, and 774.

16. *Third Committee*, pp. 398–99.

17. *Third Committee*, pp. 403–04.

18. The Chinese delegate in question was P. C. Chang, whose interpretation of *Analects* 6:22 ("Respect the Spirit as if the Spirit were there" [his own translation in an earlier publication]), was used by him to articulate a Chinese defense of humanistic tolerance for religious and philosophical pluralism against the proposed Saudi amendment. I have discussed Chang's argument and its background in some detail in an earlier essay, "P. C. Chang, Freedom of Conscience and Religion, and the Universal Declaration of Human Rights," *Chinese Studies Forum*, 3 (2002): 35–47.

19. Quotation from *U.N. Official Records, Third Session, 1948–49, Plenary*, pp. 889–91.

20. For an illuminating discussion of conservative versus liberal Islamic positions on this debate, see David Little, John Kelsay, and Abdulaziz Sachedin, *Human Rights and the Conflicts of Cultures: Western and Islamic Perspectives on Religious Liberty* (Columbia: University of South Carolina Press, 1988), pp. 33–52.

21. *Third Committee*, p. 391.

22. *Third Committee*, pp. 393–94.

23. *Third Committee*, pp. 395–96.

24. Preceding quotations from *Third Committee*, pp. 399 and 404.

25. On this last point see the preamble and chapter 1 of the 1945 *United Nations Charter* reprinted in Brownlie and Goodwin-Gill, *Basic Documents*, pp. 2–4.

26. *Third Committee*, p. 98.

27. Preceding quotations from *Third Committee*, pp. 642 and 646.

28. *Third Committee*, p. 656.

29. Preceding quotations from *Third Committee*, pp. 644 and 648.

30. *Third Committee*, pp. 659–60.

31. As I understand it, the UDHRWR is a document originally drafted by a number of scholars at a 1998 McGill University conference that is now being circulated to other scholars and religious communities for their

consideration and modification. As I am not privy to those conference proceedings—if in fact there are such (analogous to the Third Committee
debates)—I must perforce rely solely on the published declaration, together
with some subsequent commentary. See, for example, the articles in part 3 of
Runzo, Martin and Sharma, *Human Rights and Responsibilities*; notably the
articles by Arvind Sharma, Charlotte Elisheva Fonrobert, Jerry Irish, and
David W. Chapple.

32. See note 2 above.

33. Here I refer to the approach adapted from the work of John Rawls
on political liberalism by such figures as Charles Taylor and Amy Gutman,
among others. Although I myself have discussed this approach in a number
of venues, the most recent is my "History, Human Rights, and Globalization," *Journal of Religious Ethics* 32, 1 (Spring 2004): 39–70 (see especially
56–65).

34. These articles read in part (in chronological order of occurrence):

Article 8: "Everybody has the right to seek restitution for historical,
social, economic, cultural, and other wrongs."

Article 15: "Everyone has the duty to promote the emergence of a constitutional global order."

Article 24: "Everybody has the right to work and to rest . . . .The right
to rest extends to the earth."

Article 28: "Everyone has the right to socioeconomic and political order
at a global, national, regional, and local level which enables the realization
of social, political, economic, racial, and gender justice and the duty to give
precedence to universal, national, regional, and local interests in that order."

35. Here I am thinking about the numerous conventions regarding the
right to development and the draft declaration on the rights of indigenous
peoples: see Brownlie and Goodwin-Gill, *Basic Documents*, infra. I might also
mention that I have some reservations about the UDHRWR Article 28's pri-
oritization of universal, national, regional, and local interests, without further argument.

36. These UDHRWR articles read in part as follows:

Article 12: "Everyone has the right not to have one's religion denigrated
in the media or academia. It is the duty of the follower of every religion to
ensure that no religion is denigrated in the media or academia."

Article 19: "Everyone has the right to freedom of opinion and expression . . . provided that one conforms generally to the accustomed rules of
decorum recognized in the neighborhood."

37. UDHRWR Article 9 reads in part as follows: "No one shall be
restricted to arbitrary arrest, detention, or exile by the state or by anyone
else. The attempt to proselytize against the will of the person shall amount
to arbitrary detention."

38. Here I am thinking of later declarations and conventions relating to intolerance and discrimination based on religion and to the rights of minorities: again, see Brownlie and Goodwin-Gll, *Basic Documents*, infra.

39. I wish to express my gratitude to John Kelsay, Aline Kalbian, Sandy D'Alemberte, Michael Slater, and Patricia Twiss for their critical and helpful comments on an earlier draft of this chapter.

CHAPTER 5

Religion and Human Rights

A Personal Testament

DAVID LITTLE

The subject of religion and human rights is something in which I have
more than academic or professional interest. It is true I have invested
considerable time and energy to the question throughout my scholarly life.
In recent years, I have paid special attention to the more practical aspects;
namely, the degree to which states and other actors have actually complied
with the standards of religious freedom and equality enshrined in the international human rights documents. At the same time, I have come to see that
my efforts in this area are not "value-free"; in fact, they express a deeper
worldview that, for better or worse, I hold and am pleased to avow. In this
article I attempt to lay out the sources and features of that worldview.

As it happens, I am a committed Presbyterian layman, and have served
at various times as an officer in that church. That means I stand in what is
known as the "Reformed" tradition of Protestant Christianity, which stems
from the sixteenth-century French theologian and religious leader, John
Calvin (1509–1564). Calvin's general approach is summarized by the motto
ecclesia reformata semper reformanda—"the church reformed, ever reforming."
Those words signal Calvin's strong concern for church life and organization,
both as an expression of Christian commitment and as a model for social and
political life. Moreover, the motto implies Calvin's characteristic emphasis
on the obligation of Christians to act out their beliefs in institutional and
practical ways.

It was emphases like these, in addition to some much-disputed doctrines
concerning "predestination," the sovereignty of God, supremacy of scripture,

and the civil enforcement of Reformed orthodoxy, that set Calvin and his followers at odds with Roman Catholics of the day, as well as with other Protestant reformers, such as Martin Luther. Some of these predilections, including the way he implemented them, were responsible for giving Calvin what may charitably be called a controversial reputation.

During the latter part of the sixteenth century, the Calvinist movement gathered momentum, spreading throughout northern Europe to other parts of Switzerland, and to Germany, Holland, France, and Great Britain. Among other things, it had an important impact on seventeenth-century European colonial expansion, reaching far-flung places like the American middle colonies and South Africa (with some notorious consequences) via the Dutch, and the American colonies in New England via the British.

In my own case, the Puritan ancestors on my father's side settled in a town near Boston, Massachusetts, in the 1640s, and their descendents proceeded to fan out across what became the United States and to produce a prodigious number of Calvinist clergy, right up to the present. My father, recently deceased at age one hundred, was a Presbyterian clergyman, as were his father and four preceding generations before him, and as are several of my father's immediate descendents and near relatives. (When I once declared my own intention to become a Presbyterian minister—a declaration I never made good on—my father remarked that our family is in a rut!)

In Great Britain and eventually in America, Reformed Christians, known unflatteringly as "Puritans," split up into several subgroups over controversies about theology, church order, and the proper relation of the church to the state. As one of those subgroups, Presbyterians took their name from the Greek New Testament word, *presbyteros*, meaning "elder"; thus, Presbyterians are a church "ruled by elders." On the basis of Calvin's preference for a kind of democracy, elders came eventually to be elected by each local church; representatives were then selected from among those officials and they in turn were delegated to an ascending series of governing bodies. The system of church governance thus came to include a local "presbytery," a regional "synod," and a national "general assembly."

Accordingly, Presbyterians pride themselves on having been early proponents of representative democracy in both church and state, and there is some truth in that belief. At the same time, it should not be forgotten that in seventeenth-century England, Presbyterians were not unfairly regarded as staunch reactionaries who wanted—against the will of many—to force their church on the whole country, as they had already succeeded in doing in Scotland. The campaign to accomplish that end in the 1640s failed because of the resistance of fellow Calvinists (as well as non-Calvinists), some of whom favored a more liberal brand of democracy in church and state, and a more pluralistic social order, than did the English Presbyterians.

In America, Reformed Christianity, including the Presbyterian Church, has exhibited a similar pattern of internal division and tension. In the American Civil War, for example, Presbyterians, along with other churches, split over the question of slavery. Even today, Presbyterians are deeply divided into "liberal" and "conservative" wings, in part over questions of homosexuality and the role of women in the church, but also over broader theological, scriptural, and political issues.

I mention this contentious background because it provides the context within which my own Christian faith, and many of my professional interests including my devotion to human rights, have been negotiated. "Negotiated" is very much the right word. Ever since I was an adolescent struggling with questions of religious belief, I have been in dialogue with my tradition. I first became acquainted with it, of course, in my home and then at a Presbyterian school from which I graduated—the College of Wooster in Wooster, Ohio. I studied the tradition more closely at Union Theological Seminary in New York City, and more fully still at Harvard University, where I pursued a doctorate in Christian ethics and sociology of religion. At Harvard, I produced a dissertation that modified and partially defended Max Weber's famous essay *The Protestant Ethic and the Spirit of Capitalism*.[1] Weber's thesis was that Calvinist Puritanism in England and America made a decisive contribution to the rise of modern capitalist society.[2]

In many ways, my entire educational career was an exchange, and sometimes a debate, with the Puritan tradition out of which I come. Nor did things change after I completed my formal education. I have tried ever after to decide which parts of the tradition I could and which parts I could not accept. The process of negotiation is still going on. In what follows, I sketch out how that process has proceeded, and draw some conclusions about the subject before us, religion and human rights in relation to my own religious beliefs.

THE AMBIGUITY OF CALVINISM

As I have suggested, Calvinism, throughout its four-hundred-and-sixty-year history, is a deeply equivocal movement. In my view, there is much that is repulsive in the tradition, but also much that is highly appealing. The trick is to separate the one from the other.

Oversimplifying somewhat, I divide Calvinism into Reactionary and Liberal Tendencies, and briefly characterize each of them. Then I indicate where I stand and why. As might be suspected, I favor the "liberal tendencies" and identify myself with them. In fact, they constitute the framework of my own religious faith, as well as the ultimate basis of my commitment to human rights.

I emphasize that this classification *is* oversimplified, primarily because the ideas and actions of the principal figures in the tradition, including John Calvin, do not always stay put. These ideas and actions can be caught shifting back and forth between "reactionary" and "liberal" tendencies, both because of the circumstances in which the figures have found themselves, and also because of the nature of the ideas being espoused. Those ideas are open-ended and subject to different and conflicting interpretations, which produces a tradition that is both dynamic and unstable. To distinguish the wheat from the chaff is no easy task. At the same time, I have no doubt that these conflicting tendencies are present and do constitute basic elements in the tradition.

Reactionary Tendencies

Calvin, along with his Puritan descendents, has generally acquired a bad reputation in popular and academic culture. One thinks of Nathaniel Hawthorne's description in the introduction of his book *Mosses from an Old Manse*, in which he pictures the once gloomy walls of the manse's study, "made still blacker," as he puts it, "by the grim prints of Puritan ministers that hung around."[3] Puritans are imagined as a uniformly disagreeable and censorious lot, inconsolably distressed, as the saying goes, by the thought that someone somewhere might be happy.

This image is, alas, not altogether mistaken. Calvin himself presided over a Geneva that was in many ways severely repressive of both thought and action. He created a supervisory body known as the Consistory, whose business it was to snoop around all over town rooting out unorthodox belief and lax moral behavior, and to haul offenders before a magistrate to receive what Calvin and other town leaders believed to be their just (and sometimes quite harsh) deserts. And who can forget the infamous public burning of Michael Servetus for heresy, more than four centuries ago, on October 27, 1553. That verdict was the result of a civil trial in Geneva in which the public prosecutor was none other than John Calvin himself. Moved by a certain amount of pity, Calvin unsuccessfully advocated execution by sword rather than burning, but he entertained no doubts whatsoever about the propriety of capital punishment in this case. Servetus's heretical views concerning the Trinity were taken, among other things, as a severe threat to public order.

It is sometimes claimed that the significance of the burning of Servetus has been exaggerated.[4] The event was, to be sure, something of an exception; there are no other unambiguous examples of heresy executions in Calvin's career. What is more, Calvin did not suppress all forms of what he would regard as heretical or questionable literature. The Qur'an was tolerated during his time, as were various classical Roman writings, which were anything but orthodox in faith or morals.

As a matter of fact, Calvin did, in theory, have a rather robust view of the freedom of conscience and of the separation of what he called the "spiritual power" and the "power of the sword."[5] He sharply distinguished between an "inner forum," or conscience, and an "outer forum," or civil authority, and from time to time emphatically spoke of these as "two worlds, over which different kings and different laws have authority."[6] As a consequence, he asserted, the two spheres must "always be examined separately."[7] Even when, he went on, "the whole world was shrouded in the densest darkness of ignorance, this tiny little spark of light remained, that . . . recognized [human] conscience to be higher than all human judgments."[8] As we shall see, this doctrine of the sovereignty of conscience was to have important consequences for later Calvinism and for those societies that were touched by its influence. In fact, this belief may have worked to modify somewhat Calvin's record of persecution, at least as compared with more unrelenting patterns of abuse, such as those associated with the Catholic Inquisition.

Nevertheless, Calvin had an infuriating habit of taking away with one hand what he had given with the other. That was his reactionary side. Having affirmed the centrality and importance of the sovereignty of conscience, and of protecting that sovereignty from the interference of the "outward forum," Calvin turned right around and instructed the city of Geneva to enforce coercively "the outward worship of God," and to defend by the same means "sound doctrine of piety and the position of the church."[9] Or, again, having declared unmistakably that the "church does not have the right of the sword to punish or to compel, not the authority to force, not imprisonment, nor the other punishments, which the magistrate commonly inflicts,"[10] he nevertheless conspired with the Genevan authorities to enforce in numerous ways the doctrines and scriptural interpretations of the Reformed church.

And, while the public burning of Servetus may have been the only pure example of a heresy execution in Calvin's career, there were nevertheless other troubling cases, fully supported by Calvin, such as an instance of banishment for heresy,[11] or of beheading for a combination of blasphemy and sedition.[12] Still worse, from 1543 to 1545, more than twenty victims were publicly burned as witches with Calvin's acquiescence.

The same inconsistency concerns Calvin's belief in a universal moral law, which to his mind is applicable to and obligatory upon all human beings, regardless of culture or religion. Again, Calvin distinguished between two areas of human experience: the order of "higher things" (strictly religious matters) and the order of the "things of this life" (the moral and civil sphere). This distinction, Calvin thought, corresponds to the two tables of the Decalogue, namely, the "religious" commandments (1–4), and the "moral" commandments (5–10). What he called the "light of reason" or "universal impressions of a certain civic fair dealing and order," to which all human beings had natural access, apply to the moral table, but not to the religious.[13] Human reason was, Calvin believed, more severely corrupted in religious than in moral matters.

Theoretically, at least, the "power of the sword" applies to the moral sphere, but *not* to the religious. Physical force is capable, up to a point, of effectively restraining and punishing violence and arbitrary injury, which represents a persistent and fundamental threat to the universal moral order, and recurring evidence of which indelibly marks the "fallen condition" of all humanity. However, applying physical force to the "inner forum," the conscience, and to the "things of the spirit," and thereby attempting to compel religious belief, only distorts and deforms the spirit. Such enlightened ideas might—and, in the hands of others, actually did—provide the foundation for a liberal theory of religious freedom and tolerance. But that was not true, for the most part, in Calvin's case.

Again, having emphatically affirmed these ideas in theory, Calvin frequently turned his back on them in practice, disregarding the implications that would have permitted all people freedom to believe and practice as they were disposed so long as they observed the basic requirements of a common moral law. In direct contradiction to such ideas, Calvin proceeded to inspire in many followers in Switzerland, France, Germany, England, Scotland, and Colonial America the very impulses to authoritarianism and coercive repression of religious dissent that the Calvinist legacy is unfortunately famous for.

This outcome was no doubt heavily influenced by the strength of Calvin's own personality, which was unmistakably marked by an "authoritarian character."[14] Calvin became increasingly convinced that "he was acting solely by virtue of a divine mission," and therefore "did not admit discussion of his ideas—especially not about dogmatic principles, but not even about matters of personal opinion, sometimes of only the smallest importance."[15]

Liberal Tendencies

In the words of Lord Acton, Calvin's goal "was to create not a new church, but a new world, to remodel not doctrine only, but society,"[16] and one of the most important results of his efforts was to check "the reigning idea that nothing limits the power of the State."[17] Having so eloquently enunciated the two fundamental principles—the sovereignty of conscience and the existence of a universal moral law that is prior to and relatively independent of religious belief—even Calvin could not successfully inoculate all his followers against the radical implications of these principles. Thus, in addition to the reactionary side, there is, as I suggested earlier, an important liberal strand of thought—frequently a minority view, but no less powerful—that began to embrace the revolutionary potential of Calvin's two principles. This liberal strand of thought and action thereby paved the way for many of the human rights ideas we affirm today.

As Max Weber understood so acutely, sometimes in spite of itself Calvinism turned out to be a powerful social, political, and economic influence, especially in England and America. In particular, the two principles, sovereignty of conscience and an independent moral law, came to have an important impact in these countries.[18] The story is complicated, and must here be reduced to a brief sketch.[19]

Sixteenth-Century England. While Calvin was still alive, English Calvinists began applying his thought to politics with some important results. Explicating his belief in the inherent "rights of each individual" regarding matters of religion and conscience, as well as property, political participation, and civil resistance, Calvin's English followers began explicitly using the language of "natural rights."[20] These rights were understood to apply equally to each and every human being, and, above all, to protect them against arbitrary government. The rights were "natural" in the sense that they were neither earned nor achieved, nor did they depend on any particular religious belief or affiliation. Moreover, they implied a civil order with extensive built-in restraints against abuse that could support the common benefit of all citizens in respect to religion, politics, law, and economic activity. In a word, the theory implied that force might permissibly be used only in keeping with moral constraints as defined by natural rights. Violations of these moral constraints by tyrannical governments justified, in extreme circumstances, duly restrained counterforce against them.

Seventeenth-Century England: The "Puritan Revolution" (1642–1648). Just such resistance, justified accordingly, was what the Puritan armies led by Oliver Cromwell pitted against the "tyranny" of Charles I in the 1640s. The Puritans claimed that the Stuart monarchy had become grossly arbitrary, and thus thoroughly illegitimate, in part because it had systematically violated the natural rights of its citizens. In the name of restoring those rights, appeals to which had become widespread in the seventeenth century, the government needed first to be restrained by forceful means as necessary, and thereafter to be drastically restructured.

To be sure, Cromwell's reforms, which lasted until 1660, did not by any stretch of the imagination amount to a liberal democratic order, though Cromwell himself harbored conflicting views about democracy and freedom of conscience that reflected the ambivalence of the Calvinist tradition. During and after the revolution, English Puritans, as we pointed out earlier, fragmented into various parties—ranging from reactionary to very liberal. One of the extreme liberal parties, known as "the Levellers," drew up a series of remarkable draft constitutions in 1649—called "Agreements of the People"—favoring full-fledged constitutional democracy, with provisions for equality before the law, division of powers, judicial reform, the prohibition of religious tests for public office, and a revolutionary doctrine of the freedom of religion and conscience.

Leveller religious convictions recalled Calvin's distinction between the two tables of the law, and between an "inner" and "outer forum." The inner sphere is guided by the spirit and "not by the sword," they declared. "For the sword pierceth the flesh; it toucheth but the outward man; it cannot touch the inward. Therefore, where . . . a conversion is not . . . obtained [by the spirit], there no compulsive power or force is to be used."[21]

And the Levellers significantly expanded on the Calvinist commitment to democratic governance, going beyond what Calvin himself intended. In the words of one member:

> For really I think that the poorest he that is in England hath a life to live, as the greatest he; and therefore truly, sir, I think it's clear, that every man that is to live under a government ought first by his own consent to put himself under that government; and I do think that the poorest man in England is not at all bound in a strict sense to that government that he hath not had a voice to put himself under.[22]

Besides a commitment to democratic rights, Levellers and other radical Puritan sectarians of the period referred to additional human rights themes of the greatest importance today, like economic and gender rights. Levellers and their confreres would not have understood the tendency in some circles these days to disparage human rights of an economic and social kind. One writer, having affirmed political and civil rights, including freedom of con-science, went on to declare that "every man of us, in duty to our own natures and to our native country," is justified in seeking

> the recovery of our natural human rights and freedoms, that all orders, sorts, and societies of the natives of this land may freely and fully enjoy a joint and mutual neighborhood, cohabitation, and

human subsistence, . . . it being against the radical law of nature and reason that any man should be deprived of a human subsistence, that is not an enemy thereto.[23]

As to the reform of gender relations, sectarian women of the time attacked "their limited educational opportunities, their confinement to domestic duties, [and] their subjection to their husbands."[24] In line with radical appeals to equal rights in the affairs of church and government, these women and their supporters advocated full equality in marriage: "During the [Puritan Revolution] and Interregnum the very foundations of the old patriarchal family were challenged."[25]

[O]nce the religious sanction was taken away or weakened, then the whole society was subject to challenge and re-scrutiny from a new point of view—that of reason, natural right, popular consent and common interest. The Leveller principle that men and women were born free and equal and could only be governed by their own consent had implications for the family as well as for society in general.[26]

One other Puritan who emerged out of "the seed-ground" of Calvinism,[27] was active during and after the Puritan Revolution, and who, in particular, had an important influence on the liberal tradition in America, was Roger Williams. Williams was certainly a Calvinist, though a rather deviant one. He was committed in his way to the doctrines of predestination, supremacy of scripture, sovereignty of conscience, and to the idea of popular participation in church and government, but he interpreted some of these doctrines and ideas in radical ways. For example, Williams argued that if God were indeed the sole author of election, then (contrary, certainly, to Calvin's practice in Geneva) God's authority ought to be allowed to operate freely and thus without any interference from the civil magistrate.

Williams pushed Calvin's ideas of sovereignty of conscience and the separation of civil and ecclesiastical authority to the limit. In his hands, those ideas implied a system of extensive religious freedom, which Williams, at considerable personal cost, openly advocated in colonial Massachusetts in the 1630s. His more reactionary Congregationalist colleagues, John Cotton and John Winthrop, responded by exiling him to what became the colony of Rhode Island where he managed against great odds to establish "the first commonwealth in modern history to make religious liberty . . . a cardinal principle of its corporate existence and to maintain the separation of church and state on these grounds."[28]

How remarkable and groundbreaking an innovation his achievement was cannot be overstated:

> The trouble with welcoming everyone to a haven of religious liberty was that, sooner or later, everyone came. Baptists arrived early. . . . Anglicans also arrived [later, after Williams's death]. Though [Williams] strongly disagreed with and often denounced them, he would not have prevented their worship. . . . . Congregationalists appeared about the same time, too late to permit Williams the irony of a public welcome as opposed to a public trial. Jews emigrated while Williams was still alive, no doubt giving much satisfaction to one who had complained about the "incivilities and inhumanities" of England against them . . . [, and had declared the need] to make way "for their free and peaceable Habitation among us." And many others came to Rhode Island seeking only to escape religion, not to embrace it. . . . Liberty of conscience brought them all, but in largest numbers it brought the Quakers.[29]

So radical was his commitment to religious liberty that, in the name of tolerance and inclusiveness, he resolutely declined to evangelize Native Americans because, among other reasons, "[f]orced coercion was no conversion at all," as one biographer puts it.[30] "To have dominant cultures or powerful nations determine the religion of a powerless people was [in Williams's mind] to learn absolutely nothing from the history of the ancient or the European world."[31]

CONTEMPORARY HUMAN RIGHTS THINKING

A dominant belief continues to exist that modern human rights thinking is the consequence, primarily, of the European Enlightenment. That is supposed to mean that human rights are, among other things, antagonistic to religion. These conclusions are mistaken in three ways.

First, the Enlightenment itself was hardly "one thing." There are important differences, especially between the British and French versions, when it comes to the relation of religion and state.

Second, as we have been hinting, the notion of human rights—namely, *the existence of subjective claims, regarded as inborn and unearned, that are antecedent to and independent of governmental authority, and that ascribe to individuals a legitimately enforceable moral title or warrant to constrain the behavior of other people in such things as the exercise of conscience, political participation, control of property, and resistance to arbitrary injury*—goes back well before the

European Enlightenment of the eighteenth century. If our preceding suggestions are correct, the Calvinist tradition, which antedates the Enlightenment by one and one-half centuries, is crucial, although it is, of course, but one part of a much older tradition of natural rights.[32]

Third, while a careful reading of John Locke's writings themselves should have dispelled stubborn beliefs that the rights he stood for are militantly secular, the grounds for those convictions collapse completely once Locke's brand of "Enlightenment ideology" is located historically.

Locke, who is properly thought of as one of the central philosophical sources of modern views of human rights, needs to be seen squarely as an heir of the Calvinist tradition. There can be little doubt that "Locke's *Two Treatises of Government* [is] the classic text of radical Calvinist politics."[33] And recent scholarship makes abundantly clear that Locke's influential doctrines of natural rights to conscience and the "separation of church and state," as well as to property, civil resistance, and to political participation and democratic governance, are both inconceivable apart from the Calvinist legacy, and more sympathetic to the integrity of religious commitment than is conventionally understood, precisely when they are read in the light of that legacy.[34]

The very two principles that we have identified, and that Locke also believed in—sovereignty of conscience and a universal moral law relatively independent of particular religious and cultural commitments—underlie contemporary human rights thinking, and go some distance toward creating a hospitable environment for religion. Unless we see that, we cannot possibly make sense of existing human rights documents and the way they are currently being interpreted.

Both the language and the prevailing interpretation of the provisions for "freedom of conscience, religion or belief" have very little to do with the spirit of anticlericalism and suspicion of religion characteristic of the French Enlightenment and its resulting approach to questions of religion and state that has prevailed in France from the time of the revolution to the present.[35] On the contrary, authoritative interpretation of the right to the freedom of religion implies that religious and other fundamental beliefs represent *an exceptional limitation on the law* that entails special respect and protection. By suggesting, for example, that a right of conscientious objection may legitimately be derived from the provisions for freedom of religion and conscience, human rights jurisprudence can be said to reflect, not a spirit of hostility or even indifference toward religion, but, in fact, an attitude of *deference* toward it.[36]

That interpretation illuminates the pervasive provisions in human rights law curtailing all forms of "coercion" that "would impair . . . freedom to have or to adopt a religion or belief,"[37] and, accordingly, calls attention to operative assumptions concerning the "separation of sword and spirit" and the "sovereignty of conscience."

As to the relevance of an idea of a common moral law, the Universal Declaration of Human Rights sets the standard by speaking in the preamble of "the inherent dignity and of the equal and inalienable rights of all members of the human family,"[38] and by claiming in Article 1 that "[a]ll human beings are born free and equal in dignity and rights." When these words are coupled with the statement, again in the preamble, that "disregard and contempt for human rights have resulted in barbarous acts which have outraged the conscience of mankind,"[39] there can be no doubt that the terminology rests on a moral understanding favoring the universal validity and application of human rights.

Add to that the centrality in human rights literature of the principle of nondiscrimination. According to Article 2 of the Universal Declaration (which is reaffirmed in all subsequent instruments), "*Everyone* is entitled to all the rights and freedoms set forth in this Declaration, *without distinction of any kind*, such as race, colour, sex, language, *religion*, political or other opinion, *national or social origin*, property, *birth or other status*." This language appears conclusively to exclude any special religious, national, or cultural beliefs or status as a basis for being protected by or having access to human rights. Human beings are held to possess human rights, and to be accountable and obligated to live up to them, *not* because they are Muslim, or Christian, or Buddhist, or Jewish, or Hindu, or a member of any particular religious or philosophical tradition. The whole point of human rights is that they are taken to be binding and available, regardless of any particular identity or conviction.[40]

WHERE I STAND

My religious faith is best understood in relation to the two principles I have identified throughout as those underlying human rights thinking: a common moral law and the sovereignty of conscience.

As to the common moral law, the longer one ignores concrete examples, the easier it is to sustain thoroughgoing beliefs in cultural relativism, and other forms of particularism and scepticism that cast doubt on moral universals and human rights. But when such examples are considered, it becomes clear that those beliefs are mistaken. If we know anything, we *know for sure* that the genocidal slaughter or raping or expulsion of the sort witnessed during the Holocaust, or more recently in Bosnia, Kosovo, and Rwanda, *is morally abhorrent in itself*, no matter who does it, where, or on what pretext. Nor can there be any serious doubt that everyone *ought to know that*, and may, accordingly, be held accountable for acting in violation of such knowledge. Nor, finally, can it be doubted that each individual subjected to treatment of that kind—no matter what the culture, religion, or ethnicity—possesses an inherent right *not* to be so treated, and that, consequently, *everyone* thereby owns by birth a legitimately enforceable moral title to justify condemning and if possible resisting the infliction of that sort of arbitrary injury. In short, we cannot avoid the fact that we implicitly accept what can only be called a *taboo* or "sacred prohibition" against genocide and other gross forms of arbitrary injury.

Though there is, of course, more to be said about the grounds of human rights, this is for our purposes all we need to confirm St. Paul's conviction that human beings have a law "written on their hearts,"[41] according to which "the whole world may be held accountable."[42] That law is taken to be "inherent" and "inalienable" in the sense that it constitutes a prior and fixed constraint on human life. It is such a conviction, I believe, that undergirds the "human rights revolution" and ultimately disarms all forms of moral scepticism and relativism.

To the objection that, even if true, this does not get us very far, I counter with three points: First, to be satisfied that there exists, after all, some kind of basic universal moral knowledge is in the present philosophical climate *not* incidental or trivial. Second, a clear lesson of the experience with fascism, state socialism, and ultranationalism is the realization that certain basic individual interests must never be allowed to be sacrificed to the doctrine of communal domination.

Whatever concessions need be made to the independence and integrity of minority and other communities, establishing protections against the abuse of individuals perpetrated in the name of collective ideals, such as those practiced by fascists and others, remains the ineradicable foundation of human rights. Third, experiments with communal domination that have afflicted the twentieth century also leave no doubt that human beings have by no means outgrown their obstinate and perverse proclivity for violating the sacred prohibition against genocide and other forms of arbitrary injury. They have simply expanded their technical aptitude for so doing.

There is a deep problem posed by moral knowledge of this kind which Reformed Christianity, in my opinion, answers commendably. It is that, however unwavering and intense our reaction against genocide and other intolerable forms of arbitrary injury, and however clearly that reaction seems to confirm our commitment to a taboo against such practices, on reflection, we appear to lack any equally secure understanding as to *why* we react the way we do, or how we might go about *explaining* and *defending* the basis of such a reaction. We know something well enough, but we are uncertain why or how we know it.

Perhaps our reaction is, after all, simply the product of our upbringing, simply the result of a cultural bias we just happen to have inherited. There are, to be sure, all sorts of superstitious taboos. What is different about the taboo against genocide? Or, we ask ourselves, even if other cultures and religions have come to agree that genocide and other forms of gross arbitrary injury are morally abhorrent, what exactly does that prove except that several traditions happen to have agreed on something? The mere fact that a group of people (however large or small) concur that certain actions are right or wrong does not itself validate or invalidate those actions.

Or, perhaps thinkers like Freud and Nietzsche are correct that our most elemental moral convictions are the result of a pathological religious heritage—a grand illusion—from which, for the sake of our health, we must liberate ourselves. We may, in other words, begin to wonder whether our attachment to a "taboo" against arbitrary injury is rooted in psychological and social dispositions as unseemly and unflattering as are, according to Freud, our attachments to a taboo against incest.

Or, perhaps the sociobiologists are right that aversive reactions to arbitrary killing are "really" adaptive mechanisms that facilitate the survival of the species in some grand Darwinian sense. Possibly, it is simply a useful fiction for people to believe they have "certain knowledge" that genocidal behavior is wrong because it keeps them playing their proper evolutionary role. Of course, if this account is true, then our aversive reactions lose their moral force, and we are deprived of our righteous indignation in face of the genocidal behavior of Nazism or ultranationalism. For now genocide is wrong *only if* perpetuating the human race is a good thing to do, and the question must be answered: Why is that so? In other words, if the taboo against genocide depends on a prior belief in the desirability of human survival, the question is begged as to what makes *that* belief compelling.

The problem with all such theories and explanations, as well as others we might mention,[43] is that, finally, they "reduce away" the essential character of our primary moral reactions, such as our commitment to the taboo against genocide. A special virtue of religious positions, by contrast, is that they *reinforce* and *undergird* in one way or other the "sacredness" of our primary moral reactions—the sense of awe and immutability that accompanies those reactions—rather than undermining or distorting that sacredness. In that way, religious positions provide what is in my estimation a more convincing account of our real moral experience than the reductive approaches we have mentioned.

Reformed Christianity, in particular, gives high priority to the sacredness of the moral law. It might be argued, in fact, that a belief in a universal moral law that is prior or "given" is the linchpin of the entire system. Without "natural" or commonly available knowledge of the basic rights and obligations of human existence, for which human beings are assumed to be responsible, the central emphasis on human disobedience and transgression, which in turn evokes a compensating need for the restoration and rehabilitation of humanity, would not make sense. For it is the belief that human beings are profoundly impaired, spiritually and morally, and that they therefore need assistance in order to recover their moral and religious competence, that lies at the heart of Reformed theology.

Assistance comes in two forms. Political assistance, including the possibility of coercion, is necessary up to a point, in order to help restore competence by guiding and goading human beings to meet their fundamental moral responsibilities. These responsibilities are identified in the "second table" of the Decalogue, and spelled out more specifically as basic "natural" (human) rights, namely, provisions for protecting such things as conscience, property, and political participation, and ensuring freedom from tyranny. These rights certainly focus on political and civil matters; and, especially among the liberal Calvinists, on constitutional democracy in state and church. However, the rights are not only civil and political; they also address issues of economic and gender equality as well. At bottom, the essential function of all these "natural" rights and duties is to prevent or restrain the infliction of arbitrary injury upon any and all human beings.

Above and beyond political assistance, however, religious assistance is also required. Particularly for the liberal Calvinists, that form of assistance is distinctly noncoercive. It presupposes a "realm of freedom," a sphere of "sovereign conscience," where every person is at liberty to negotiate fundamental beliefs as it seems fitting to do. It is a place where beliefs and practices (so long as they do not violate the common moral law) are scrutinized and evaluated in accord with the "laws of the spirit," not the "laws of the sword." This way of thinking, of course, lays a foundation for the "freedom of conscience, religion, or belief," which underlies contemporary human rights thinking.

For the (liberal) Reformed Christian, the image of Jesus as a radical political innovator is at the heart of things. Repeatedly defying expectations as to what sort of messiah he was supposed to be, Jesus sets forth the revolutionary notion that his "kingship is not of this world"; if it were, he says, his followers would fight to protect him.[44] Instead, his mission has no other objective than "to bear witness to the truth," and to perform that witness in a decidedly nonviolent, noncoercive way,[45] though that meant submitting himself to severe abuse—"even death on a cross."[46] The "truth" in question concerns human rehabilitation achieved through divine demonstrations of "mercy," "grace," and "forgiveness," which are intended to dissolve the barriers of hostility, defensiveness, and vengefulness that accompany and further entrench the disposition to violate and disobey the common law of humanity. As "gifts," they are in their nature uncoerced and voluntary; unless they are offered and received willingly, they lose their point.

The essential message of a liberal Calvinist like Roger Williams is thus that everyone should be left free to embrace the claim of truth I have described, or not to embrace it. If the claim is rejected, people should be completely at liberty, without threat of violence or coercion, or other civil penalty or disadvantage, to choose any one of myriad alternative claims. This approach provides an arresting model of religious communication, one that by implication sharply restricts the coercive functions of the state and liberates a sphere of "religion and belief" where conscience is sovereign.

At the same time, if religion and morality are distinguished in the way this approach suggests, there are, nevertheless, at least four ways, on Calvin's understanding, in which, religious conviction "reaches out" and instructively supplements moral thought and practice. I affirm versions of all four convictions, and they might readily be applied to human rights thinking and practice.

First, even though basic moral knowledge is firmly implanted in the human heart, human beings try to find ways to avoid the imperative force of the moral law. People may claim, for example, that since we cannot on reflection really be sure there are any moral constants, such uncertainty excuses noncompliance with or indifference to the moral law. According to Calvin, theological conviction that moral knowledge is part of the structure of the universe undergirds and reaffirms the bindingness of primary moral reactions. It dispels doubt, and emboldens action "in the paths of righteousness."

Second, religious conviction overcomes other sorts of doubt that can enfeeble moral commitment. When, Calvin says, we see the righteous

> laden with afflictions . . . , stricken with unjust acts, overwhelmed with slanders, wounded with abuses and reproaches; while the wicked on the contrary flourish, are prosperous, obtain repose with dignity and that without punishment, we must straightway conclude that there will be another life in which iniquity is to have its punishment, and righteousness . . . its reward.[47]

Anticipating Kant, Calvin seems to be saying that if the moral law is part of the structure of the universe, and if profiting by victimizing the innocent is a violation of that law, it will be necessary to long for and to believe in a final vindication. If there is no confidence of that kind, then, in the ultimate sense, justice is a delusion and innocent suffering pointless. Whatever the details of a belief in eternal life, there must be some underlying conviction that cruelty and victimization are not the last word in the human story.

Third, religious knowledge for Calvin supplements moral insight in that it helps to illuminate the task of applying general principles to specific circumstances. People, as a rule, are well aware of general moral principles (such as the wrongness of arbitrary injury), but things get less clear as one is required to put principles into practice. "The adulterer will condemn adultery in general, but will [forget that principle when it comes to] . . . his own adultery."[48] For Calvin, the Bible and informed preaching can be of great assistance in guiding people in particular circumstances.

Fourth, religious conviction provides motivation for living up to the demands of morality in face of weakness of will. People may at times know well enough what they are to do, but lack the "perseverance" to carry it out. Religious encouragement and "mutual counsel" in association with committed fellow believers is of great value at that point.

CONCLUSION

This account is one person's way of linking religion and human rights to personal religious commitment. It suggests that the liberal Calvinist tradition provides a particularly strong historical and theological foundation for a belief in human rights.

At the same time, this treatise can by its nature be nothing more than a *recommendation*. In the spirit both of liberal Calvinism and contemporary human rights understanding, fundamental beliefs in things like the "foundations of human rights," or the "theological resources for human rights thinking," however fervently embraced, are nevertheless matters of "conscience, religion or belief," and as such they are subject to the conditions of "the sovereignty of conscience" and the "laws of the spirit." Other people are clearly at liberty to propose alternative ideas, and it is hoped that resulting exchanges will contribute to the indispensable process of what Roger Williams called the "chewing and weighing" of fundamental beliefs.

NOTES

Reprinted from the *Journal of Law and Religion* vol. 18 with permission.

1. The dissertation was published as David Little, *Religion, Order, and Law: A Study in Pre-Revolutionary England* (San Francisco: Harper & Row, 1969), and was republished in 1984 by the University of Chicago Press.

2. Max Weber, *The Protestant Ethic and the Spirit of Capitalism* (New York: Scribner, 1958).

3. Nathaniel Hawthorne, *Mosses from an Old Manse* (London: Hurst, 1850), p. 7. Hawthorne goes on: "These worthies looked strangely like bad angels—or, at least, like men who had wrestled so continually and so sternly with the devil that somewhat of his sooty fierceness had been imparted to their own visages."

4. *See* most recently Marilynne Robinson, *The Death of Adam: Essays on Modern Thought* (Boston: Houghton Mifflin, 1998), p. 200.

5. *Calvin: Institutes of the Christian Religion* (2 vols.) bk. 4, ch. 11, § 8, p. 1220, ed. John T. McNeill, trans. Ford Lewis Battles, Library of Christian Classics vols. 20–21 (Louisville: Westminster Press, 1960); see id. at p. 1220 n. 15.

6. Id. at bk. 3, ch. 19, § 15, pp. 847–48.

7. Id.

8. Id. at bk. 4, ch. 10, § 5; p. 1183; cf. "human laws, whether made by magistrate or by church, even though they have to be observed (I speak of good and just laws), still do not of themselves bind the conscience." Id. at p. 1184.

9. Id. at bk. 4, ch. 20, § 2, p. 1487.

10. Id. at bk. 4, ch. 11I, § 3, p. 1215.

11. Jerome Bolsec, an ex-Carmelite monk, was banished in 1551 for denouncing Calvin's doctrine of predestination. See John T. McNeill, *The History and Character of Calvinism* (New York: Oxford University Press, 1954), p. 172.

12. In 1547 Jacques Gruet, a member of an anti-Calvin Genevan family was beheaded in part at least for holding what were regarded as blasphemous views, though charges that he was involved in a seditious plot may also have influenced the decision; see Francois Wendel, *Calvin: The Origins and Development of His Religious Thought*, trans. Philip Mairet (San Francisco: Harper & Row, 1963), p. 87.

13. *Calvin: Institutes*, supra n. 5, at bk. 2. ch. 2, § 13, pp. 272–73.

14. See Wendel, supra n. 12, at 82.

15. Id.

16. Lord Action, *Lectures on Modern History* (New York: Meridian Books, 1961), 132.

17. Id. at 136.

18. In what is otherwise a provocative and original collection of essays, Marilynne Robinson surrenders, unfortunately, to a one-sided and uninformed interpretation of the writings of Max Weber, particularly his essay on the Protestant ethic. See Robinson, supra n. 3, at 23–24, 180–81. As I contend in *Religion, Order, and Law*, Weber's treatment of Calvin and the Puritans *is* deficient in some ways, as are some of the details of his attempt to demonstrate the connection between Puritanism and the rise of modern

capitalist society. However, with appropriate revision, based on a fuller and more sustained investigation of the theology and social thought of Calvin and the English Puritans, together with a careful analysis of the relevant economic and legal developments of the period, as well as a more nuanced and systematic deployment of Weber's own theoretical proposals, much of what Weber argued for in the essay on the Protestant ethic can after all be vindicated.

For compelling confirmation of Weber's basic insights regarding the connection between "ascetic Protestantism" and modern capitalism, *see* David Landes's magisterial volume on economic history, *The Wealth and Poverty of Nations: Why Some Are So Rich and Some So Poor* (New York: Norton, 1998), especially pp. 174–79. Weber's general perspective regarding the connection between culture and economic behavior in fact underlies Landes's whole approach. (Incidentally, there are also fascinating suggestions scattered throughout Landes's book regarding the important connection between religious tolerance and economic development, which demand further reflection and examination, and which are related to some of the themes of this chapter.)

19. See David Little, "A Christian Perspective on Human Rights," in *Human Rights in Africa: Cross-Cultural Perspectives* Abdullahi Ahmed An-Na'im and Francis M. Deng, eds. (Washington, DC: Brookings, 1990), p. 59, for a fuller account.

20. There has been considerable misunderstanding of this usage in the scholarly literature; see id., especially pp. 76–97 and, in particular, nn. 40, 41, and 82, for criticisms of Quentin Skinner, *The Foundations of Modern Political Thought* (2 vols.) (New York: Cambridge University Press, 1978), and for criticisms of Richard Tuck, *Natural Rights Theories: Their Origin and Development* (New York: Cambridge University Press, 1979). As I attempt to demonstrate, Skinner and Tuck (along with others like Jeffrey Stout who trade on their ideas) have rather seriously misrepresented the character and range of Calvinism regarding natural rights ideas, including freedom of conscience and religion.

21. Richard Overton, "An Appeal from the Commons to the Free People" (1647), in *Puritanism and Liberty: Being the Army Debates (1647–1649) from the Clarke Manuscripts with Supplementary Documents,* ed. A.S.P. Woodhouse, 2d ed. (Chicago: University of Chicago Press, 1951), pp. 323, 332.

22. "The Putney Debates," in *Puritanism and Liberty,* supra n. 19, at 53.

23. Overton, Woodhouse, *Puritanism and Liberty,* p. 333.

24. Keith Thomas, "Women and the Civil War Sects," *Past and Present* 42, 55 (April 1958): 13.

25. Id. at 55.

26. Id. at 54.

27. "Calvinism [is] itself, the main seed-ground of the Puritan move-ment," A.S.P. Woodhouse, "Introduction," in *Puritanism and Liberty*, supra n. 19, at 36.

28. Sydney E. Ahlstrom, *A Religious History of the American People* (New Haven: Yale University Press, 1972), p. 182.

29. Edwin S. Gaustad, *Liberty of Conscience: Roger Williams in America* (Grand Rapids: Eerdmans, 1991), pp. 175–76.

30. Id. at 30.

31. Id.

32. See the writings of Brian Tierney; for example, *Religious Rights: An Historical Perspective*, in *Religious Human Rights in Global Perspective: Religious Perspectives* John Witte, Jr. and Johan D. van der Vyver eds. (Providence: Martinus Nijhoff, 1996), p. 17.

33. Skinner, supra n. 18, at vol. 2, p. 239.

34. See Little, supra n. 17. *Cf.* Richard Ashcraft, *Revolutionary Politics and Locke's "Two Treatises of Government"* (Princeton: Princeton University Press, 1986), for an emphasis, especially, on the connection between the Levellers and Locke (pp. 149–65). See Ashcraft's important, but partially misguided, essay "Religion and Lockean Natural Rights," in *Religious Diversity and Human Rights* Irene Bloom, J. Paul Martin, and Wayne L. Proudfoot, eds. (New York: Columbia University Press, 1996), p. 195; and a brief response that is both appreciative and critical, in David Little, "Rethinking Human Rights: A Review Essay on Religion, Relativism, and Other Matters," *Journal of Religious Ethics* 27, 1 (Spring 1999): 151, 167–68.

35. On a recent trip to France for the purpose of investigating the strong antisect/anticult position taken at present by the French government, I was told repeatedly that the persistence of the "laicist" or anticlerical tradition dating back to the French Revolution causes French people, and especially the government, to look with great apprehension upon expressions of religious fervency, such as the sects and new religious movements represent, particularly if they seem to be exerting significant public influence.

36. See David Little, "Studying 'Religious Human Rights': Methodological Foundations," in *Religious Human Rights in Global Perspective: Legal Perspectives*, Johan D. van der Vyver and John Witte, Jr., eds. (Providence: Martinus Nijhoff, 1996), pp. 45, 50–52.

37. *International Covenant on Civil and Political Rights* Art. 18, § 2 (Dec. 16, 1966), 999 U.N.T.S. 171.

38. Universal Declaration of Human Rights preamble (Dec. 10, 1948), U.N.G.A. Res. 217 A(III) <http://www.un.org/Overview/rights/html> (accessed on Mar. 23, 2002).

39. Id.

40. The above two paragraphs are taken, in modified form, from Little, *Rethinking Human Rights*, supra n. 32.

41. Rom. 2:15 (R.S.V.) [hereinafter, all biblical quotes refer to the Revised Standard Version Bible].

42. Id. at 3:19.

43. For example, versions of Pragmatism and Hobbesianism, some of which are widely influential these days.

44. John 18:36.

45. Id. at 18:37.

46. Phil. 2:8.

47. *Calvin: Institutes*, supra n. 4, at bk. 1, ch. 5, § 10, p. 62.

48. Id. at bk. 2, ch. 2, § 23, p. 282.

CHAPTER 6

Interreligious Dialogue and Human Rights

TERRY C. MUCK

Can interreligious dialogue contribute to the human rights project? Apparently many people think the answer to that question is yes.[1] Academics have associated the two: the Bruggerman Center for Interreligious Dialogue at Xavier University, for example, lists human rights as one of the primary subjects with which its dialoguers deal.[2] United States political groups have begun to see the association: for a number of years now the United States Institute for Peace (USIP) has commissioned extensive social scientific studies of religion-related human rights violations in various countries around the world and published the resulting monographs. Church groups have seen the connection: The World Council of Churches has made religiously rooted violence one of its principle topics of interreligious dialogue. And of course the United Nations Declaration on Human Rights not only identified freedom of religion as an essential indicator of human rights compliance, the document itself was supported and developed with religious ideas at its base.[3]

In addition, there is no shortage of books dealing with the two subjects. *The Ethics of World Religions and Human Rights*, edited by Hans Kung and Jürgen Moltmann (London: SCM, 1990), deals with both subjects throughout, as does *Human Rights and Religious Values*, by Abdullahi A. An-Ma'im, Jerald D. Gort, Henry Jansen, and Hendrik M. Vroom (Grand Rapids, MI: Eerdmans, 1995). It is true that the more common subject in these books is the theoretical relationship between human rights as an ideology and its historical and theoretical rootedness in the religions of the world. Still, implicit in such discussions is the idea that religions should not just provide the mandate and justification for a commitment to human rights. Religions, these books argue, should also provide practical help in making sure that human rights moves beyond theory and becomes ever more fully implemented in societies and cultures of the world.

Thus, when one talks about interreligious dialogue and human rights, one is tipping the question toward the practical implementation of human rights, using dialogue among adherents of different religious traditions as a means of promoting human rights. To write about this subject, one usually stipulates that (1) human rights are a good thing and (2) religions should promote them, since religions (at their best) are advocates of human flourishing in all its forms. Interestingly, in order to discuss and advocate this subject, one does not have to, strictly speaking, agree that human rights are rooted, both historically and theoretically, in religious thinking, although almost all who are involved in the use of interreligious dialogue to promote human rights would do so (as we will in this chapter).

Once this stipulation is made, the question becomes more focussed: How can interreligious dialogue contribute to the human rights project? Or even better, How *does* interreligious dialogue contribute to the human rights project?

This question is worth asking for three major reasons, one theoretical, one historical, and one pragmatic. Theoretically, it is important to identify just what it is about interreligious dialogue that has the potential to further the cause of universal human rights. Historically, it is worth asking because it has not always been self-evident that religions have contributed positively to the human rights agenda. And pragmatically, just how to use interreligious dialogue to promote human rights is a skill that must be learned and practiced in order for positive benefits to result.

WHAT ARE HUMAN RIGHTS?

The most official document regarding human rights, the United Nations Declaration of Human Rights, adopted as policy by the member countries of that body in 1948, defines human rights as the "rights a person has simply because he or she is a human being."[4] This basic definition explicitly emphasizes the universal nature of human rights and it implicitly emphasizes the culture-specific character of the actual "rights," that is, the legally enforced entitlements each of the world's cultures have come to believe are expressions of what every human being should see as their human birthright. The modern discussion of human rights in the Western world has been characterized by these two ideas, universality and cultural specificity.

The Universality Principle

Many authors have noted that the idea that everyone is entitled to certain human rights simply because they are human beings is a modern innovation.[5] Human rights, according to this view are not denied to any human being, regardless of their age, sex, race, religion, ethnicity, nationality, social class, caste, education, wealth, health, or ability. Of course, the universality principle does not pretend that any human society has ever lived up to this total concept of human rights. Without exception all have fallen short of even the ideal set out in the United Nations Declaration on Human Rights. All have and do discriminate in practice. But it is only with modern times that universality has even been embraced as an ideal, and growing numbers have endorsed the universality principle not only in theory and law, but in practice.

The Cultural Specificity Principle

It is difficult to overestimate the importance of the idea first introduced into modern intellectual discourse by late nineteenth and early twentieth-century anthropologists, that all ideas are culturally embedded and in that sense are unique. As expressed by these early scholars, the idea of cultural specificity deemphasizes the practice of applying universal principles of behavior and understanding to all cultures everywhere, and instead insists that each culture be allowed to speak for itself and express its own ideals unencumbered by principles applied by outside observers. In this view, human rights, at least in their behavioral expressions, must be seen as culture specific, determined by each culture in practice.

It does not take a great deal of imagination to see that the Universality Principle and the Cultural Specificity Principle have the potential to conflict with each other. One culture's sense of what constitutes a universal human right entitlement may be seen by another culture as nothing more than a fascinating quirk. As one reads, for example, Mary Ann Glendon's book *A World Made New: Eleanor Roosevelt and the Universal Declaration of Human Rights*, one is struck by the insight that a very high percentage of the discussions generated by the process of producing the document can be traced to precisely this concern.[6] The genius of the document is that it seems to arrive at a balanced conclusion that there are universal human rights, but great latitude must be given to individual cultures in how those so-called universals are expressed in those cultures, thereby honoring the cultural specificity principle.

The Individual/Communal Balance

A third idea (and perhaps the major unresolved conflict) emerges as one reads the UN Declaration. It is the idea that a careful balance is needed between considering human rights as legally enforced entitlements that each and every individual must be given access to, and considering human rights as matters of public policy, both civil and economic, public policy that has the effect of leading to overall human flourishing of the community. That is, the word "human" in the phrase "human rights" refers to both individuals and to communities of human beings (and, finally, the community of all human beings).

Countries that have refused to sign on to the United Nations Declaration of Human Rights (that is, voted against it and/or have resisted its full implementation among their constituencies) did/do so most often using the rationale that the document is overly Western. By this they may mean many things, but the core complaint is that the document overemphasizes the individual nature of human rights at the expense of their understandings of communal rights that lead to overall human flourishing—sometimes at the expense of individual rights.

The modern understanding of human rights, then, includes a careful balancing of two spectrums of understanding, one a spectrum ranging from universal principles to specific cultural mores, the other ranging from an individual understanding of human rights to a communal understanding (see figure 6.1). Human rights discussions get off the track when any one of these four poles are either underemphasized (or ignored) or overemphasized so that any one of the other three are ignored. Implementation of a human rights document like the United Nations Declaration of Human Rights, then, demands careful discussion and negotiation, so that cultural differences can be honored, and, in cultures where the individual reigns supreme, the common good is not forgotten and in communal cultures the disenfranchised or ostracized individual is fully protected. That is, proper implementation of any human rights program demands a great deal of dialogue.

WHAT IS INTERRELIGIOUS DIALOGUE?

A useful definition of interreligious dialogue was published in 1981 by John Taylor, a Methodist bishop in Africa: "Interreligious dialogue is a sustained conversation between parties not saying the same thing and who recognize and respect contradictions and mutual exclusions between their various ways of thinking."[7] Three specific ideas emerge from this definition.

FIGURE 6.1
The Universal/Specific Spectrum and Individual/Communal Balance.
Effective human rights initiatives must fall within the Human Rights Circle.

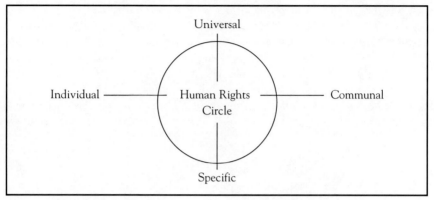

Intentionality

A sustained conversation is one to which both parties commit over a specified length of time. That is to say, dialogue is not a haphazard, one-time, or one-sided discussion. Further, intentionality implies that the topics of discussion are mutually agreed upon.

Disagreement

Dialogues are unnecessary if the two parties agree on everything. One can have very good conversations among people with whom one agrees of course. But these are not dialogues. Dialogues begin with the premise and expectation of disagreement, and it is understood that at the end of the dialogue, disagreements may still remain. Disagreement is not a sign of unreadiness, it is an expectation of dialogue. Informed disagreement is not a sign of failure of dialogue, but simply an acknowledgment of increased understanding.

Respect

A dialogue is neither an argument nor a competition. A dialogue turns into an argument when one or both partners become uncomfortable with the basic expectation of disagreement. It becomes a competition when the

search for common ground in the midst of ongoing disagreement is abandoned. The basic questions being asked in a dialogue are *Where do we disagree? Where do we agree?* and, *Is the ground of the agreement wide enough on
which to build common understandings and intercultural behaviors?*

These three points—intentionality, disagreement, and respect—apply
to all dialogues. What distinguishes interreligious dialogue from other dialogues is the subject matter, and, to some degree, the style of argumentation
used. Interreligious dialogue is dialogue about disagreements that in some
sense are religious. And the warrants and rationales of interreligious dialogue
not only do not exclude the transcendental, but one expects frequent resort
to nonempirical warrants.

A BRIEF HISTORICAL TOUR

Is interreligious dialogue a necessary or at least useful tool in promoting
human rights? This is a legitimate question. Religion throughout history
seems to have been both one of human rights' biggest endorsers and one of
human rights' biggest violators. One can with all seriousness ask the question
Why should we attempt to involve the world's religions and religious people
in the human rights project at all? Indeed, many in the human rights movement see religion as a drawback to human rights rather than as an ally. It
may be convincing to argue that *dialogue* itself is an important methodology
in adjudicating the two spectrums, the universal/particular and the individ-
ual/communal, they might say. But why *interreligious dialogue?*

Consider some of the world's most populous religions: Christianity,
Islam, Hinduism, and Buddhism. On the human rights minus side, Christians led a military campaign against Muslims in the Middle East in an
attempt to recapture the Holy Land, led an internal purge against heretics
that involved torture and murder of its own adherents, and in modern times
forcefully imposed Western civilization on Asian and African societies.
These are all clear violations of human rights as defined by the United
Nations Declaration of Human Rights. On the other hand, Christian missionaries almost single-handedly raised the world's health quotient to
unprecedented heights, have been responsible for laying the groundwork for
entire modern educational systems in many two-thirds world countries, and
often have been in the forefront of movements for social reforms such as pro-
scriptions against widow burning in India. These are all clear examples of the
championing of human rights issues throughout the world.

Other religions have equally ambiguous records when it comes to
human rights. Muslims have throughout their history led military campaigns

against infidel nations, and sometimes insisted on indigenous people's conversion to Islam at the point of a sword. On the other hand they have shown themselves to be humane rulers, giving protection to even non-Muslims in lands they control and establishing social institutions that have been models for other nations. Hindus regularly attacked Buddhists in Sri Lanka in an attempt to establish the teachings of the Vedas in that island nation, and the abuses of the Hindu-based caste system in India have been copiously documented. Yet Hindus have been models of religious tolerance when it comes to diverse teachings in their own land and have contributed an enormous amount of spiritual wisdom, particularly in the areas of religious philosophy. Buddhists, for their part, were equally aggressive in attacking Hindus in Sri Lanka and South India. Yet it is arguable that the Buddha, more than any other Indian religious leader, mitigated the excesses of caste, and in the modern world there are no more admirable champions for human rights than engaged Buddhists fighting for social justice on a number of fronts around the world.

An ambiguous record indeed. One almost wants to ask for the real religions to stand up and be counted: Are you for or against human rights, in the modern sense? That is, universal human rights for all people, not just adherents of your own particular religion. Why the ambiguity?

There seem to be two major reasons. The first has to do with self-advocacy. All of the religions mentioned have been very aggressive in promoting themselves and their teachings to people who do not belong to their tradition. Buddhist, Christian, and Muslim dharmadhatus, missionaries, and dahwists have aggressively spread the substance of their teachings to new cultures throughout their histories. Hindus have come late to the self-advocacy enterprise, but have made their mark on the modern with an energy befitting the scope and resources of the second most populous nation in the world. Although self-advocacy in itself is not a violation of human rights (indeed, the United Nations Declaration of Human Rights considers a religion's right to advocate its teaching to others a fundamental human right),[8] the methods used to self-advocate have often trampled on other important human rights, such as freedom of religious choice and freedom of speech. Too often there has been a disconnect between the peaceful messages of brotherhood and sisterhood of Christianity, Islam, Hinduism, and Buddhism, and the methods used to communicate those messages.

The second reason has to do with the incestuous relationship throughout world history between spiritual power and political power, between church and state, mosque and state, temple and state. In Christianity, Islam, Hinduism, and Buddhism, this relationship has never been an easy one. It has frequently led to abuses of power, usually in the nature of establishing one religion as the official religion of a country, meaning freedom of religious choice has been abrogated. This has led to the religions teaching on the one hand that human beings must be free to choose and practice their own religion, and on the other hand giving either tacit or explicit support to political regimes that insist on uniformity of religion. In such scenarios, human rights are often trampled upon.

This ambiguous history notwithstanding, there is reason to hope that modern political and economic conditions will gradually emphasize religion's positive role vis-à-vis human rights and diminish its negative potential. Religions are waking up to the fact that if they want to retain their rights to self-advocate in a world increasingly hostile to religious institutions, they will have to make sure that the methods they use for self-advocacy are more consistent with their messages of peace and love, or at the very least do not violate the competitive market rules that govern all other modern forms of human exchange.

Politically, the separation of church and state, the creation of religiously plural democracies as the political forms of choice, are beginning to defuse the highly volatile mix of religion and politics that seems to so often lead to human rights abuses.

But these are negative reasons why religion and interreligious dialogue need to be involved in the human rights project. Two essential positive reasons make the involvement of religion and interreligious dialogue in the human rights campaign mandatory.

THE UNIVERSAL DEMANDS THE TRANSCENDENT

It is entirely understandable that proponents of the modern idea of human rights, that is, universal human rights, would want to endorse universal human rights without appealing to any universal principles underlying them. When one looks at the dismal history of the universal ideas of the twentieth century—Hitler's final solution, Stalin's ideas of worldwide Soviet sovereignty, Pol Pot's social engineering in Cambodia—it is understandable that one would become highly suspicious of anyone who comes forward with an idea that is good for all times, all places, and all people—that is, "my idea."

Yet it is equally understandable that in a century of so much abuse of large groups of the most vulnerable people everywhere—the poor, women and children, the ethnic other, the religiously different—that one would want to insist on universal patterns of protection for these ignored, silenced, and disenfranchised. When a choice is forced between a cultural endorsement of the subjugation and abuse of women, for example, and the universal idea that all women everywhere should have equal rights before the law and in comparison with men, we must choose the universal idea. And, indeed, there have been other notable attempts at implementing universal ideas in the twentieth century that seem admirable, such as the human rights movement itself.

The choice, then, is not between universal human rights ideas and no universal human rights ideas. The choice has to do with what warrants we use to argue for specific universals: Do we argue for specific universals based on specific cultural ideas? Or do we argue for specific universals based on religious warrants that claim some kind of transcendent or supracultural referent? Our argument is this: In order to have universal human rights, one must appeal to universal justification, and the only kind of universal justification that will work is the way religions understand the transcendent.

All human conceptions have elements of both a universal idea and culturally specific expressions of those ideas. There is no purely abstract idea in terms of what human beings can understand. And there is no way a human being can understand a discrete, culturally conditioned datum without putting it in the context of a wider set of ideas. For some reason, (and theorists disagree on the reason) human beings think in ways that incorporate both universals and particulars. Kenneth Burke thought it was a function of human (and especially religious) thinking to be always pushing ideas to their totalized end point.[9] Michael Polyani taught that human beings, for whatever reason, tend to hold ideas with "universal intent":[10] if something is good for a few then it is probably good for all. Traditional religious thinkers of course assign the source of universalistic thinking to God or the gods or dhamma, some underlying universal principle. For all of them, however, the idea was that in order to have a truly universal idea, that idea must be the ground of all, outside of the usual ways of empirical or logical justification, a presupposition, an unproved assumption. One cannot have a set of universals that apply to all, nor can one have only individual cultural systems, incommensurable with one another, each deciding on their own unique set of human rights. One must have somewhat unique cultural patterns of human rights that express universal human rights that can only be expressed in somewhat unique cultural patterns.

The obvious problems with the false universals, the totalitarianisms of the twentieth century, is that they were/are culturally specific ideas masquerading as universals. Not just masquerading as universals, but imposed on others, against their will, through the use of coercive power. The obvious problems with the systems of culturally specific choices presented in the twentieth century (whether the cultural relativisms of the anthropologists or the postmodernisms of the philosophers) is that they are based on single transcendent ideas (there are no cultural universals, there is no single universal metanarrative) that are themselves universally applicable, systemically essential foundations to these systems of thought—even as the systems themselves deny that such exist.

What is needed is a way of recognizing the existence of the transcendent as the ground of universal human rights, without reducing that transcendent to just one more in a long series of proposals by political theorists, ethicists, or philosophers, that, in turn, prove to be just one more in an almost endless series of competing justifications for various human rights systems. Some have called this "domesticated transcendence," that is, transcendence that turns out to be just a human program for doing it my way. Where might one find systems of thought that teach us how to comprehend and use a true conception of transcendence? Of universally based ideas? The religions, of course.

THE WAY RELIGIONS UNDERSTAND THE TRANSCENDENT

The religions understand that their transcendents, whether God or the gods or an underlying reality like the dhamma, are not, in the end, subject to the same kinds of justification processes as other parts of our reality. They are not finally subject to empirical justification, as scientific data must be; they are not finally subject to popular support as political ideas must be; they are not subject to logical consistency as philosophical systems must be. Of course, the religions do believe that their transcendents are manifested in empirically measurable positive ways, that they last a long time because they contribute to human flourishing and thus people support them, that they are logical and rational in their human expressions. But the religions believe their transcendents are transcendent precisely because they are supraempirical, revelatory, and suprarational (not irrational). They go beyond the scientific, political, and philosophical.

It is interesting to look more closely at the historical instances of when religion became a counterproductive force in terms of the human rights project and ask Why was that so? It was almost always so because religion succumbed to the temptations of domesticated transcendence. Crusading Christians decided to use political means to achieve spiritual goals. Christian inquisitors turned to "science" (if torture and mental abuse can be called that) to persuade "heretics" to become orthodox.

The religious contribution to the human rights project lies in its ability to understand the true nature of transcendence, and its realistic ability to help people understand true transcendence in culturally specific ways. Since this is not science or politics or philosophy, the methodology used to com-

municate this contribution is not experiment, nor vote, nor logic, but dialogue, a give and take between a religion's best understanding of the transcendence and the cultural forms in which that understanding must be
embedded. No other human institution can do this—or even wants to. Thus,
all other appeals to universal justification end up being disguises for a limited
cultural understanding—that is, not truly universal, but just what each pro-
ponent would like to be universal.

Thus, the first contribution of interreligious dialogue to the human
rights project is a way of talking about universals that avoids the dangers of
either totalitarianism or cultural relativism. In this understanding, religion is
a way of talking about universals in ways that do justice to cultural specificity. The transcendent in such conversations remains truly transcendent. It
cannot be too precisely defined because by definition it goes beyond definition. Yet the transcendent cannot be too specifically tied to cultural expressions, because cultures are different and thus the expressions of the same
transcendent in different cultures will look both the same and different.

In a way, this contribution, this dialogue, is a conversation between religion and the secular human powers necessary to the implementation and
enforcement of human rights. Religion supports human dignity, and it helps
cultures discover ways to human dignity through their cultural forms. It is up
to the cultures themselves, and to the human community as a whole, to
implement and enforce the human rights project.

THE SPECIFIC DEMANDS OF THE RELIGIONS

Interreligious dialogue makes a second major contribution to the human
rights project. It not only facilitates the necessary negotiation between religion and society in trying to implement true transcendence as a basis for culturally specific human rights, but it facilitates the necessary negotiations
among the religions regarding the differences that are evident among the
various religions' understandings of the transcendent. Put simply, the religions don't always agree. Some of the most obvious human rights violations
in the world today are carried out in the name of religions seeking to impose
their understandings of the transcendent and the world on people who have
different understandings of the same.

In addition, religions don't stop in their contribution to human rights
with a positing of the transcendent and the methodology for making the
transcendent accessible to specific cultures. The religions of the world all
have specific programs of what can be considered human rights: Christians
have the ten commandments, Buddhists the various lists of *sila* or moral
rules, Hindus the Manusmriti, and so on. Although a great deal of good work

has been done by several groups to show that in their essence these "human rights programs" are the same, the differences are still there and religions themselves do not consider the differences to be minor.[11]

Thus, interreligious dialogue contributes to the human rights project by providing a forum (or forums) where the religions of the world can discuss their differences and hopefully arrive at both religious and cultural expressions of human rights in various places at various times that will be acceptable to all the religions represented in that area. The tension addressed here is not between the religions and secular culture, but among the religions themselves. The results of these dialogues can be divided into three classes: continuing disagreement, compromise, or complementarity.

Continuing Disagreement

As we have seen above, interreligious dialogue does not always eventuate in agreement. Dialogue takes place because there is disagreement, and sometimes ends there. When this is the case, sometimes the human rights category in question has to be drawn larger in order to incorporate two or more understandings of it that are operative in the same culture. Religious groups that wish to educate their children in private schools are allowed to do so, but must follow general educational guidelines provided by the state and determine ways to incorporate their religious interests in pedagogically acceptable ways, for example. In a sense, two sets of guidelines are operative in such a case.

Occasionally, a group's religious scruples cannot be accommodated by a society. Christian Scientists in the United States who don't believe in giving medical care for certain categories of disease, and reject that care for their children, are often forced to provide that care under penalty of law, because the wider culture deems it necessary. The concern is not for just the religious individuals involved, but for the wider culture. Some religious groups, such as Jehovah's Witnesses, reject inoculations against disease, but when the danger of the spread of the disease threatens the whole society, courts have insisted on the inoculations in spite of the violation of the human rights of the specific groups.

Compromise

Sometimes it is possible for a single solution to be arrived at through dialogue. When Muslims want their female children to wear veils in public schools, sometimes an agreement can be reached where a form of the veil can be used that does not violate the spirit of either the Koran or public school policy. In certain communities, different religious groups have often gotten together to decide on a fair way to accommodate celebration of the different religions' holidays. Similarly, in some communities interreligious groups have gotten together to agree on guidelines for how to teach the sometimes ticklish subject of religion in the public schools. It is often possible to incorporate all the religions' interests in win/win agreements, instead of insisting on a unilateral, single religious solution.

Complementarity

Because different religions view different human rights issues using different theoretical/theological lenses, it is sometimes possible for the religions to each contribute insights to the issue that make for a stronger human rights statement than one religion alone could produce. The potential for such an understanding (still unrealized, perhaps) is the issue of human rights we discussed earlier between the importance of individual human rights and the importance of communal human rights. We suggested that a balanced human rights program must take into account both the individual and the community. Interestingly, if one looks at the world religious scene, Western religions, in particular Christianity, have tended throughout the history of their cultural manifestations to emphasize the individual nature of human rights, while Eastern religions, in particular Chinese religions, have tended throughout the history of their cultural manifestations to emphasize the communal nature of human rights. It seems that the global human rights project can benefit from incorporating insights from both of these religious traditions. Instead of seeing them as mutually exclusive, they could be seen as complementary, eventuating in a much stronger course of action when they are both allowed to contribute to the project.

Interreligious dialogue of this sort should be seen as a way of contributing information to secular bodies that ultimately carry out the implementation and enforcement of human rights programs. This type of dialogue does not create policy, it creates information and possible courses of action that can help policy makers make decisions. Actually, dialogue is made easier by removing religions from policy-making authority in human rights discussions.

CONCLUSION

Interreligious dialogue is crucial to the human rights project. It is societies' way of insuring that human rights can be truly universal without imposing one culture's interests on another. It is the mode of choice in insuring that both universality and cultural specificity are honored.

Interreligious dialogue also ensures that the common religious interest in the transcendent can be communicated to global secular culture without losing the specific interests of the different religions themselves. Dialogue is a means of allowing religious difference to positively inform the human rights discussion instead of making such differences the occasion for lessening the universality of the human rights agenda.

Interreligious dialogue does not replace other modes of action necessary to a successful human rights program. Cultures are still needed to implement specific human rights programs, cultures that operate through the power of honor, shame, and relationship. Political and legal systems are still needed to enforce the demands of human rights programs, systems that operate through the power of national and international law. Religion oversteps its role when it attempts to become overly involved in either implementation or enforcement. Revelation becomes destructive when it is reduced to the forms of the secular and the mundane.

But cultures and legal systems become equally destructive when they ignore the revelatory aspect that religions bring to human rights discussions.

NOTES

1. An internet Google search for "interreligious dialogue" and "human rights" turns up over 7000 hits. Search on November 15, 2003.

2. www.xu.edu/brueggeman_center

3. See Walter Laqueur and Barry Rubin, *The Human Rights Reader* (New York: Meridian, 1979), pp. 3–16.

4. See Laqueur and Rubin, pp. 197–201.

5. See Max Stackhouse, "Some Intellectual and Social Roots of Modern Human Rights Ideals," *Journal for the Scientific Study of Religion* 20, 4 (December 1981): 301–309.

6. Mary Ann Glendon, *A World Made New: Eleanor Roosevelt and the Universal Declaration of Human Rights* (New York: Random House, 2001).

7. *Mission Trends #5*. Gerald Anderson and Thomas Stransky, eds. (Grand Rapids, MI: Eerdmans, 1981), p. 94.

8. See Article 18.

9. Kenneth Burke, *The Rhetoric of Religion: Studies in Logology* (Berkeley: University of California Press, 1970), pp. 7–42.

10. Michael Polyani, *Personal Knowledge: Toward a Post-Critical Philosophy* (Chicago: University of Chicago Press, 1974).

11. See Hans Kung and Karl-Josef Kuschel, eds. *A Global Ethic: The Declaration of the Parliament of the World's Religions* (New York: Continuum, 1993). From a religion's point of view see Arvind Sharma, Joseph Runzo, and Nancy Martin, eds., *Human Rights and Responsibilities in the World Religions* (Los Angeles: OneWorld Publications, 2003).

PART II

Christian Perspectives on Human Rights Issues

CHAPTER 7

The End of Man

Human Rights, Christian Theology,
and the Rights of Human Persons

STEPHEN G. RAY JR.

INTRODUCTION

This chapter will be concerned with reconceiving the basis for human rights in the context of the twenty-first-century United States. Specifically, I will challenge the presumptive basis of most human rights theory in the United States—the preamble to the Declaration of Independence—and in its place offer the rudiments of a theory grounded in the well-being of human bodies. The goal of this chapter is not to present a fullblown theory of human rights but, utilizing the thinking of Martin Luther King Jr., to identify a more compelling conceptual ground upon which such work might be accomplished.

Before I begin it seems important to clarify why I am concerned with the conceptual basis from which we think about human rights. Lest it seem that I make too much of the power of an idea, let me assert that ideas are the imaginative currency that gives meaning to our world and our interactions in it. We formulate our convictions about ourselves and others and, consequently, about our respective places in creation based upon the ideas that structure our worldviews. So, if people of goodwill in our particular context work with ideas about human persons that allow rights to be abstracted into principles and certain persons to be objectified into bodies, it should not be surprising that people find themselves ever fighting for the rights of those bodies. Nor should we be surprised when the language of that struggle is easily coopted by forces very much opposed to its intent. The ways that ideas are rendered can have the power to motivate good people to challenge systems that work to destroy human persons or, conversely, the power to mystify persons into becoming silent bystanders. It is precisely this power which inheres in ideas that makes examination and renovation of their foundation so important. This chapter is concerned to do just such a task. What I hope to accomplish by contending for a commitment to the well-being of bodies as a basis for theorizing about human rights is the creation of a foundation for a conceptual matrix that will not allow persons to be superceded by principles or their well-being to be abstracted from the concrete conditions of their everyday living.

The thought of Martin Luther King Jr. can be used to flesh out this idea of conceptually grounding human rights in the well-being of bodies. To use the language of King, I am advocating an approach that recognizes the "somebodiness" of every "body." That is to say, I am seeking a discourse in which bodies are not beside the point in talking about rights, but, precisely the site at which that discourse finds a home.

HUMAN RIGHTS AS EPHEMERA: A REFORMED CHRISTIAN TAKES ON THE PROBLEM

Respect for human rights is a good idea that, like many good ideas, is looking for a market. While it is undeniable that we humans, as a race of beings, have made great strides in this area, it is also clear that these strides have been ephemeral and elusive. The slightest geopolitical dislocation or economic calamity and the first thing on the "chopping block" is the commitment to human rights. We see this transient commitment to human rights enacted by global powers, national and regional governments, rebel and guerilla groups, and on down the line to local police departments. One can only conclude that, at this point in our evolution as a species, the idea of human rights as a necessary end in itself has not quite caught on. There are many ways to explain this situation.

From a Reformed Christian viewpoint, an explanation for the halting and meandering journey toward a general commitment to human rights can be found in the recognition of the depravity of human beings. While this word—depravity—may conjure images of fleshly delights, its more mundane yet most profound meaning points to the inescapable entanglement of most human beings with some form of self-interest. This entanglement may be interpreted as pride when gazing upon the doings of power and privilege, apparent self-loss when sojourning with the experiences of marginalized and oppressed persons, or some variant of the two. Whichever of these definitions one prefers, the idea of depravity points to the seeming inability of human beings to achieve the type of self-transcendence requisite for a realization of the relationality conjured by the word *agape*—the experience of relationship in which one loves oneself adequately, one's neighbors properly, and God appropriately—which is a prerequisite for a meaningful commitment to human rights.[1] Moreover, this lack of situational self-transcendence feeds a false interpretation of the needs of self-preservation which then mitigates against the final realization of the dream of universal human rights by subordinating the well-being of others to one's own perceived self-interest.[2]

The idea of depravity also serves to highlight the dual character of the problem; it is by nature both universal and contextual. What is at stake in the concern for human rights is something universal—the guarantee of well-being to human persons simply because they *are* human persons. At the same time that guarantee must be achieved and mediated contextually (i.e., specific locations, eras, and cultures). Thus, a Christian account of the widespread problem of approaching human rights as ephemera, which takes seriously the category of depravity, would suggest that the matter is most effectively dealt with, both conceptually and materially, when attention is paid to both universal and contextual dimensions of the problem. In what follows, I offer an analytic description of why the idea of human rights enjoys only an episodic status as a worthwhile end in a particular context in a way that takes seriously the situational character of the problem and likewise notices the universal quality of the solution.

UNSTABLE GROUND: HUMAN RIGHTS AND THE LANGUAGE OF THE RIGHTS OF "MEN"

The context that I am focusing on is that of the contemporary United States. I will therefore draw upon the cultural, political, and religious ideas that have significant currency in the late modern United States. With this as a basis, I turn now to words which, in this context, have a singular currency when thinking about the rights of human persons.

> We hold these truths to be self-evident that all men are created equal and are endowed by their Creator with certain inalienable rights, among them life, liberty and the pursuit of happiness.
> —Declaration of Independence, July 4, 1776

These are perhaps the most important words ever written in the history of the United States. This simple epigraph has served as the theoretical framework through which we, as a society, have conceived and understood the idea of human rights. The threefold matrix of life, liberty, and the pursuit of happiness has been the touchstone for our nation as it has tried to understand and interpret its obligations to its citizens and to other human beings around the world.³ These words have also provided the language that people have used throughout our history as the clarion call to the nation to return to its roots when it has strayed. Who can forget the stirring words of Martin Luther King Jr. during his great speech on the steps of the Lincoln Memorial when he intoned the words, "I have a dream that one day this nation will rise up and live out the true meaning of its creed: 'We hold these truths to be self-evident: that all men are created equal.'"⁴ These simple words have been the beacon light of America's thinking about human rights.

While recognizing their historic power, I want to raise the question of whether these words are up to the task of being the primary foundation for thinking about human rights in our contemporary context. My way of approaching this concern will be by asking the following question: Do the imagistic referents of these words support the ideas that they reference? As the question may suggest, I will be engaging in a rhetorical analysis of these words, but this is not simply a linguistic exercise. Because I believe that there is an inextricable link between words and actions, I want to ask whether these words can motivate the type of actions necessary to give the idea of human rights flesh. So, with this question I am asking whether this particular configuration of language is effective in theorizing about human rights.

Before I begin my analysis of the phrase, let me make explicit several assumptions that underlie this project. First, although the preamble has been widely interpreted as a political statement, I agree with Michael Perry that this is an explicitly theological statement about an incontrovertible religious idea.⁵ The use of the term "Creator" makes this point rather clearly. Thus, my critique will interpret this phrase as a theopolitical statement. The significance of this mode of interpretation will be made in the final section of this chapter.

The second assumption that I am working with is that our cognitive engagement with language, as such, is one that has inherent connection to the varied array of images that comprise our imagination. It is my belief that all of our written and spoken communication relies upon visual images that serve as referents for whatever is being expressed in a particular communication. For example, the very first introduction that many of us had with math, that most abstract of disciplines, was with a bowl of fruit. We initially learned about quantity and its manipulation by some concrete image that became a part of our mental schema. This was then replaced by a symbol. It is important to remember that, even though the symbol comes to mind, there is still a material referent which gives the symbol meaning. This material referent is what I am terming the "imagistic referent." My presumption is that behind almost all meaningful communication is such a material referent.

The third assumption is that the imagistic referents behind our language create for us a space of appropriate meaning. That is to say, they signal to us what in our vast array of possible responses is appropriate to the occasion. In essence, we conclude which mental space we should occupy in order to provide a response that fits the situation. For instance, if I ask you what you would like with your tea, you would hardly say A1 Steak Sauce. Why? Because the word tea, and the ideas related to it, invite us into a mental "cupboard," if you will, in which steak sauce is not on the shelf. Sugar perhaps, creamer maybe, steak sauce, not likely. Words, written or spoken, rely for their meaning not only on simple imagistic referents, but also on complex matrices of related images and meanings.

The fourth assumption is that these spaces of meaning are contextualized by history and contemporary experience. Words do not manufacture meaning. Rather, they rely on some matrix of preexistent meaning and contemporary applications for their expressive power. As long as words have the power to express meaning, these matrices live with them. This is not to deny that words have the power to create new spaces of meaning; yet, even here, the new relies upon the old. Without some preexistent meaning to which a new interpretation can be added there is little hope that a meaningful advance can be made. An example of this is the idea of "Women's Rights." Without some preexisting framework that gives the ideas "women" and "rights" meaning, this becomes a fairly vacuous term.

By beginning my critique of these opening words of the Declaration of Independence (hereafter simply noted as "the preamble") with a brief description of the relationship between language and image, I hope to sidestep an issue that attaches to a usual way that this document is critiqued, namely, that the history of our nation has given lie to them from the very beginning. While it is a well-established historical point that when these words were written the only persons contemplated as referents for them were men of Anglo-Saxon descent, there has been a substantial enough utilization of these words to underwrite the expansion of the rights to many marginalized groups (i.e., the modern Civil Rights Movement) that this analysis seems somewhat dated to many residents of the United States. In fact, it may seem to many that this language is eminently serviceable in a new context—that of human rights—precisely because of these recent expansions in application. I want to question this last assumption on the grounds that it does not take seriously enough the inherent matrices of meaning that attach to these words and, consequently, presumes a facility for the task that does not exist.

Let me begin my critique by looking closely at the language itself, with the aim of identifying the matrix of meaning within which the words exist. When the words "We hold these truths to be self-evident, that all men are created equal" are used as a warrant for some purpose there are immediately two aspects of this matrix of meaning that come to the fore—the invocation of natural law and the construction of a normative subject. When the preamble invokes the concept of self-evident truth what is accomplished is that that which follows is rendered as transhistorical and universal truth—a type of natural law. Certainly, we can quibble with the idea of anything being self-evident—critical theory has done much to demonstrate that all truth is learned and culture based, but, let us remain focused on the rhetorical function of these words.

For a moment let's think about what is intended when propositions are claimed to be rooted in natural law. To do that it is necessary to define natural law. A simple way to understand natural law is this: whatever proposition is being posed is a part of the very fabric of nature. That is to say it may be violated, but it can in no way be denied as truth. Thus when the assertion "all men are created equal" is invoked, what is being asserted is that there is an inherent "equality" of all "men," which, though it may be functionally transgressed, it cannot conceptually be denied. It is this aspect of transhistorical equality which I believe leads many to embrace this passage as an adequate basis for talking about human rights.

I want us to notice something about this language that I think will begin to betray its fundamental weakness. Conceptually, there is a funny thing that happens when these words are deployed: That which is purported to be an article of natural law is demonstrably untrue. Put another way, human experience denies the validity of this affirmation. It is not simply rationally deniable but patently untrue that all people are created equal. People are born with varying physical abilities, significantly different intellects and aptitudes, and with substantially different morphologies. So, how then can this seeming falsehood be posed as transhistorical truth? To answer this question we need to focus on the cognitive shift that these words anticipate and the basis of warrant they contemplate.

The cognitive shift these words anticipate is a simple one. The phrase anticipates the hearer immediately contextualizing the claim being made. That is to say, the truth being proffered is one that self-evidently has a basis of truth that is not immediately apparent. There is some further implicit presumption that is necessary to provide appropriate meaning for the phrase. In this particular case, there are two alternatives that immediately come to mind. The first is that the truth of the statement presumptively refers to some principle beyond experience which has the requisite universality not found in material reality. Alternatively, the truth of the dictum relies on a presumptive limited applicability of the claim, that is, there are unexpressed but nonetheless necessary limitations on the claim. In the case of these particular words I believe that both of these alternatives are conceptually at work, and that the internal contradiction of their union debilitates the power the ideas have to underwrite claims for human rights. Let me explain.

In the first instance, the verbiage of the preamble invokes a set of principles not immediately verifiable in material reality upon which to make their claims. This is clear by the invocation of the idea that men are created. People are born, manufactured goods are created. We might make another sort of assessment if an explicit theological claim was being made, which recognized the metaphorical nature of such claims. That, however, is not the case with this language. So, this language immediately signals to us that we are operating in the realm of speculative principle because, given what we know about human beings, they are not fabricated entities. Here we are helpfully reminded by Hume that whenever claims are made whose evidence is beyond material existence those claims must be received as propositions of principle and not as demonstrable law. The following may help clarify the difference. A demonstrable natural law is that human beings and deer require water to live. A propositional principle is that human beings have a "right" to water that supercedes the need of deer. Notice the difference. In one case there is a simple observation about the mechanics of the natural world. In the second there is a qualitative judgment which, while related to the natural observation, does not logically flow from it. The preamble relies upon the principle that there is some unifying quality that "men" share which can be the basis of a set of rights.

In the second instance, the preamble assumes a limited applicability for these principles. Inherent in the understanding of the claim itself is the notion that the truth to which it refers is provisional and not universal. The intent of the author and signers of the Declaration of Independence was never that these principles should have universal applicability. This is apparent given the evidence of material existence. It is this certain presumption that allowed Chief Justice Taney to find in the Dred Scott Decision of 1847 that "The framers of the Constitution believed that blacks had no rights which the white man was bound to respect" and "it is too clear for dispute" that regarding the language in the Declaration of Independence that includes the phrase, "all men are created equal, . . . that the enslaved African race were not intended to be included, and formed no part of the people who framed and adopted this declaration." Even a cursory glance at the history of the United States will reveal that Taney's interpretation was not an aberration. Clearly, there was no recognition of any universal quality that bore notice.

So then, we have these competing, and in many ways contradictory, meanings that attach to the preamble. Let's state clearly what the conflict is: on one hand, you have the assertion that the claims of the preamble are rooted in some quality that inheres to all men, while on the other you have the assertion that the claims of the preamble are explicitly not applicable to all people. How might we adjudicate, or make sense, of their immediate conflict?

The first step is to recognize that the words mean what they say and contemplate no such conflict. What the preamble does is to rhetorically construct a normative subject, a "man" if you will, who shares with other such "men" an inherent equality from which flows certain rights. The claims being made are therefore not universal, per se, in the way that we presume, but rather universally applicable to these rhetorically constructed subjects. This is precisely the cognitive shift that the framers of these words anticipate. The words were never intended to have applicability beyond this normative subject. Who might this normative subject be? To answer this question let us look for a moment at the primary imagistic referent proffered by the language—men. My argument will now turn to a central point, that this term has had, continues to have, and will have for the foreseeable future—a specific content that cuts against the value of this verbiage as the basis for human rights.

There are two types of excavations that I want to do on this point, the first historical and the second conceptual. An analysis of the content and contextual matrix of meaning for the word "men" begins with the recognition that primordial linguistic referents never quite fade away, they always inform how we hear and understand words and phrases that seek to conjure reality. So, if, as in the case of the United States, during the formation of a society the phrases "man" and "men" had a specific content, it is likely that the echoes of that image will persist throughout the life of that society. Contrary to the protestations of the opponents of inclusive language, at least in the United States the language of man is not, and has not been, gender neutral and only rarely has it been ethnically and racially inclusive.

Moreover, this gender and racial/ethnic specificity that has presumptively excluded women and racial/ethnic minorities has in intent and purpose similarly excluded them not only from the second part of the phrase "created equal" but also from the final clause "endowed by their Creator with certain inalienable rights." This exclusion is fleshed out not only in the earlier mentioned Dred Scott decision but also in the Minor vs. Happersett case (1875) in the Supreme Court which declared that even though women were indeed citizens, they did not have unqualified rights within American society. Additionally, it is fairly clear in the continual violation of the persons and territories of Native Americans that they certainly had no such unalien-able rights. So then, as a historical matter, the echoes that accompany these words is that they properly have a very specific range of meaning and a very discrete referent within the population. I do not deny that the application in contemporary American society has had some expansion, but I would argue that these gains are ever and always tentative. It is instructive that the lan-guage of "strict contructionism" viz-à-viz the Declaration of Independence and the Constitution in law is most often used in matters that contest the rights and inclusion of segments of our society that have traditionally been marginalized. This is the problem of historical signification—the word "men" has had a very limited range of applicability within our society. There remains the conceptual problem.

The conceptual problem is this: we cannot long equivocate about uni-vocal language. As much as we may want the word "men" to have a generic human referent, it does not. It is precise in its meaning. Its imagistic referent is specific—the male of the human species. So, without some immediate clarification the conceptual referent will immediately exclude all women. And as previously mentioned, the term includes only certain types of males.

Taken together, the historical echoes and the precise imagistic referent which comprise the matrix of meaning for the preamble contend strongly against the type of universal applicability that most human rights language depends upon. Precisely because they rely historically and conceptually on a specific normative subject, these words lose their force when applied to other types of subjects. My point here is a simple one—the rhetorically con-structed "man" contemplated by the preamble cannot provide the founda-tion for any type of sustained struggle on behalf of human beings because, by definition, his presence prima facie denies their existence as subjects worthy of rights. If we are to take seriously the project of contending for the human rights of marginalized persons, it is necessary, as Carol J. Adams contends, to deconstruct this "man of reason."[6]

Before turning to the next part of my argument, let me outline a broader critique that I have of our reliance on the preamble for our thinking about human rights. As just outlined above, reliance upon a normative subject is problematic in itself, but perhaps even more problematic is the reliance on an abstract set of rights that adhere to this subject. The trouble is that the instability of this subject renders these rights unstable at best. If it necessary to make a conceptual shift away from material reality to make sense of and understand these rights, it becomes that much more difficult to unequivo-cally lay these claims upon systems of privilege and the persons who main-tain them. For example, in times of war, it is not unusual for the state to circumscribe the rights of its citizens. The rationale is usually that the state is the grantor of such rights and consequently has the power to control them. The recent cases brought by the government under the auspices of the "Patriot Act of 2002" are just such examples.

This type of reasoning is only possible because the rights so circumscribed are viewed as principles and not as inviolable inheritances due to all people. So, in an odd sort of way, the very conceptual warrants that are posed by the preamble (abstract principles attaching to an abstracted normative subject) make the rights mentioned eminently violable. This inherent violability is the critical reality that diminishes the capacity of the preamble to be a meaningful basis for human rights.

A FALSE DICHOTOMY: THE DIMINUTION OF THE BODY IN RIGHTS THEORY

If we step back for a moment and look at human rights per se, the well-being of bodies is inescapable. We notice the violation of human rights by seeing the violation of human bodies. Conversely, we notice the observance of human rights by seeing the flourishing of human bodies. So, the material condition of the body should be central to any theorizing of human rights, yet it is not. We do well to ask why not.

American society and culture, while something of a polyglot of many global cultures and the innovation of new contexts, is yet a Western society. The cultural and intellectual heritage of the United States is linked primarily to the history of ideas in Western Europe. I am not making any claims about where those ideas came from initially, only that they come to us in America through the prism of developments in Western Europe. A significant part of that heritage is the recognition of a radical disjuncture between mind and body.

This psyche/soma dichotomy views the human person as primarily a creature of intellect that only secondarily inhabits a physical body. In this scheme the real person is that part of the human being which is associated with some animating principle, such as personality, intellect, or spirit. The body is the vehicle for that animating principle while it traverses the material landscape that we call life here on earth. This pervasive view is evident in the theological, cultural, and political common senses extant in our society. Theologically, we see it in the preponderance of concern that many in the Christian faith have with eternal life—as if trying to navigate this life isn't difficult enough. Culturally, we see it in the significant entertainment industry that has grown around images of the violation of human bodies for our entertainment. Politically, we see it in the propensity of elected officials to be more concerned about principles and people's "thinking" than about the material well-being of their constituents. These examples illustrate the prevalence of this dichotomous view of the body and animating principle which exists within our society.

That dichotomy creates a particularly troublesome context in which to try and talk about human rights. While there are several significant facets to this troublesome context there are two that I want to specifically notice: the creation of a culture space in which persons can be reduced to their bodies and the exclusion of those persons from the discursive matrix in which human rights has meaning. Both have to do with how human persons are assessed vis-à-vis the right to have rights. Both of these facets also connect with the presumptive right that persons have to participate in the systems in their context that guarantee the respect of human rights.

Before I turn to that analysis, let me emphasize the significance of bodies for human existence. An integral part of how we experience our existence as human beings is the experience of being embodied creatures. From something as simple as the smell of a rose, which can transport us through time, to something as complex as preparing a multicourse meal with only taste and sight as measure, our experience of our bodies is crucial for our experience of what it means to be a human being. To the extent that our bodies physically and/or socially inhibit our ability to fully participate in the benefits of our society, they impair our capacity to enjoy our full humanity in those contexts. Moreover, our very sense of ourselves *as* human beings is linked to the way the world responds to our bodies. A significant piece of our esteem for ourselves, our abilities and the possibilities for our existence, is profoundly affected by the messages that we receive about ourselves from others who share our world. Those messages are inextricably bound to the bodies that carry us through life. All of this is to simply say that the dichotomous approach to human persons that is a bedrock assumption of our intellectual culture is not only counterintuitive, it is wrong because it denies the fundamental reality that human persons experience reality as integrated beings. Let me outline the significant dangers that attach to this dichotomous view of human persons.

The first problematic facet of the dichotomous view is that it fails to take seriously enough the propensity of our culture to reduce certain persons to their body—the practice of identifying some physical characteristic of a person, or persons, and ceding to it a power of definition that exceeds mere optical description. A scheme that demeans the body in the exaltation of the mind also demeans the persons involved. Let me explain what I mean by persons reduced to their bodies. I will use experience of gendered and racialized persons as my example.

The experience of women in American society and culture is that they are more often judged by the substance of their morphology than by the content of their character. Perhaps the largest single industry in American society is one that manufactures substances, plans, and programs the sole purpose of which is to alter the female body. The pervasiveness of this industry reflects something fundamental about American society and culture and its view of women: namely, they are synonymous with their bodies. While clearly a primal aspect of our society, this reductive objectification of women to their bodies has a long heritage in Western culture. We can trace its development from the Ancient Near Eastern philosophers such as Plato in the *Republic*, on through the work of Thomas Aquinas and works following in that stream.

There are three primary ways that this objectification is expressed. The first, which most directly comes from the ancient sources, asserts that the realm of human affairs that requires rationality or "mind work" is created for and best fulfilled by men. Those spheres that deal with the passions—synonymous with the body—are associated with women. Here women are objectified by a prima facie exclusion from the world of the intellect because of morphology. A second way this objectification is expressed is through the inordinate focus on a woman's fecundity, the reduction of a woman to her womb. Here, as contemporary debates about reproductive choice clearly demonstrate, there is a pervasive common sense notion that the body of a woman has a status, being, and raison d'etre that can be differentiated from her as a whole integrated person. Furthermore, that status as body can, in the final analysis, trump the claims of that integrated person. However one feels about the contemporary debate about reproductive rights, it should not escape observation that the entire debate circles around the reduction of women to their bodies and who has the final claim on those bodies. A third way this objectification is expressed is in the undeniable reality of the "pornographic glance" that characterizes much of America's film, television, and print media and other venues of entertainment. The magazine racks of supermarkets are replete with scantily clad women, the airwaves are awash with images of women navigating the world with their "looks" as their only asset, our video stores are chock full of action flicks with the requisite sexually enticing heroine. And who can fail to notice as they travel the highways and byways of our nation the numerous signs for the "gentlemen's" club just a few exits up? All of these bespeak a culture in which women are primarily rendered and interpreted as bodies and only secondarily as integrated persons. It should not go without notice that in conflicts all around the world the primary mode of violence against women is rape—the final reduction of a woman's humanity to a collection of orifices. Clearly, in a context like this a consideration of human rights must take seriously the integrity of the body, even when the dominant cultural presumptions make no such recognition.

Another instance of the reduction of human persons to simply objectified bodies is in the workings of race as cultural discourse and reasoning. In this case, the objectification becomes apparent in the pervasive cultural assumption that some knowledge can be had of a human person simply by the observation of the melanin content of their skin, or some vague knowledge, no matter how erroneous, of the geographic origin of their ancestors. An additional feature of this misguided objectification is that it leads to the further presumption that one can make intelligent decisions about behaviors and social policies constructed upon this specious knowledge. As with the case of women, this practice of objectification has a long heritage in Western culture. Its most pronounced effects were not felt, however, until the encounter of the "Old World " with the new. With this encounter, the reduction of human persons to bodies took on a powerful and tragic force.

Three significant examples of this type of objectification and its consequences can be seen in the experiences of Meso-Americans, Africans, and persons of Asian descent. In the case of Meso-Americans one has but to look to the disputation in 1550 between Las Casas and Sepulveda on the intellectual and spiritual status of the "Indians," in which the humanity of the Meso-American was being disputed on the grounds that the only thing they shared in common with "men" were their bodies. The point at issue was whether their status as simply creatures with human bodies granted them freedom from slavery and the routine violation of their persons.[7] In the case of Africans, a similar reductionism was practiced, both as an authorization for the institution of chattel slavery and for the subsequent exclusion and marginalization of African Americans in American social and cultural life. Paradigmatic of this history is the book by Charles Carroll, *The Negro a Beast?*, in which he makes an argument much like Sepulveda's that the only thing shared in common between "the Negro" and men was a body, with the consequent assessment that "the Negro" had no claim on the society of men.[8] In the case of persons of Asian descent this reductionism has taken the form of the exoticization of them and their community into the "Oriental." This exoticization has effects every bit as pernicious as in the previous cases. In the context of American culture, this has taken the form of a presumption of the eternal immigrant, as Asians are relegated to permanent outsider status in American life and culture.[9] These examples suggest that there are very real consequences that follow from the reduction of persons to bodies in a culture whose heritage is one that objectifies and denigrates the body.

OBJECTIFICATION TO EXCLUSION

The consequence that I want to take up now is the conceptual exclusion of these persons from the rhetorically constructed universe in which much of the language of human rights in the American context is grounded. Let us revisit again the self-evident truths of the Declaration of Independence. To recall, the language is: "We hold these truths to be self-evident that all men are created equal and are endowed by their Creator with certain inalienable rights, among them life, liberty and the pursuit of happiness." I want to note, specifically, the nature of the rights invoked. Only the first has specifically to do with embodied existence. The latter two, which perhaps hold the most sway, have to do with intangibles of human existence.

Before delineating them a bit more let me clarify why I believe the second and third propositions are most important for this conversation. The first unalienable right identified is one that, I believe, is sufficiently cross-cultural that it provides a foundation for all thinking about human rights. In common with most human societies, our society views life as a basic human right. I do not include this one then in the realm of contextually defined rights. I do, however, include the last parts. Liberty and the pursuit of happiness are contextually very significant categories in American culture. They are also the most abstract of the principles outlined and for that reason the weakest and most unstable of these self-evident rights. Let me explain the weakness I am suggesting.

At first glance, the word "liberty" in the context of the self-evident truths would seem to point immediately to bodily freedom. We know that this was not, and is not, the case because the Declaration of Independence had no immediate impact on the institution of chattel slavery that was a pervasive reality throughout our nation. How might one explain this historical paradox? An explanation is possible if we take notice of both the historical and religious environment in which these words were written.

Earlier I brought attention to the fact that as a historical matter the word "men," which serves as the referent of the right of liberty, had a very specific meaning. The word was not intended to have universal application. Neither was the universal application of rights that adhere to this referent contemplated. That was, however, only part of the story. The religious context was one that had a significant influence on the applicability of these rights.

When the Declaration of Independence was written our nation was in the midst of the nascent period of what would become the explosion of the Evangelical movement. A hallmark of that movement was the idea of spiritual freedom. While the intent of this focus was to contest the then prevalent Calvinist views of the predestination of souls, the lingering consequence was to open a cultural space in which liberty could primarily have meaning in relation to the soul and *not* the body. This cultural space was crucial for resolving the paradox just noted. Many of the proslavery treatises of the eighteenth and nineteenth centuries based their arguments on just this thesis. As Garth Baker Fletcher observes: "Such a stance effectively separated the salvation and freedom of Blacks' souls from the release of their bodies from physical bondage. Thus, by the mid-eighteenth century Americans had finally achieved the theological justification necessary to ensure the institutional longevity of slavery by separating soul freedom from physical bondage."[10]

For a culture that had already embedded within it a dichotomous and hierarchical view of bodies and their animating principles, the consequences of this religious discourse were substantial. Perhaps most notably, for persons reduced to their bodies in public discourse, there was little or no court of appeal for them to contest the violation of those bodies. Even the movement to abolish slavery did not in any substantial way enshrine the right of black bodies to exist unviolated or to exercise the presumptive liberties of American society. One has but to reflect on the wave of unpunished lynchings that swept the nation after Reconstruction and take notice of the many black laws that forbade settlement of freedmen in places like Indiana, Ohio, and Illinois to see the want of protection for those identified with dark bodies.

The paradox of the cultural centrality of the principle of liberty and the social reality of violated bodies illustrates the weakness of the "self-evident" right to liberty. I want to make a further claim as well; namely, that the cultural space that was opened to resolve this paradox still exists, and with it the debilitating relegation of bodies in a discussion of liberty.

A similar problem inheres in the principle right of the "pursuit of happiness." Beyond the fact that the term is so thoroughly subjective in nature that it offers little in the way of direction for material reality, it is primarily rooted in an emotive/intellectual category. That is to say, the word "happiness," as it has been given form in Western/American culture is one that operates almost exclusively in the realm of intellect. This form was early given it by Aristotle in the *Nichomachean Ethics* in which he says, "The good of man, happiness, is some kind of activity of the soul in conformity with virtue."[11] Notice that by this definition both the proper realm and the final measure of happiness have to do with the soul and are evidenced in intellectual disposition. The idea of the body as the site from which this right emanates does not exist.

The two rights that are most contextually relevant to our situation then, liberty and the pursuit of happiness, are both grounded in and replicate a worldview in which the body is of only secondary concern. I suggest that this approach to the idea of human rights is flawed because it provides

little conceptual foundation to argue for the rights of those who are exclusively identified with their bodies—women and racial/ethnic minorities.[12]
Objectification of those groups as bodies leads to their exclusion from the
constructed universe in which human rights discourse operates in the Western context.

SACRED GROUND: "SOMEBODINESS" AS
THE SITE OF HUMAN RIGHTS DISCOURSE

Let us review the argument to this point. I have contended that much of our
thinking about human rights in the American context is flawed because it
relies on an unstable conceptual basis; namely, the self evident truths laid
out in the Declaration of Independence. The flaw that I identified was that
these truths are neither self-evident nor universal in our context. I then
went on to suggest that any value that may have attached to them is further
undercut by the dichotomous understanding of human persons as first minds
then bodies. That understanding of much of our intellectual tradition holds
and is still very prevalent today. Taken together these flaws create a context
in which it is extremely difficult if not impossible to adequately conceive of,
much less advocate unequivocally for, the rights of all human persons. What
then do I propose as an alternative?

A distinctly Christian alternative to the preamble, yet one which is not
exclusionary, must take up the preeminent difficulties outlined above. First,
it must take seriously the issue of integrative bodily existence and resist the
impulse toward the creation of a normative subject whose cultural/discursive
existence militates against the well-being of those not identified with this
subject. Second, this alternative grounding must resist any discourse of rights
that decontextualizes, dehistoricizes, or spiritualizes the well-being of human
persons and their bodies. In essence, a helpful alternative must bring about
the "end of man" so that embodied human persons may flourish. I believe
that a nascent statement of this grounding can be found in the thought of
Martin Luther King Jr., specifically, in his ideas about somebodiness and dignity. King provides a helpful theory that utilizes a theopolitical rhetoric, particularly compelling in late modern America, to which I now turn.

In a speech given in 1962 King coined the phrase "somebodiness" to
describe the transformation that was taking place for many black people as
they struggled to attain their civil rights:

Probably the most powerful force, however, in breaking down the
barriers of segregation is the new determination of the Negro him-

self. For many years the Negro tacitly accepted them. He was often the victim of stagnant passivity and deadening complacency. While there were always lone voices in the Negro community crying out against segregation, conditions of fear and apathy made it difficult for them to develop into a mass chorus. But through the forces of history something happened to the Negro. . . . He has come to feel that he is somebody. And with this new sense of "somebodiness" and self-respect, a new Negro has emerged with a new determination to achieve freedom and human dignity what ever the cost may be.[13]

In this statement King deals with both the subjective and objective aspects of "somebodiness." The subjective aspect is that the achievement of the feeling of being somebody, the objective aspect is the material recognition by society of that status. What King is pointing to here is the idea that persons must be recognized as "somebodies" in order for the idea, or application, of rights to have any meaning. King also brings our attention to an important point—the reality that is encapsulated by the idea of somebodiness is not simply an imputed status, it is also and perhaps more importantly an achieved sense of the worth and dignity of oneself. These are important categories for thinking about human rights because the assault on those rights never operates simply on the objective level, it operates on the subjective level.

Forces that deny the human rights of persons are never satisfied to objectively remove and violate those rights; it is also their purpose to create a conceptual matrix in which it appears evident that these violated persons never had a claim to those rights in the first place. One can look at Nazi Germany, South Africa under apartheid, or the American South under Jim Crow to see instances of entire regimes of knowledge being constructed that not only explained why persecution and exploitation were being visited on certain persons, but which also legitimated these death-dealing practices as right and proper. Those regimes of knowledge were almost always built upon the objectification of people to bodies—bodies that could then be exploited and destroyed. In the case of Nazi Germany it was the reduction of Jewish persons and communities to the culturally manufactured trope: *the Jew*. Any perusal of the popular propaganda literature of the early years of the regime reveals the effort expended to first conceptually construct *the Jew*, and then to inflict a "social death" on Jewish persons so that they might then be physically destroyed.[14] In South Africa and the southern United States this process was also carried out with the construction of the cultural trope *the Negro* and the abstraction of all persons of African descent into it, for the purposes of exploitation of actual bodies. So, what we have then is an objective and subjective violation, both of which focus on the body—conceptually and materially. Therefore, a focus on the body is crucial when conceiving human rights. The body is the primary site of violation.

King makes a further recognition in his statement—the dialectical character of somebodiness. The assault on human bodies that characterizes the assault on human rights is also an assault on the human spirit. It is an assault that seeks to destroy the personal unity of human beings by denying the integrated nature of their existence. The spirit is destroyed by its total reduction to the body. King characterizes this assault on the spirit as an assault on persons' dignity.

In identifying dignity as a primary category for conceptually grounding the struggle for human rights, we run the risk of creating a principle similar to the self-evident truths, with all of their attendant weaknesses. King, however, almost exclusively focused on both the condition and actions of bodies. King's career as an orator on behalf of justice can overshadow the reality that his rhetoric was focused on bodies—their violation and the proper response to that violation. A quick glance at the Civil Rights Movement bears this out.

The Montgomery Bus Boycott began in response to the enforced placement in a specific location of scorn and ridicule—the back of the bus. The boycott began because Rosa Parks would not move her body from a seat. When the boycott was successful, the first thing she and King did was to place their bodies in previously forbidden seats. The struggle to integrate Little Rock High School was a conflict over which bodies could be present in that building. The contest for voting rights was fought over the material reality of which bodies could be in the voting booth to select other bodies that would govern *every body*. Housing desegregation was about which bodies could inhabit structures in particular geographic locations. We often lose sight of the centrality of bodies in the Civil Rights Movement and overprivilege the principles and ideals that were being contested.

King's concern for the material condition of bodies was evidenced in all of the struggles in which he was involved, including the last one from which he took a side trip to visit Memphis: the Poor People's March. He was also concerned with the vocation of bodies to struggle against systems of law and custom and the regimes of knowledge on which they were based—systems that created disintegrating conditions in which bodies were forced to exist. The vocation of struggle was based upon the conviction that bodies that express and live out the proper unity of purpose and being create the material reality for which human beings were created. This unity was achieved only by the liberation of all bodies from those systems of disintegration. For an adequate understanding of King's vision of the proper condition for bodies, it is necessary to turn to the Christian roots of his anthropology.

The background of King's vision of humanity is the creation story found in Genesis 1 and 2 of the Christian scripture. In this narrative there are three significant aspects that characterize the creation of human persons—the creation of a body, the imbuement of that body with the spirit of God, and a founding relationship between that living soul and God. In his sermon "Three Dimensions of a Complete Life," King contends that all three of these aspects are necessary to reflect the proper condition for which humanity was created. It is the disruption of this integrated existence which is the mark of sin and the alienation of humanity from itself and God.[15] King also hearkened to the Pauline notion that sin, once unleashed upon the world, was a power that worked to the destruction of humanity by confounding this unity of existence. In his context King talked about this as the power of prejudice, racism, and hate. These, for King, were not simply words but names much like "legion" which had the power to cloud the minds of persons in a way that would allow them to perpetuate all manner of evil on the bodies of their fellow human beings. This is why the struggle was so important for King—because the objective encounter of these powers of evil worked to free the subjective reality of human beings of their power—both in the case of the violator and the violated.

Dignity is the word which best describes what King envisioned as the final category of proper respect for human persons and it is the one I choose to ground my rhetoric of human rights. What might a respect for the dignity of human persons look like as a basis for a discourse of human rights? I begin by brief observations of what dignity is not.

Dignity is not an abstract transhistorical principle that relates to an abstract set of rights due to an abstract normative subject. Dignity is not a cultural value. Dignity is not something imputed to somebody. Dignity is not a category that can be definitively narrated through a single set of experiences—there is no normative subject in whom dignity inheres. Dignity is not something we obtain as a possession. How then do I describe dignity?

First, dignity is a contextually experienced reality known by human bodies that enjoy well-being. By this I mean that the character of dignity changes from context to context and the respect for it likewise changes. In one context the respect for dignity might manifest itself as the proper provision of food for bodies that are starving. In another it might be the replacement of unhealthy foods that serve nothing but corporate interests at the expense of the long-term health of children. The well-being of bodies in a specific context is the measure of the experience and respect of human dignity.

Second, dignity is something that, while experienced within culture, is not defined by culture. Human culture is contaminated in every place, on every level, by the workings of what the Christian tradition calls sin, but others might call systemic injustice. Human culture evolves routinely to protect and further the privilege of those who hold the power to manufacture and control cultural meanings and significations. Not surprisingly then, when we allow dignity to be proscribed by culture, it is almost always in ways that appeal to a set of principles that either have little to do with the condition of bodies or that seeks to find dignity in those conditions no matter how debased. Dignity is the experience of, and respect for, whatever it is in that particular culture which brings about wholeness and well-being for bodies in that context.

Third, dignity is the right of every human being in their particular context to experience, and to have respected, the well-being of their body. Too often, when we talk of human dignity we do it in such a way that it seems a gift that is bestowed on persons by some benevolent power. The problem with this type of evocation is that it implies that it can likewise be taken away. Dignity, when rendered in just this way, is something that finally belongs to someone else and is only provisionally granted. This characterization is one that conceptually distances the idea of dignity from bodies as the site of its meaning.

Fourth, because of its contextual nature, dignity cannot be narratively defined by one experience. The narrative of the subjective experience of dignity is as varied and unfinished as are the narratives of all human beings. We often want to lionize the experience of some as they struggle to achieve the experience of dignity and in so doing freeze in time that experience as normative. This holds two significant dangers: (1) it creates a context in which the evolving struggle for dignity can be confounded by antiquated definitions and meaning. A prime example of this is how present-day opponents of minority rights hearken to words used in an earlier time, evoking those earlier meanings, in order to circumvent aspirations that are substantially the same but altered to fit a new context; and (2) it stifles the creativity required for facing new contexts. An example of this is the continued use of the term "civil rights" in a context where economic and human rights are what are at stake. New wine requires new wineskins.

Finally, the experience of dignity is something that is achieved through the struggle for the respect of our bodies and the bodies of others. We have seen all too often the way abstracted rights are routinely denied to certain human persons, even when they are putatively identified as being applicable to everyone. We have seen in many instances the way that persons and communities achieve a sense of dignity and worth as they struggle against those systems of marginalization. King's entire premise in his approach to the Civil Rights Movement was the idea that not only was justice restored by overcoming segregation, but also that *through the movement of bodies* those involved were restored to their full sense of dignity and humanity. In the final analysis, that category of dignity as achieved and respected formed the core of King's work. It is this idea of dignity that I take to be an adequate ground upon which to theorize human rights.

CONCLUSION

My recovery of King's idea of "somebodiness" mediated through the motif of dignity as a grounding for theorizing about human rights has sought to recenter the discourse on the well-being of human bodies. Beyond this intervention, this recovery also reminds us that a concern for human rights must also take seriously the rehumanization of oppressor, oppressed, and bystander alike. By joining the subjective and objective dimensions of respect for dignity, I suggest that the project of striving for human rights is a struggle against the powers of alienation and disintegration that inscribe themselves not only on the bodies of the violated but also on the souls of all involved. In a sense, what I am contending for is a grounding for human rights discourse that, interpreted through Christian symbols, reclaims the Edenic vision of human wholeness and integrity and proleptically claims the eschatological vision of the New Jerusalem in which the children of God "shall hunger no more, neither thirst any more . . . and God will wipe away every tear from their eyes."[16] Isn't this vision, after all, the goal of human rights discourse—no more needless suffering, no more needless tears?

NOTES

1. Martin Luther King Jr. "Three Dimensions of a Complete Life," in *A Knock at Midnight*, Clayborne Carson and Peter Holloran, eds. (New York: Warner, 1998), pp. 117–40.

2. Before going on it is important that I clarify what I mean by situational self-transcendance. Reinhold Niebuhr, Paul Tillich, and a number of twentieth-century theologians have provided helpful redux of Calvin's category of pride as the primary impediment to the proper use of self-transcendence. These descriptions have been rightly critiqued by Feminist and Womanist theologians who note that the aptness of these accounts depends on a particular position of social privilege and power and are, consequently, of only limited value in describing the corruption of human relationality per se. The result of these critiques has been that general statements of corrupted self-transcendence have largely fallen out of vogue. Although I agree that the reductionist claims attached by Niebuhr et al. to their descriptions of corrupted self-transcendence—that pride is the primary category of interpretation—is appropriately critiqued, I also believe that Howard Thurman was

correct in noting that surrender of one's dignity in toto as the price for physical survival is likewise a corruption of self-transcendance (*Jesus and the Dis-
inherited*, Richmond, IN: Friends Press, chaps 2 and 3). Consequently, I
believe that an interpretation of corrupted human relationality properly
includes this idea of distorted self-transcendance with the proviso that attention is paid to the social and economic location of the subject, hence my use
of the term "situational self-transcendence."

3. Ian McFarland. *Difference and Identity* (Cleveland, OH: Pilgrim
Press 2001), p. 2.

4. Martin Luther King Jr. *A Testament of Hope: The Essential Writings
and Speeches of Martin Luther King, Jr.*, ed. James M. Washington (San Francisco: HarperSanFrancisco, 1986), p. 219.

5. Michael J. Perry. *The Idea of Human Rights: Four Inquiries* (New
York: Oxford University Press, 1998), chapter 1.

6. Carol J. Adams, "Beastly Theology: When Epistemology Creates
Ontology," in *Divine Aporia: Postmodern Conversations about the Other*, ed.
John C. Hawley (Lewisburg, PA.: Bucknell University Press, 2000), p. 229.

7. Bartolome de Las Casas, "Are Not the Indians Men?" in *Witness:
Writings of Bartolome de Las Casas*, ed. George Sanderlin (Maryknoll, NY:
Orbis, 1971), pp. 66–79, 137–42.

8. Charles Carroll. *The Negro: A Beast? or, In the Image of God* (St.
Louis: American Book and Bible House, 1900).

9. Henry Yu, *Thinking Orientals: Migration, Contact and Exoticism in
Modern America* (New York: Oxford University Press, 2001).

10. Garth Kasimu Baker-Fletcher, *Xodus: An African American Male
Journey* (Minneapolis: Fortress, 1996), p. 50.

11. Aristotle, *Nichomachean Ethics* (Indianapolis: Hackett, 1985), p. 22.

12. While certainly one can point to the Bill of Rights contained in the
Constitution as an instance of rights that take embodied persons seriously, I
contend in our context the self-evident truths expressed in the Declaration
of Independence have a far greater conceptual public currency than does the
Constitution and is therefore of greater consequence for thinking about
human rights.

13. Martin Luther King Jr. "The Case against Tokenism," in *A Testament of Hope: The Essential Writings of Martin Luther King, Jr.*, p. 108.

14. Orlando Patterson, *Slavery and Social Death* (Cambridge: Harvard
University Press, 1982), chap. 1.

15. Martin Luther King Jr. "Three Dimensions of a Complete Life," in
*A Knock at Midnight: Inspiration from the Great Sermons of Reverend Martin
Luther King, Jr.*, pp. 117–40.

16. Revelation of John, chapter 7, verses 16–17. Revised Standard
Version.

CHAPTER 8

Persons, Politics, and a Catholic Understanding of Human Rights

JEAN BETHKE ELSHTAIN

Human beings are soft-shelled creatures. All bodies are fragile. But some bodies in some circumstances are more vulnerable than others.

In Argentina, during its period of the so-called dirty war in the late 1970s and early 1980s, young people were the most vulnerable—most likely to be "disappeared"—a horrible and dreaded word that then entered the political vocabulary as part of the gallery of horrors of human mistreatment of other human beings. Young men were the most vulnerable of all. Over two-thirds of the "disappeared" were men.

Those who rose to protest these disappearances were women, Las Madres, The Mothers of the Plaza. Because of the potency of the symbol of "the mother" in Catholic societies, women had not only symbolic authority but at least partial insulation from the violence of the regime. How would it look to attack a group of mothers looking for their lost children? Mothers weren't exempt, of course, but mothers openly marching in a public place were more difficult to assault than a group of men, of fathers. The language in which Las Madres protested these disappearances was double and universal in each instance: the language of a mother's grief and the language of human rights. We see in such circumstances how necessary are rights, albeit a weak reed when tyrants are determined to harm and to harm egregiously. Nevertheless, we cannot do without the cry that takes shape as a cry that one's rights, one's very dignity as a person, is under assault.

Take a second example. In her powerful prison memoirs, *Eyes of the Tailless Animals*, so called because prisoners in North Korea's extensive gulags and torture centers are called "tailless animals" and reduced to less than

139

human status, Soon Ok Lee writes of a prison cell in which she found herself after she had survived a series of horrendous tortures:

> Six pregnant women were lying on the cold cement floor, which was not even covered with a mat. I thought, even animals receive better treatment outside this prison. The women were giving birth to their babies. The babies were supposed to be stillborn. Because Kim Il Sung had ordered that all anti-Communists be eliminated within three generations, prison policy said that prisoners, who were considered anti-Communists by definition, could not have babies in prison. When pregnant women came to prison, they were forced to abort their babies. Poison was injected into the babies cuddled in their mothers' wombs. After the injection, the pregnant woman suffered tremendous pain until the babies were stillborn about twenty-four hours later. Medical officers walked around the pregnant women and kicked their swollen bellies if they screamed or moaned.
>
> Miraculously, some of the babies were born alive. They cried like normal babies do. When a live baby was born, a medical officer said to the medical prisoners, "Kill it! These criminals don't have any right to have babies. What are you doing? Kill it right now!"
>
> The mothers of these newborn babies just laid on the floor and sobbed so helplessly while a medical prisoner's shaking hands twisted the babies neck. The babies struggled for a short second, but they died so easily. Male prisoners wrapped the babies in rags and dumped them into a basket.
>
> I was shocked. This was the most cruel human behavior I had ever heard of in my life. Even today, I dream about the women who had just given birth to their babies.[1]

Soon Ok Lee is one of the few to survive the North Korean gulag. Most prisoners die within four months. She entered a bewildered if convinced communist, wondering why she had been singled out (evidently the local commissar simply had a quota to meet and trumped up some charges against her because he was irritated with her for refusing him a favor), and she escaped a committed Christian. She became a Christian while in prison because she saw how Christians were particularly singled out for abuse, men and women and children, yet how they loved one another, even in that hell on earth.

Why? Because, thinking of those babies who survived attempted coerced abortion, crying feebly, their necks wrung—*They Died So Easily*—

she yearned for a way to lift up human dignity. Whether in the gulags of North Korea or the torture centers in Buenos Aires or in any of the other hells on earth past and present, human dignity needs a guarantee. There are particular violations meted out to helpless prisoners, like those fragile new-borns and their crying mothers, that the language of rights, even a powerful account of rights, seems inadequate and puny when measured up against such horrors. Something so deep is being violated—something intrinsic to and constitutive of our humanity. Pope John Paul II insisted repeatedly over the course of his great human rights pontificate that, when we find ourselves face to face with another human being, we must "pause at the irreducible." Many do not pause. Many do far worse.

But what sorts of rights? Let me turn to alternative versions of rights. Let's ask ourselves: First, what version of rights yields what sorts of rights cultures and, second, what culture of rights most deeply recognizes our intrinsic dignity and our sociality? And why, therefore, is such a rights culture more open to the particular concerns of my overall topic than any other?

What construals of rights and rights-talk underlie, or are consistent with, what versions of a human rights culture? There can be a human rights culture in which "things just happen to have worked out this way" and rights are turned into a kind of shopping list. Rights keep proliferating and it is difficult to keep up with them as different groups of claimants push claims they choose to couch in the language of particular rights that apply specifically, even exclusively, to that group of claimants; all of this by contrast to rights that apply to all human beings without exception.

Do we really require *separate* rights that pertain in light of what I learned in graduate school to call "ascriptive characteristics," those things about us that are accidents of birth? Race and gender would be two examples. To be human, by contrast, is no accident of birth: it is definitional of it. Humanness is the great leveler: who belongs definitionally within the category human? Have we lost confidence in our humanness to do the necessary legal and political work?

Let's let these questions hang in the air as I turn to an argument defending the power and robustness of a version of human rights that flows from Catholic social teaching. The great social encyclicals are addressed to "all persons of goodwill" and are said to apply to "all without definition." These arguments are offered up to and for Christians and non-Christians alike as a way to articulate and to defend a human rights culture that sustains that culture for all persons.

I begin with *Dignitatis Humanae*, 1965. The document proclaims "the dignity of the human person" and goes on to insist that that dignity involves enjoying and making use of responsible freedom not driven by coercion" [but]"motivated by a sense of duty."[2] Duty and the rightful exercise of rights are not severed from one another—this by contrast to much of our regnant "rights talk" from which any correlative notion of duty has been expunged.

Indeed, much contemporary "rights talk" equates rights to wants and preferences derivable from the presuppositions of contractarianism that posit the self as primordially free, understood, in the classic works of Thomas Hobbes and Jean-Jacques Rousseau, at least, as a condition of asociality. Freedom means to be free from external impediment in one's unimpeded forward motion, for Hobbes. Rousseau has a version in which our entanglements (with women, certainly) wind up corrupting us, sapping us of our original natural vigor and liberty.

Hobbes and others associated with radical nominalism saw persons as entities driven by irresistible desires and a power urge—a "restless seeking of power after power that ceaseath only in death."[3] Any rights culture derived from such premises becomes a way we confront and are protected from one another. There is no orientation toward freedom in this view whereas, in Catholic social teaching, the context within which rights are located is undeniably teleological in the sense that there is a good toward which we tend and there is an intrinsic connection between truth, reason, and human rights and freedom.

Let's deepen the contrast between nominalist "rights talk" that emerges in light of primordial human urges and the alternative I have begun to unpack. There are three parts here: (1) anthropological presuppositions, or understandings of the human persons; (2) the concept of rights itself, and, finally, (3) the good toward which rights tend. If my argument is in any way compelling, it helps to reveal a late modern dilemma: we cannot do without rights, but the ways in which rights are generalized and universalized may not be capable of sustaining those rights at the most fundamental level because too much of the deep background and justification for rights has been jettisoned along the way.

ANTHROPOLOGICAL PRESUPPOSITIONS

When I was in graduate school it was still possible to talk about contrasting views of human nature without being accused of that most dire of all contemporary sins, essentialism. Perhaps we have thrown out way too much by clapping a strict censorship over words like nature and the natural in the erroneous assumption that all those who evoke nature or the natural are committed to the view that human beings are not shaped in any fundamental way by their social and political worlds and their historic time and place. This is balderdash. When we speak of anthropology, we talk about what sorts of creatures we are and we can do this without smuggling in a strict determinism of any kind.

You need some sort of view of human persons in order to speak coherently of human rights. You can do this by acknowledging, as I did at the outset, our fragility; by speaking of our dignity and uniqueness; and by going an Augustinian route and talking about how deeply we are "pressed" by the world. You can do all of this even as you frame considerations of human political life with a strong notion of the good toward which human being tends and the plural goods that reflect a higher good and draw us closer to it.

To evoke anthropology in this way is open to cultural and historical specificity and the role of contingency in human affairs. So, for example, if one argues that rights require the conviction that every human being is sacred and inviolable in some basic sense, this has the status of a given. What sort of person? An intrinsically, not contingently, social creature. We are born to relationality. Rights are lodged in a presupposition of human dignity. Rights locate us in a world with others: that is why rights and duties are linked in the Catholic tradition of "rights talk." I should note here that, although this dignity of the self cannot be entirely dehistoricized, there is a necessary moment of abstraction (if you will) as we speak about human persons as such.

Thus: the modern social encyclicals affirm with even greater emphasis the importance of rights and their centrality to a defense of the dignity of persons. And these rights are not spoken of primarily as individual claims against other individuals or society. They are woven into a concept of community that envisions the person as a distinctive part of overlapping communities. Rights exist within a historic and social context and they are intelligible in terms of the obligations of persons to one another within that context.

This helps us to steer clear of excessive individualism without, at the same time, submerging persons into an indiscriminate social "blob" such that they cannot be seen for the distinctive beings they are. Within this vision, commonality is on some level assumed and solidarity is an achievement. What wants explaining is not solidarity but isolation. By contrast, those oriented to the views embedded in nominalist "rights talk," strain mightily to figure out how such essentially selfish creatures as human beings might actually relate to one another in relatively decent ways.

There is an undeniable individualist thrust within contemporary culture. This way of thinking—if taken to extreme—sees us as complete unto ourselves. The self is sovereign and has proprietary interest in itself. Our speech is a monologue and not a dialogue. In the abortion debate, you find this way of talking prevails. But does self-sovereignty really serve any person and his or her needs? There is, to be sure, an insight in these self-sovereign accounts worth preserving, namely, that we really do become, in some profound sense, what we have chosen.

But the problem with choice in much contemporary debate is that it is impoverished by being reduced to wants and preferences without any necessary reference to goods, ends, and purposes and how one might distinguish the more from the less worthy. There is no normative ordering of goods. This sovereign self casts a pall of suspicion over ties of reciprocal obligation and mutual interdependence with which women and their lives have long been associated and, I submit, such presuppositions over time erode friendship, families, civil society, polities, even markets. This erosion of civil society institutions invites what political theorist William Galston calls "the plenipotentiary state, an entity that must accrue more power unto itself and knows not when, and where, and why to stop.[4]

Catholic social teaching speaks throughout of "responsible" freedom realized through multiple, plural associations with their respective authoritative claims. Our dignity can neither be repealed nor negated. *Dignitatis* also declares that the right to religious freedom, for all persons, is first and foremost because this right speaks most pointedly to the ur-ground of rights, namely, our very selves geared, on this view, to seeking the truth as a principle of our natures. Creating immunities from state control over religious conscience makes possible a form of human flourishing that is unattainable if there is no freedom in the area of religion.

RIGHTS, UNDERSTOOD HOW

Human rights are by now inevitable, as I have already claimed. But the gravamen of rights differs widely. In the American Constitution, the first noticeable mention of rights was the Bill of Rights and these revolved largely around civic freedoms—assembly, press, speech—and concerned primarily what government cannot do to you. It is surely no accident that the first amendment concerns religion: free exercise plus nonestablishment. Free exercise assumes communities of believers free from external control. It suggests, does it not, that the regime of rights cannot be sustained by rights alone? One needs selves and communities of certain kinds.

Yet "me and my rights" seems to be where we have arrived in much rights-talk. The human will is made absolute. Rights are deployed in order to institutionalize the sovereignty of the human will. To recognize any limit to the exercise of will is deemed a diminution of the self and appears to us as a form of self-abnegation. Pope John Paul II addressed this issue at a Plenary Assembly of the Sacred College of Cardinals in 1979 when he observed that

> Very often, freedom of will and the freedom of the person are
> understood as the *right to do anything*, as the right not to accept any
> norm or any duty that involves commitment. . . . But Christ does
> not teach us such an interpretation and exercise of freedom. The
> freedom of each individual creates duties, demands full respect for
> the hierarchy of values, and is potentially directed to the Good
> without limits, to God. In Christ's eyes, freedom is not first of all
> "freedom from" but "freedom for." The full enjoyment of freedom
> is love, in particular the love through which individuals give
> themselves.[5]

Within Catholic teaching, this freedom is underwritten by religious freedom. *Dignitatis* proclaims religious freedom a "civil right" in accord with the dignity of persons, being lodged in a very principle of our natures insofar as we are endowed with reason and free will; hence, we are propelled by a "moral obligation to seek the truth, especially religious truth."[6] As Pope John Paul II argued: *Dignitatis* expresses "not only the theological concept of the question but also the concept reached from the point of view of natural law, that is to say from the 'purely human' position, on the basis of premises given by human experience, human reason, and our sense of human dignity."[7]

This right to religious freedom is not a subjective claim but an objective truth or the civil recognition of such. At the same time it must be said that this way of talking and thinking is unintelligible to many of our contemporaries within a shared culture—the contemporary West—this despite the fact that religious freedom is a bulwark of the rights lexicon. Without some account of the human good, however, it is hard to know what this right is all about. Telling us what rights are all about—the explicit recognition of our intrinsic dignity—provides a good bit of the heft and lift of the argument here sketched.

A shopping list of rights distorts the matter by putting all declared "rights" on a par: in this way a right to state-paid vacation is just one right on a par with the right to religious and political freedom or the right to be free from torture. Without a way to sift and winnow rights, rights easily become distorted and even trivialized: a most unfortunate development indeed.

RIGHTS, PERSONHOOD AND WOMEN

In a world defined by rights as adversarial possessions, human identity is flattened out. We are all said to be nothing but bundles of needs and claims. What separates us from one another is not our human distinctiveness, in this view, but the fact that some are always cast as powerful; others always are cast as powerless; some as hegemonic; others as victims. Rights are what we use to "get ours." We lose a rich notion of human plurality and distinctiveness in this process as well as a recognition that all are sinners, all in need of grace and forgiveness.

Let's refract this issue with special reference to whether men and women are treated (1) as by definition inferior in relation to superior, that is, women as inferior, men as superior; or, (2) as identical in a way that flattens out distinctiveness and negates embodiment; or, alternatively, (3) as analogical beings who work out their identities over time in relation, the view that most comports with Catholic understandings of rights. Here we must part company with those of our Christian forebears who saw in man the most perfect representation of what it meant to be created in the image of God.

In an interesting series of essays on "integral sex complementarity," Sr. Prudence Allen writes: "In light of contemporary understandings, the writings of Pope John Paul II are illuminating, for he states explicitly that woman and man equally reflect the image of God."[8] Allen concludes that it is "hard to overestimate the significance of this shift in emphasis and what it is bringing to the Church's understanding of man and woman as persons."[9]

This shift in understanding is significant because it gestures toward an understanding that puts together in a single frame rights as markers of human dignity and a view of male and female in relation. Not every problem is hereby resolved; rather, a theological basis for understanding rights is enhanced and proffered in a way that provides ample ground for disputation over the implications of this view for male and female standing, offices, and identities.

In a 1994 "World Day of Peace" message, John Paul II offered reflections on "Women: Teachers of Peace." His starting point was clear: "If, from the very beginning, girls are looked down upon or regarded as inferior, their sense of dignity will be gravely impaired and their healthy development inevitably compromised. Discrimination in childhood will have lifelong effects and will prevent women from fully taking part in the life of society."[10] The ground here is an ontology of human dignity that yields strong conclusions against invidious comparisons and ill use. This is a position at once old and new. It goes back to Trinitarian understandings of a commune of separate yet one person(s). Male and female are from the beginning embodied beings who display both the marks of solitude and a communion of persons.

Surely Christians of all peoples are obliged to take up the question of rights, sex, gender, participation, and power from a standpoint of theological distinction and argument enriched by philosophy. In our own time, rights have been driven more and more into a corner in which they are seen as a way to get and to hold power: this is more reflective of Machiavellian

thought than Catholic social thought and it invites simplistic oppressor/
oppressed scenarios. It flattens out distinctiveness. It pushes for a harsh
politicization of all human relationships. It undermines the dialogic "working" of men and women as creators and sustainers of one another under or
within the frame of a transcendent principle that brings an appropriate
humility to all human projects.

Rights as markers of human dignity is not compatible with rights as
vehicles to attain dominion. In fact, rights are the way we limit and chasten
dominion. This more "horizontal" notion of rights is dependent upon a
shared "vertical" relationship to God through Christ's incarnation and passion, through creation, fall and redemption. In this world, men and women
are different yet equal in dignity and worth. And unjust rule is a form of
dominion that privileges and dignifies one sex to the deprivation of the
other. It signifies a fundamental disordering of human life.

CONCLUSION

Thus we are borne full circle back to our central imperatives. The ends
toward which rights tend cannot be evaluated absent a recognition that one
must begin with some understanding of the human person and her and his
fragility. The Universal Declaration of Human Rights affirms the "inherent
dignity" of all persons. This dignity is not free floating, not an arbitrary principle picked up on and found useful; rather, human dignity is lodged in the
fact that human beings are creatures of a certain sort. Catholic social teaching fleshes this out by insisting that, if contemporary society has great difficulty figuring out an intelligible and defensible way to articulate and to limit
rights, this is because it has embraced a nominalist construal that admits of
pragmatic adjudication only when it comes to all the difficult questions, thus
affording little guidance as to what counts as an offense, an act of violence,
in the first instance, or what is a basic entitlement, in the second.

In the words of John Paul II: "Truly, one must recognize that, with an
unstoppable crescendo from the Old to the New Testament, there is manifested in Christianity the authentic conception of man as a person and no
longer merely as an individual. If an individual perishes, the species remains
unaltered: in the logic established by Christianity, however, when a person
dies, something unique and unrepeatable is lost."[11]

Michael Ignatieff points out in an article, "Human Rights: The Midlife
Crisis," that a "cloak of silence" has been "thrown over the question of God."
Ignatieff's reference point is the deliberations that led to the Universal Declaration itself. In Ignatieff's words: "The Universal Declaration enunciates
rights; it doesn't explain why people have them."[12] Communist and some

non-Communist delegations, at the time of the drafting, rejected explicitly any reference to human beings as created in God's image. Even "by nature" failed to pass muster.

So "secularism has become the lingua franca of global human rights, as English has become the lingua franca of the global economy. Both serve as lowest common denominators, enabling people to pretend to share more than they actually do."[13] Can this pretense be kept up? Or will it lead, over time, to watering down or detioration of a culture of rights? We cannot predict a future with great confidence. Ignatieff, for one, is undaunted, for it is none too clear to him, at least, "why human rights need the idea of the sacred at all. Why do we need an idea of God in order to believe that human beings should not be beaten, tortured, coerced, indoctrinated, or in any way sacrificed against their will?"[14]

These insights, he insists, derive from a certain version of moral reciprocity, a secularized Golden Rule. He calls this a minimalist anthropology. But just how reliant is this notion of moral reciprocity absent a substantive notion of persons and their moral standing? Will it stop abuses of the sort we saw in Taliban-dominated Afghanistan where women's life expectancy plummeted and girls were kept illiterate? Where women could be summarily executed for alleged sexual infractions? This is what happens when women are construed as lesser beings in a particular sort of "religious" context. Secularism has its own version of the denigration of women.

There is a lot more work to do in this area. What sort of human rights culture? One tethered to moral dignity and equality or one cut loose from it? One in which rights proliferate but human dignity plummets? Current state-mandated euthanasia movements would be one case in point. Rather than discussing the terms under which the healing profession might be prescriptively required to end a life on demand, states should be respectful as they stand before fundamental rights, rights that have their source in the presumption of inviolable human dignity and moral equality. The state did not create these rights or the ur-ground on which they stand. It either recognizes them or it does not. It is either their guarantor or their denigrator.

You cannot think intelligibly about persons, rights, and Catholic social thought without tending to these matters.

NOTES

1. Soon Ok Lee, *Eyes of the Tailless Animals: Prison Memoirs of a North Korean Woman* (Seoul: Living Sacrifice, 1999), pp. 90–91.

2. "Dignitatis Humanae," appears in *The Pope Speaks* (vol. II, no.1, winter, 1966).

3. Thomas Hobbes, *The Leviathan*, ed. Michael Oakshotte (New York: Collier, 1966); see especially his jumores or infamores—chapter 13 on the "war of all against all."

4. Galston speaks of "The Plenipotentiary state" evoking Abraham Kuyper, the great reformed theologian, on the theme of "sphere sovereignty." See *The Practice of Liberal Pluralism* (Cambridge: Cambridge University Press, 2004).

5. Giorgio Filibeck, ed., *Human Rights in the Teaching of the Church: From John XXIII to John Paul II* (Vatican Lity: Liberin Editrice Vaticans, 1994), pp. 161–62.

6. "Dignitatis Humanea," p. 86.

7. *Human Rights in the Teaching of the Church*, p. 321 (from "Redemptor Hominis").

8. Sr. Prudence Allen, "Integral Sex Complementarity and the Theology of Communion," *Communio* 17 (Winter, 1990, pp. 523–44, 542–43).

9. Ibid., Sr. Allen.

10. Pope John Paul II, *Origins* (24, no. 28, 1994), pp. 465–69.

11. John Paul II, "To a General Audience," 1984, in *Human Rights in the Teaching of the Church*, p. 51.

12. Michael Ignatieff, "Human Rights: The Midlife Crisis," in *New York Review of Books* (May 20, 1999), pp. 58–62, 58).

13. Ibid.

14. Ibid, p. 59.

CHAPTER 9

Human Rights and Asian Values

KAM WENG NG

RENEWING THE DEBATE ON ASIAN VALUES AND HUMAN RIGHTS

Pundits may recall that in the nineties Western powers took to task several Asian governments for alleged abuse of human rights. Western governments publicly criticized China for violating human rights in the wake of its violent repression of the student demonstration at Tiananmen Square in 1989. Diplomatic pressure was applied to Indonesia to stop its military aggression in East Timor. Concerns were raised regarding draconian security laws that empower the Malaysian government to detain its citizens without trial. Even President Clinton intervened when a Singapore court sentenced a wayward American youth, Michael Fay, to be caned for vandalizing cars.

In response, Asian governments mobilized their public intellectuals to the defense. In particular, Asian leaders proposed that human rights should be formulated within a framework of Asian values. The leaders of the Asian values framework have especially been associated with countries in East Asia: China's Marxist leaders who have been historically antagonistic toward the West, Lee Kuan Yew who represents the "Singapore School" which seeks to legitimize its social engineering to shape a modern nation anchored on Confucian tradition, and Dr. Mohammad Mahathir, known for his vitriolic criticism against Western values and his vigorous efforts to present Malaysia as a model of Islamic modernity.

It should be noted that the term "Asian values" assumes that there exists a set of common values throughout an obviously vast region that encompasses a plurality of cultures and religions including Islam, Buddhism, and Confucianism. It is therefore tempting to dismiss the Asian protagonists on grounds that their concept of Asian values is an artificial construct deployed to legitimize authoritarian governments and that the ruling elite's ideology is not even accepted by local grassroots intellectuals. Still, one should acknowledge their concerted effort to construct common grounds, beginning with the Bangkok Governmental Declaration (1993). The influence of Asian delegates was evident in the Vienna Declaration on Human Rights (1993). In any case there is sufficient agreement among Asian leaders at least in mounting a challenge to Western hegemony in the discourse on human rights.

International relations underwent a significant shift since the Al Qaeda terrorists attacked the World Trade Center in New York on September 11, 2001. Since then, the American government has seen the need for the cooperation of Asian governments in its war against the Al Qaeda global network and feels obliged to relax its criticism against human rights abuse by Asian governments. The United States government has even passed new security laws that grant authorities sweeping powers to conduct surveillance and detain terrorist suspects on its own soil. This effectively undermines the moral authority claimed by the United States to censure human rights abuse elsewhere. The consequence is an increasing tendency for the United States to close one eye to and mute its earlier criticism of repressive laws in Asian countries. Local Asian activists can only react with dismay when human rights become relegated to the back burners of diplomacy and international relations.

Ironically, this loss of interest in human rights issues comes at a time when Asian governments have also lost the grounds for justifying their authoritarian rule. They had asserted their freedom to define human rights in terms of Asian values. They acknowledged that the Asian approach to human rights might be more restrictive compared to the Western approach. Still, they argued that their approach was self-legitimating and worthy of respect since Asian values were evidently responsible for the astounding economic development in Asia. However, the financial crisis in 1997 has shattered this smug confidence.

Asian governments may welcome the reprieve that has come, now that Western governments no longer call them to task over human rights abuse. However, in the process, the debate on human rights and Asian values has faded. Not surprisingly, issues on human rights seem relegated to secondary columns in the mainstream newspapers today. Social activists are even beginning to wonder if we are witnessing the end of the era of human rights that enjoyed its apex in the nineties.

Asian activists can no longer hope for support from Western governments in their campaign for human rights or expect that political pressures will be brought to bear on Asian governments to restrain their abuse of human rights. Their only recourse is to deploy moral resources to sharpen their critique. For this reason, it is important to keep the debate on human rights and Asian values alive precisely because Asian governments continue to rely on Asian values (albeit implicitly) to justify authoritarian governance.

We shall explore the arguments deployed by Asian leaders to challenge Western discourse on human rights. Special attention will be given to the common arguments underlying their challenge. It is noted, however, that the Asian critique does not mean that human rights as a basic value is being rejected. What Asian leaders seek is to qualify these rights so that they become congruent with Asian history and tradition.

We will further explore how these conflicting concerns may be harmonized in a multitiered modernity anchored in local history and tradition. For example, analysis of Asian Islamic societies, which are traditionally regarded as centrally controlled societies, reveals cracks and openings in the social structure that make these societies vulnerable to the disruptive forces of modernity.[1] In turn, such disruptions may allow for the emergence of a new ethos that is supportive of human rights development.

THE CONTEXT OF THE DEBATE

Asian leaders have continued to protest that Western governments are cynically exploiting human rights issues to justify their interference with the internal affairs of Asian societies. In 1994, Dr. Mahathir criticized Western governments in a keynote address on human rights:

> Much later the Cold War ended and the Soviet Union collapsed leaving a unipolar world. All pretense of non-interference in the affairs of independent nations were dropped. A new international order was enunciated in which the powerful countries claim a right to impose their system of government, their free market and their concept of human rights in every country.
>
> In the eyes of these critics, geopolitical interests rather than moral ideals determine how significant human rights issues should figure in East-West relationships. For example, many Asians wonder why the USA makes human rights an issue with China, but ignores the absence of such rights in oil producing countries like Saudi Arabia.[2]

Mahathir complained bitterly that the Western governments stood by when Serbs went on with their butchering of the Bosnians.

In contrast, Western powers are also seen to be imposing their human rights demands without sensitivity to the complexities and historical backgrounds of Asian societies. Western critics of China's forceful handling of new religious movements must remember that in Chinese history religions have served as platforms to mobilize political rebellion. Then again, implementation of human rights policies must take into account the need for conflict management to maintain social harmony in Asian countries, many of which comprise diverse ethnic groups artificially bonded together when they gained independence from their colonial masters. We should note that maintaining unity and cohesion is a nightmare for authorities having to oversee a far-flung archipelago like Indonesia. Singapore relied on aggressive social engineering when its existence was hanging on tattered strings of survival in the initial years after its expulsion from Malaysia.

It is granted that there is a need for a more thoughtful and nuanced application of human rights in Asia. Still, one wonders if some Asian governments have not themselves exploited the gravity of the local situation to justify their own abuse of power. Can one justify detention of human rights activists without trial under Malaysia's Internal Security Act that was originally designed to counter armed insurrection? Can authorities suppress free-trade unions in order to please foreign investors? Should widespread corruption be ignored when corporate governance degenerates into kleptomaniac governance?

To be sure, Asian critics offer more sophisticated arguments than expediency in their resistance against demands for greater implementation of human rights policies. Of the various arguments voiced by Asian governments I shall focus on four: (1) that human rights are culture specific; (2) that community takes precedence over individuals; (3) that social-economic rights have priority over civil political rights; and (4) that the implementation of human rights should be respected as a matter of national sovereignty.

THE ARGUMENTS FOR ASIAN VALUES EXAMINED

Argument 1: Human Rights Are Culture Specific

It is claimed that human rights are the outcome of particular social and historical circumstances. The Bangkok Governmental Declaration (1993) stresses that "while human rights are universal in nature, they must be considered in the context of a dynamic and evolving process of international norm setting, bearing in mind the significance of national and regional peculiarities and various historical, cultural, and religious backgrounds."

Response to Argument 1

In dichotomizing the East from West, Asian values apologists have ironically adopted the strategy of the Western intellectual construct of Orientalism. They subscribe to the myth of Asian identity as a monolithic cultural entity. In actual fact, however, Asia is even more diverse religiously and culturally than Europe or the United States.

Let it be noted that current human rights talk about any person's entitlement for protection and social goods is based on the simple fact that that person is a human being.

> To claim that there are human rights is to claim that all human beings, simply because they are human, have rights in this sense. Such rights are universal, held by all human beings. They are equal: One is or is not a human being, and thus has or does not have (the same) human rights, equally. And they are inalienable: One can no more lose these rights than one can stop being a human being, no matter how inhuman the treatment one may be forced to endure.[3]

Human rights belong to all human beings, whether they are Western or Asian. The fact that the current concept of human rights originated from the West does not mean that it cannot and should not be applied in Asia. After all, Asians have no reservation applying Newtonian principles and quantum physics even though these physics originated from the West.

Argument 2: Community Takes Precedence over Individuals

Asian officials like to contrast the Asian emphasis on duty and social cohesion with the selfish individualism of the West. They argue that Asian values—with their emphasis on a sense of community and nationhood, a disciplined and hardworking people, strong moral values, and family ties—result in a harmonious society [Lee Kuan Yew]. On the other hand, it is suggested that the present breakdown of society epitomized by widespread drug abuse, increasing crime, and racial tension in the West is due in large part to the emphasis on individual rights and adversarial politics.

Mr. Goh Chok Tong, former Prime Minister of Singapore asserts:

> For success to continue, correct economic policies alone are not enough. Equally important are the noneconomic factors—a sense of community and nationhood, a disciplined and hardworking

people, strong moral values and family ties. The type of society determines how we perform. It is not simply materialism and individual rewards which drive Singapore forward. More important, it is the sense of idealism and service born out of a feeling of social solidarity and national identification. Without these crucial factors we cannot be a happy or dynamic society.[4]

In 1994, Dr. Mahathir, in a speech at the Senate House, Cambridge University, cited a survey that found six societal values most valued by East Asians: "First, having an orderly society; second, societal harmony; third, ensuring the accountability of public officials; fourth, being open to new ideas; fifth, freedom of expression; sixth, respect for authority." He contrasted these values with the six most important values for Americans: freedom of expression, personal freedom, the rights of the individual, open debate, thinking for oneself, and sixth, the accountability of public officials. Mahathir commented wryly, "Interestingly, slightly more East Asians emphasized the importance of 'new ideas' and public accountability than did Americans."

Implicit in these responses to the Western concept of human rights is the rejection of its foundation based on individualism. A. M. Hussein argues, "Any emphasis on individual human rights, apart from the rights of the community in which this individual lives, is sheer nonsense. In real history, human rights for the community come first, and human rights for any individual are conditioned by a healthy environment and appropriate social institutions.[5] The underlying perspective is the view that society is an organic whole whose collective rights prevail over the individual and that man exists for the state rather than vice versa. Individual significance is defined by the role the individual plays in a community based on family and kinfolk relations.[6] It is therefore wrong to attribute absolute value to human rights since these rights are bequeathed by the state.

Chandra Muzaffar, a prominent Malaysia public intellectual, judges the West as having failed to observe human rights even by its own standards. He cites such cases in white racism, widespread violence in Western societies, and family disintegration because creative individuality has degenerated into vulgar individualism, the divorce of rights from responsibilities. He questioned further whether the dominant Western concept of rights is itself particularistic and sectional since it emphasizes only civil political rights and downplays economic, social, and cultural rights. He wondered, "How can a concept of rights confined to the nation-state respond to the challenges posed by an increasingly global economic, political, and cultural system? Isn't it true that the dominant Western approach to human rights fails to recognize the role of global actors—like UNSC, IMF and MNCs—in the violation of human rights?"[7]

He concluded with a rhetorical question: "What are human rights if they are not related to more fundamental questions about the human being?" In other words, the West has failed to promote higher goals of human dignity. Such a view is echoed by Chinese critics Xie and Nui who stressed that "None is entitled to put his individual right above the interest of the state, society, and others. This is a universal principle of all civilized societies."[8]

Response to Argument 2

Proponents of East-West dualism ignore the reality that the debate/tension between communitarian and individualistic liberalism is not one divided geographically between Asia and the West. We note that Western philosophers (Charles Taylor, Alasdair McIntyre, Michael Walzer, and Michael Sandel) have argued vigorously for a communitarian social philosophy. Likewise, elements of individualism are not alien to Confucianist philosophy with its emphasis on individual self-development and critique of power abuse. While Confucius rejected blind allegiance, he also required officials to tell the Prince the truth even if it offends him. [Asian censorship boards should take note of this when they seek to limit freedom of the press.] His wisdom was evident when he counseled, "When the (good) way prevails in the State, speak boldly and act boldly. When the State has lost the way, act boldly and speak softly."

Amartya Sen cites Emperor Asoka as a paragon of tolerance and Buddhist universalism, citing the *Edict of Erragudi* that "a man must not do reverence to his own sect or disparage that of another man without reason. Depreciation should be for specific reason only, because the sects of other people all deserve reverence for one reason or another."[9]

Sulak Sivaraksa from Thailand, suggests that Buddhism offers resources although its texts speak of duties rather than rights. Still, human rights values may be inferred from the core principles of Buddhism. He suggests the following: *dana* (generosity); *sila* ("the ability not to exploit oneself or others"), and *bhavana* (cultivating "seeds of peace within the mind"). His suggestion, however, cannot evade the observation that Buddhism makes little reference to political life—whether democratic or authoritarian—and thus not surprisingly, there is no impact at the grassroots level in Thailand. Perhaps too much is made of a religion that concentrates on the spiritual and meditative path. It may be more honest to admit that perhaps human rights values are derived from other sources.[10]

However, it would be claiming too much to say that historical Asian societies contain traditions of human rights. What may be conceded is that there were elements in these traditions that affirmed tolerance and positive support for human freedom and that these elements should be retrieved in the development of a comprehensive framework for human rights in contemporary Asia.

Argument 3: Social-Economic Rights Have Priority over Civil Political Rights

Asian governments insist that they lend support to demands for human rights, but their approach would place the greater priority on the right to subsistence and economic development as a precondition to the full enjoyment of all other human rights. Giving priority to human rights over economic development results in unproductive labor conflicts and social tension. In contrast, giving priority to economic rights enables countries like the Asian Tigers to achieve unprecedented economic growth.

Response to Argument 3

Amartya Sen, the Nobel Prize winner for economics from Harvard, retorts that there is no empirical verification for the idea that limiting civil and political rights supports economic growth. Asian critics have been selective in providing evidence to support their case. (Why limit examples to China and Singapore and ignore Africa, Latin America, or nearer home, other Asian states like Burma and Pakistan?)

In contrast, one may argue that market liberalization leads to economic growth, which was the case in India. Greater economic productivity results from openness to competition, land reforms, and higher literacy and education. One may argue that increased economic productivity results because robust economic institutions and efficient workers are nurtured in an ethos where human rights are upheld. In any case, political freedom and civil liberties should be seen as rights that are valued in themselves. There is no justification for the suppression of these rights in the name of economic rights. Quite rightly, human rights activists insist that human rights form a seamless whole, whether economic or civil-political.

Argument 4: The Implementation of Human Rights Should Be Respected as a Matter of National Sovereignty

Dr. Mahathir complains that Western powers, in the wake of their victory in the Cold War, now expect all countries to adopt the liberal view on human rights as conceived by the Europeans and the North Americans and implement a Western style of multiparty system of government. He adds, "It would seem that Asians have no right to define and practice their own set of values about human rights. What, we are asked, is Asian Values? The question is rhetorical because the implication is that Asians cannot possibly understand human rights, much less set up their own values." The demands of the West in effect violate the principle that every nation has a right to self-determination, especially over how human rights should be implemented in its domestic affairs. Indeed, one may argue that demands for universal human rights merely mask Western imperialism and its subversion of economic development of Asian nations.

Xie and Nui asserted: "Imposing the human rights standard of one's country or region on other countries or regions is an infringement upon other countries' sovereignty and interference into other countries' internal affairs." This is asserted regardless of the fact that the issue at hand is the Universal Declaration of Human Rights, which surely can lay claim to acceptance far beyond the West.[11]

Response to Argument 4

It is ironic that Asian leaders should appeal to the concepts of state sovereignty and nation-state (which are Western concepts) to defend their negligence of human rights. At the same time, they overlook the fact that historically human rights became prominent in the West because of the rise of the centralized nation-state. Human rights were emphasized precisely because of the need to limit the awesome power that a centralized state can wield. Social reformers insisted on inalienable human rights rather than just positive rights (which may be conferred by national laws and, by the same token, may be revoked by the state).

TOWARD CONSTRUCTIVE ENGAGEMENT

The discussion above suggests that the arguments based on so-called Asian values fail to challenge the fundamental premise for the universal application of human rights that should include Asia. Perhaps the failure of their critique is not surprising. For if, indeed, human rights are accorded to any individual simply because one is human, then all humans, whether Western, Asian, or otherwise, deserve these rights. What is really at issue is *how* human rights may be implemented in a particular locality. In other words, there should be no necessity to choose between universal and local.

The debate also alerts us to the fact that human rights are not abstractions. They are wedded into local history and cultural traditions. It is therefore both sensible and legitimate that Asian governments be allowed to develop human rights in ways that address the complexities and tensions of local societies. Asian governments should be more consultative in the decision-making process if they are honest with their claims of Asian values. Freedom of speech will be exercised in ways that are more sensitive toward and indeed intolerant toward hate speech.

Western critics have forgotten the fact that human rights gained prominence in the West because of the rise of independent commercial cities and the business class. These provided alternative social capital capable of checking the power of authoritarian governments. Should they expect human rights in Asia to flourish without the support of a vibrant economic class? More recognition should be given to so-called economic rights and development priorities in Asia.

It is appropriate to focus on culture since a paper constitution cannot guarantee human rights in the long term unless it is ingrained in the social ethos and implemented through social institutions. In particular, human rights must be sustained by a culture of pluralistic democracy and tolerance and a vibrant civil society. It should be noted that in principle even detractors defending Asian values would want to support human rights and democratic principles. The question is how these should be qualified or adapted in the Asian context? Masakazu Yamazaki in his essay "Asia, a Civilization in the Making," *Foreign Affairs* 74, no. 3 (May/June 1995), has provided a splendid suggestion on how to reconcile the tension between universal human rights with Asian history and local cultural traditions. Yamazaki first notes that Western civilization results from a synthesis between Judaic and Hellenic traditions under the umbrella of the Roman Empire and the unifying framework of Christian civilization. Subsequent developments led to "a World civilization that would encompass national and ethnic civilizations and cultures alien to one another. The crucial factor in the process was that no single nation claimed the supranational umbrella as its own."[12]

Local nationalists have always been defensive and reluctant to accept new foreign ideas. But Yamazaki adroitly suggests that such a defensive stance is unnecessary because he envisages a final synthesis that will harmonize the universal with the local.

> The peoples of East Asia . . . can be said to partake of modern Western civilization at the topmost stratum of their world, to retain their national civilizations and nation-states in the middle stratum, and to reserve their traditional cultures in their day-to-day lives. In political affairs, human rights and democratic principles belong to

the first stratum, distinct bodies of law and political institutions to the second, and the political wheeling and dealing to the third.[13]

In Yamazaki's model, the second level assumes diversity of local cultures shaping local institutions. One may envisage how the state may regulate the economy in different ways, taking into account local customs in business dealings and depending on what priorities have assumed importance at a particular juncture of nation building.

In summary, it should be insisted that human rights are nonnegotiable and that there can be no justification for government restriction on human rights. They are, after all, not gifts from any particular government but the inherent possession of every single person by the mere fact of his being human. The goal is to indigenize human rights so that they are expressed in forms that resonate with local cultural sensibilities and respect the historical relationships between various communities in a local region or nation. Hopefully, the insights from Yamazaki's discussion on multitiered modernity will encourage Asian activists to campaign for human rights and deflect the suspicion that they are unwitting agents of Westernization. On the other hand, local activists should intentionally shape local institutions so that human rights may be practiced in a manner appropriate to local culture.

RELIGIOUS INSTITUTIONS AND HUMAN RIGHTS

The many-sided nature of the debate on human rights should not lead us to overlook the fact that human rights are not just ideals but the outcome of political power, law, and public policies enforced through social institutions. In particular, Asian activists are conscious that religion continues to play a significant role in fostering community spirit and legitimizing social institutions in Asia. In particular, Asian Christians are keenly aware that religion in general and Christianity in particular provides moral resources for social critique. The challenge is for Christians to develop social institutions in civil society that will promote a culture of human rights that is resilient and resistant to encroachment by authoritarian governments seeking to restrict human rights.

A case study on such possibilities in the Muslim society of South East Asia should be instructive. Preliminary observation suggests that the social fabric of a regulated Muslim society is not necessarily a seamless whole that is immune to forces of change. Two characteristics are particularly relevant. First, Muslim society itself comprises diverse social groupings with varying levels of commitment to its religion. A well-known example popularized by Clifford Geertz is found in Java. Here, believers are divided into the

FIGURE 9.1
Shifting Centers of Power

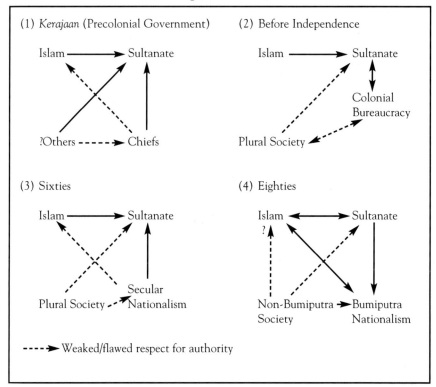

categories of *priyayi* (nobility), *santri* (scripturalists), and *abangan* (folk religionists) (*The Religion of Java*, Glencoe, IL: The Free Press, 1960). The lack of homogeneity in Islamic society arose because of its historic modus operandi of adhesion and conversion in the propagation of religion. Hence, the continual tension between folk Islam and Scripturalist Islam.

Wang Gang Wu has helpfully outlined how competing power groups have dynamically evolved in the Malaysian context.[14] The different configurations (see figure 9.1) highlight how centers of power are continually shifting. The dynamic situation should not lead the analyst to overlook the foundation of Malay/Muslim society, which has remained unchanged through history. The identity of this society is essentially grounded on the politics of ethnic nationalism. In particular, Malay identity is founded on a political memory of the Malacca Sultanate in the fifteenth century. The State was founded on an ideology where the citizens submit to the sultan as their "Protector," without concern for the morality or immorality of his exercise of power so long as he successfully provides for the well-being of his subjects.

The legitimacy of the sultanate is expressed through a theater of rituals and symbols of power. Historians have noted how the "invention of traditions" seek to "inculcate values and norms of behavior through repetition, which automatically implies continuity with the past . . . with a suitable historic past." These traditions confer legitimacy to the social order as "rooted in the remotest antiquity, and the opposite of constructed, namely human communities so 'natural' as to require no definition other than self-assertion."[15] The power of the sultan was further reinforced when, with the advent of Islam, he came to be regarded as the shadow of Allah.

Under these new circumstances the power of the sultan may well acquire the trappings of absoluteness. But Anthony Milner in his book *The Invention of Politics in Colonial Malaya* (Cambridge, UK: Cambridge University Press, 1995), pointed out that in the absence of a state bureaucracy, his power was limited. The sultan depended on the cooperation of feudal chiefs to implement his rule. More significantly, with the advent of colonialism and new educational institutions a new class of elite emerged which was able to mobilize itself to formulate new social ideologies. They were even able to disseminate in the media views that were contrary to reigning court ideology.[16]

Following the historical analysis outlined above, social activists today should analyze how current forces of globalization shaking social institutions and current political ferment generate opportunities for social engagement. There is no fixed formula although the following dynamics should be kept in mind: First, social analysis brings out cracks and openings in a social order that appears to be so uniform that it is immune from disruption. Second, historical analysis challenges the legitimacy of the hegemonic order which presents itself as the order that best preserves the essential qualities and integrity of a unique society and should therefore be accepted as it is. Both of these moments help in the formulation of an agenda of human rights that takes into account the continuities and changes specific to Malaysian society. Naturally, such an agenda will address concrete social issues related to local society. Activists should be alert and opportunistic in building shifting alliances that are supportive of human rights.

Historically, the church—with its social philosophy of human dignity and covenant as social contract and limited government—helped contribute to the rise of freedom and human rights. An exemplary case may be found in the church in Korea. The church gained credibility when Christians were in the forefront in the fight for nationalism and fundamental rights of the Korean people.[17] The Korean church can even boast of its martyrs for this social cause. Is it any surprise that we witnessed an explosion in the growth of the church in Korea?

Christians may envisage the church as one of the institutions of civil society that mediate between global values of human rights and local culture, as envisaged in Yamazaki's second stratum of modernity. We are always mindful that authoritarian governments seek to take full control of institutions of civil society. Under such circumstances, it is vital that the church functions as a bastion where truth, freedom, and justice become articulate and materialized in a visible way. This brings to mind how Vaclav Havel advocated for a parallel society at a time when repression was total in Czechoslovakia.

On the one hand, the church is a community that embodies relationships that affirm human dignity and mutual respect. As such the presentation of the Gospel must go beyond verbal proclamation if it is to be credible and relevant. That is to say, the claims of the Gospel should be consistently interwoven into the fabric of interpersonal relationships of the church as a consensus-based community. On the other hand, the church must be reminded that it cannot fight only for the rights of Christians but for all fellow citizens of the country. Human rights and social justice cannot be the exclusive privilege of any one community. They are, rather, inalienable expressions of human dignity. All matters genuinely related to human dignity are universal rights and any claim to have them must not be motivated by self-interest but by a concern and responsibility for the world.[18] To this extent, the emancipatory interest of the Gospel demands that the church abandon its narrow self-interests and contribute to the common good.

We need to be challenged by the words of John De Gruchy, "the church cannot expect of the state what it cannot achieve in its own life. The witness of the church to the state is severely compromised when its own behavior contradicts the message it proclaims, when resolutions are denied in practice, when words lack conviction and commitment. The church has no right to be heard when it speaks without competence, or when it says nothing worth saying."[19] It is unacceptable for the church to remain as a bystander in the debate and struggle for human rights. The church will earn respect and recognition if it demonstrates sacrificial service and solidarity with fellow citizens.

NOTES

1. I shall include in the concept of modernity the following components:

(a) epistemology: the autonomous self in judgment; (b) ethics: the imperial self that bows only to its self-created ethical standards; (c) social structures: differentiated and specialized institutions; (d) economics: instrumental rationality based on calculability and efficiency; (e) bureaucracy: an iron-cage administration; (f) politics: progress in democracy and social justice.

2. Mahathir's keynote address in *Human Wrongs: Reflection on Western Global Dominance and Its Impact upon Human Rights* (Just World Trust, 1996), pp. 7, 11.

3. Jack Donelly, "Human Rights and Asian Values: A Defense of 'Western' Universalism," found in Joanne R. Bauer and Daniel A. Bell, ed., *The East Asian Challenge for Human Rights* (New York: Cambridge University Press, 1999), p. 61. See Donelly's extended discussion in his book *Universal Human Rights in Theory and Practice* (Ithaca: Cornell University Press, 2002).

4. Goh Chok Tong, "Singapore Values, Singapore Style," *Current History* (December 1994), p. 417.

5. Joanne Bauer and Daniel Bell, *The East Asian Challenge for Human Rights*, p. 77.

6. Jack Donelly, p. 113.

7. *Human Wrongs*, pp. 272–73.

8. Donelly, p. 114.

9. Amartya Sen, "Human Rights and Asian Values," *The New Republic* (July 14–21, 1997).

10. Found in web site by Carnegie Council on Ethics and International Affairs. http://www.cceia.org

11. Donelly, p. 108.

12. Masakazu Yamazaki, "Asia, a Civilization in the Making," *Foreign Affairs* 74, 3 (May/June 1995), p. 109.

13. Ibid., p. 116.

14. Wang Gang Wu, *Community and Nation* (Sydney, Australia: Allen and Unwin, 1981), pp. 228–31. We should refer to the landmark study by Max Stackhouse in, *Creeds, Society and Human Rights* (Grand Rapids, MI: Eerdmans, 1984). It is significant that Stackhouse analyzed American liberal society along with Marxist totalitarianism and the Hindu caste society. The significant absence of a similar study on Islamic society remains an unfilled lacuna today. See also Todung Mulya Lubis, *In Search of Human Rights: Legal-Political Dilemmas of Indonesia's New Order, 1966–1990* (Jakarta: Gramedia, 1993).

15. Eric Hobsbawn and Terrence O. Rangers, eds., *The Invention of Tradition* (New York: Cambridge University Press, 1983), p. 14. See also Bernard R. Anderson, *Imagined Communities* (London: Verso, 1983).

16. Anthony Milner, *The Invention of Politics in Colonial Malaya* (New York: Cambridge University Press, 1995).

17. See Kenneth M. Wells, *New God, New Nation: Protestant and Self-Reconstruction Nationalism in Korea 1896–1937* (Honolulu: University of Hawaii Press, 1990).

18. A point stressed in Vaclav Havel's courageous and humane book, *Living the Truth* (London: Faber, 1986), p. 102.

19. John De Gruchy, *The Church Struggle in South Africa* (Grand Rapids, MI: Eerdmans, 1979), p. 227.

CHAPTER 10

Changing One's Religion

A Supported Right?

MARGARET O. THOMAS

The United Nations Universal Declaration of Human Rights 18 (1948) and the Universal Declaration of Human Rights by the World's Religions 18.2 (1998) contain language explicitly asserting the right of the individual to change religion. Is this a right that can be supported by social and religious institutions?

The religious communities' own answers are ambiguous. This article uses selected material from bilateral Christian-Muslim consultations convened internationally by the World Council of Churches (hereafter WCC) as a case through which to illuminate the question.

THE SITUATION: POTENTIAL FOR CONFLICT

The complex personal, social, and legal issues accompanying a change of religious identity and affiliation can result in misunderstandings and collisions of values that perpetuate mistrust and stimulate conflict, even though the number of persons who change religion is frequently not statistically significant.

Awareness of the concern comes before the U.S. public. Debate in the media explores the possible impact of any Christian conversionary activity that might accompany Western humanitarian relief for Iraq (Educational Broadcasting 2003). The effect of immigration/refugee policies and practices

167

on Christian converts of Muslim background is scrutinized (Refugee Reports 1996). The government's choice between official punishment and quiet diplomacy toward nations accused of religious persecution is evaluated (Seiple et al. 2002; Horowitz 2003), frequently masking special interest in converts.

Local/regional dynamics affect the way religious choice issues unfold around the world. In the United States, religious status is not a public concern, and changing from one religion to another has comparatively few social consequences. Yet change elicits strong reactions in parts of the globe where religion is a major personal/communal identity factor or where power struggles between religious communities are sharp. In the Middle East, the heartland of Islam, the vast majority is Muslim and historic Christian churches preserve quite self-contained communities. Christian mission from the West has frequently created pressure through its obvious expectation that individuals should be able to move from one religious community to another, and social repercussions of conversion into the Christian church can be severe.

HUMAN RIGHTS DISCOURSE: USING A SETTING OF BELIEF AND RESPONSIBILITY

WCC experience has shown that religious freedom can be a subject in the religious dialogue of an international group of Christians and Muslims who gather intending to trust one another and to overcome misuse of religion for political ends. Engaging in human rights discourse, however, has required confronting the perceived problems created by Western humanistic influences and the selective implementation of human rights by Western powers.

Over the span of more than a decade, the WCC office of interreligious relations convened Muslims and Christians from around the world for a series of consultations broadly focused on religion, law and society, religious freedom and mission.[1] Discussants who met in 1994 (Berlin) and 1995 (Malta) concluded that Islam and Christianity, rooted in their belief in God's will for creation and humanity,[2] offer resources and commitments that can "expand and deepen the impact of human rights principles on the everyday lives" of their communities (Mitri 1996, 111); human rights can be the basis for common work with the objectives of establishing advocacy, awareness building, and further reflection. A number of broad bases underlie this consensus (and are applicable to discussion of changing religion as a right):

- Human rights vocabulary should not be used by Christians and Muslims to attack each other.

- Trustful mutuality requires that neither Muslims nor Christians ask of the other what they would not be willing to give.
- Rights exist within the context of community (with the rights of the community and of the human person constantly interacting for the well-being of society).
- People in each place should be able to exercise responsibility for their own community "in communion with other communities worldwide" (Mitri 1996, 107f).
- The broad variants within both the Muslim and the Christian religious traditions place upon each the responsibility to engage in intrareligious dialogue, including discussion about human rights concerns.

In 1995, the dialogue group prepared a draft that recognized the right of "freedom of religion and conscience" without further definition. In October 2002 (Geneva), a WCC-convened meeting on "dialogue and beyond," attended by key Christian and Muslim leaders,[3] spoke in greater detail. Its final report says:

> We together affirm the fundamental rights of individuals and groups as expressed in the UN Declaration of Human Rights and the reciprocal duties which flow from those rights. We assert that all . . . are entitled to full and equal citizenship rights and freedom of expression and religion in whatever country they may belong to. We especially confirm that the equal participation of religions and religious communities in public affairs locally, nationally and internationally is not only a right but also a duty. . . . *It follows that we also affirm the freedom of the individual to adhere to the religion of his or her choice,* and that it is the function of the state to protect the full and equal right of all religious communities to organize themselves and to participate appropriately in public affairs. (Emphasis mine; CD 40:23)

To create what goes on public record, persons from two different religious traditions achieve a convergence around the particular points they can say together to both their own constituencies and the world. In this case, the values of *belief* and *responsibility* appear to be fundamental pegs on which both can hang commitments. The language of individual *choice* is used, not the language of *change*.[4] Interestingly, a subgroup that worked on the issue of human rights had included in its report to the consultation plenary "the right of every person to change his or her religion, without sanctions" (CD 40:33).

THE LANGUAGE OF RELIGIOUS TEXTS:
ENTERING OR LEAVING A COMMUNITY

Christian sensibilities are built into the international language of religious freedom. At the founding WCC Assembly (Amsterdam, 1948), Christians defined religious freedom (including the right to change religion or belief) as a fundamental human right based on their understanding that "God's truth and love are given freely and call for a free response." This right soon became a part of UDHRUN (*Common Witness* ¶A3).

UDHRWR 18.1 begins with Muslim sensibilities, using a direct quote from the Qur'an in English translation: "There shall be no compulsion in religion" (2.256a,[5] Pickthall trans.). A document intended for general use cannot assume that all readers will understand a quotation according to its original meaning, but certainly its own community's interpretation will resonate in the new setting.

The Islamic teaching about compulsion rests on the assurance that humans have been created to discern between the right and the wrong ("Truth stands out clear from Error" 2.256b) and that faith/belief cannot be forced by human activity[6] ("No soul can believe, except by the will of Allah" 10.100a, Yusuf Ali trans.).

The Cairo Declaration on Human Rights in Islam 10 (1990) is, in effect, a commentary on 2.256: "Islam is the religion of unspoiled nature. It is prohibited to exercise any form of compulsion on man or to exploit his poverty or ignorance in order to convert him to another religion or to atheism." The warning against playing on vulnerabilities to induce conversion is consonant with Islam's understanding that no one should be compelled to *enter* its community (become a believer) and the reality that *leaving* the community is almost impossible; personal and/or institutional sanctions work internally to guard against disloyalty and unacceptable religious deviance.[7] At the same time, according to the Universal Islamic Declaration of Human Rights 10, 12–13 (1981), everyone should have the right to express belief, within the general limits set by *shari'a*, if public outrage is not incited or slander and disrespect not used; religious minorities should be able to maintain themselves in accordance with the principle of 2.256.[8] Christians do not consistently cite a particular scriptural text or set of texts for guidance on religious compulsion. *Dignitatis Humanae* (Vatican II, 1965) states that the individual right of religious freedom "has to do with immunity from *coercion in civil society*," leaving untouched the "traditional Catholic doctrine on the *moral duty* of men and societies toward the true religion" (¶1,2; emphases mine).

The importance Muslims give to staying within the community is echoed, in different form, in historic Christian assumptions about maintaining the community of faith. The Anglican *Articles of Religion* 33 (1563) speak of persons who "by open denunciation of the Church [are] rightly cut off from the unity of the Church" and thereafter seen as "heathen" unless they are again received into the church. Nevertheless, *entry* into the Christian community, while welcomed, is usually a more complex process than in Islam; and *leaving* the community, while undesirable, is more possible in theory and in practice.

KEY GUIDANCE: REDUCING TENSION TO ENABLE GROWTH

Two key principles articulated in WCC-convened dialogue are intended to open up space for constructive struggling with living human rights issues, including religious freedom. First, conflict should be deglobalized in order to avoid its spread and to allow a contextualized resolution. Second, in each community authentic witness should respect the integrity of others and abstain from competitive proselytizing methods.

Deglobalizing Conflict in an Age of Globalization

Population shifts, pluralism, and ethical confusion accompany the economic and communication globalization of recent years. These forces challenge exclusivist claims of religion—be they theological, social, political, or legal—and, in turn, produce greater exclusivism as well as greater pluralism.[9] Hence globalization brings closer relationships between peoples; conversely, it also promotes stereotyping in which acts committed in one situation create enmity elsewhere (*CD* 40:17, ¶8). Issues around changing religion are ready fuel for such demonization of others when a religion is deemed to have unfairly taken in new adherents in some part of the world or to have mistreated those who have left their community of origin.

The document *Striving Together in Dialogue* (developed in Amersfoort, Netherlands, 2000) brings together Christian-Muslim discussions for publication. It speaks about "*de*-globalizing" tensions, stating that solutions to specific local causes of conflicts can best be found by addressing those local causes. Persons outside a local area should not respond uncritically to calls for solidarity but can be helpful in offering general principles. The aim is "to release Islam and Christianity from the burden of sectional interests and self-serving interpretations of beliefs and convictions." (¶19).

Former WCC general secretary, the Rev. Dr. Konrad Raiser, used this principle in a speech after September 11, 2001, in which he said that the churches should "seek to 'de-globalize' the conflict and even be careful with the effort to identify particular root causes which provide a comprehensive interpretation" (WCC web report on "Beyond 11 September: Implications for the Churches," 2001).

In WCC-convened dialogues, Muslims and Christians have also looked at the diplomacy of "reciprocity"—a search for a kind of global symmetry between the Christian and Muslim communities whereby a privilege is demanded of a majority community in a specific place as the condition for giving what should be understood as a right in another place where the community's members are a minority (e.g., a church building somewhere in the Middle East as a requirement for erecting a mosque in a European location). This approach not only fails to deglobalize but also contradicts "the unconditional universality of the value of justice" (*Striving* ¶34).

Witnessing to Faith in the Face of Temptations to Proselytize

The primary motivations for moving from one religion to another—related to spirituality or morality, integrated belief, or theology—may be joined (or occasionally superseded) by other factors: for example, making a new start to avoid oppression or limitations; escaping secular ideology or unsatisfactory practice of a religion of birth; altering social or economic status; achieving educational or professional goals; enabling marriage or family adherence to a single religion; allying with a group which has shown compassion; turning to or from a majority or ruling religion.[10]

The *Striving Together* document states the conviction that "people of faith can enjoy the liberty to *convince and be convinced* and, at the same time, respect each other's religious integrity, faithfulness . . . and loyalty" (¶32; emphasis mine). Thoughtful Christians and Muslims are aware that neither can ask the other to abandon the witness of mission/evangelization/evangelism[11] and *da'wah*[12] in the name of avoiding mutual stress, since witness and invitation are integral to the faith of both. But WCC-convened dialoguers have also acknowledged the need for a mutually agreed, tough ethic of witness. Standards of this ethic effectively set limits upon the means used by a religious community to attract converts, recognizing the complexity of the decisions involved when a person moves from one religious community to another. These include agreeing that legitimate witness must be separated from unacceptable proselytism and that inequalities in power relations between religious communities should never be exploited to attract others (Hartford 1999).[13]

Two general resources for discussion of these standards have been especially highlighted:

1. From interreligious dialogue: the final statement and proceedings of a significant Christian-Muslim conversation on mission and *da'wah* held in Chambésy (Switzerland) in 1976, under both WCC and Islamic sponsorship (Chambésy, also Brown 1989, 82–86).

2. From intrareligious dialogue: documents growing out of Christians' discussion of their internal tensions about evangelism among Christians (most recently, *Towards Common Witness: A Call to Adopt Responsible Relationships in Mission and to Renounce Proselytism*, adopted, WCC Central Committee, 1997). These focus on the actions and intentions of the ones making witness, rather than on those to whom witness is made, and are therefore appropriate for interreligious use.[14]

Proselytism, the interfaith Chambésy final statement says, uses "purposes other than holy" to add members who come from another community "for reasons other than spiritual" so that, for example, "any service [*diakonía*] which has degraded itself by having any purpose whatever beside *agapé* (love for God and neighbor)" is a "propaganda instrument" (¶6). *Towards Common Witness* (section B) calls proselytism "a perversion" of authentic witness "and thus a counterwitness."

Both *Common Witness* and Chambésy cite ways proselytism plays upon divisions and destabilizes situations, including:

- Exploiting vulnerabilities of personal and social circumstance (often related to another community's problems and weaknesses), e.g., ignorance, poor health, young or old age, poverty, political instability, lack of national power relative to another nation.
- Offering educational or humanitarian services that are otherwise unavailable.
- Using historical, political, economic, cultural pressures and arguments.
- Caricaturing beliefs and practices of others without dialoguing with them about their understandings.
- Comparing the best in one's own tradition with the weak in another's; disparaging or stigmatizing others.
- Harassing and badgering others about one's own superiority (including spiritual threats), either in person or through the media.

The harsh judgment upon proselytism implies that it is not possible, at one and the same time, to engage in authentic witness and use proselytizing methods. In actuality, there is a wide range of possible mission activities and, essentially, the judgment upon proselytism stands against any form of encouraging change of religious affiliation based upon competition,[15] cultural superiority, or the perquisites of political power — activities that, in the spirit of UDHRWR, could be characterized as forms of compulsion.

In contrast, the intra-Christian WCC document *Towards Common Witness* (section C2) offers practical proposals for "responsible relationships [among Christians] in mission" that have their counterpart in ways Christians and Muslims can treat one another when they are engaged in evangelism/*da'wah*:

- Hold deeply the conviction that mission is God's, not ours, and we are God's co-workers.
- Reach out through listening, walking with, resourcing, receiving from one another.
- Help people who want to change their religious identity to discern their motives, worthy or unworthy.
- Extend the understanding of different, even contradictory, views in two communities about common assertions.
- Repent of failures; reflect self-critically.

A 1992 analysis of Christian-Muslim relations, addressed by the WCC to its own member churches, says, "[D]*iakonía* is a form of witness that has its own integrity. Therefore, Christians are constantly called to preserve that integrity, and to be seen as engaged in disinterested and loving service" (*Issues* III.7). In turn, the Chambésy group spoke about the possibility for cooperation on behalf of the common good, setting it over against the reality of the long alienation between Christians and Muslims. The implication is that authentic witness seeks the well-being of all without any condition or expectation.

One of the difficulties today is the identification of Christianity with colonial, neocolonial, and globalizing powers who are viewed by others as oppressors rather than promoters of the common good. Muslims often suspect the motives of Christians whom they so identify; many Western Christians, in turn, swim in the waters of their own culture and nation, scarcely able to see how these may violate others. Among the Chambésy recommendations (¶7) are two that are exceptionally painful:

- That Christian churches and organizations "suspend their misused *diakonía* activities in the world of Islam" until Muslims and Christians can convene to consider the methods of mission/*da'wah* in accordance with each's faith.

- That, wherever possible, Christian churches and organizations from outside a region distribute material assistance through, or in cooperation with, local governments and communities.

The second of these proposals has been implemented to some extent, although Christian churches and organizations also maintain self-standing distribution of material aid, citing unresolved logistical difficulties and the wishes of financial contributors. The first proposal was not carried out. It seems unrealistic in terms of implementation and is, therefore, the more striking for the urgency of its spirit.

MEASURES OF ACCEPTANCE: THE INDIVISIBILITY OF HUMAN RIGHTS

The integrity of a human right's acceptance can be tested by the standard of indivisibility: Is it possible, in practice, to adhere to a particular human right and also to maintain other rights that have been articulated? Several freedoms need to be particularly examined in relation to the activity of governmental, social, familial, and religious institutions as these affect the right to change religion. These include, in a given society:

- *Conscience* (UDHR 18). Is there acceptance that diversity in culture and religion will be created by, or manifest through, the promptings of conscience? May those who choose to be members of a particular religious community live in accord with its religious values? (see *Striving* ¶31)
- *Manifesting religion in community, in private or in public* (UDHR 18).[16] Does the right to change one's religion include the right to live freely as an adherent to the newly adopted religion? May a convert become publicly integral to a new community of faith and its activities?
- *Non-discriminatory equal protection before law* (UDHRWR 7). Will society's legal institutions protect a convert from the reactions of others who view him/her as having committed an unacceptable act in making a change of religion? How does this relate to the duty to maintain public order? (see, e.g., UDHRWR 19, 20)
- *Cultural participation* (UDHRWR 27). How do the cultural changes that often accompany change in religion affect an individual's ability to remain in cultural solidarity with the social

community of his/her birth? Are missionaries from outside the society unwelcome as agents of cultural change?

- *Nationality* (UDHRWR 15). If religion is part of legal identity, may a new convert change the community to which she/he legally belongs, with all attendant rights? Or will she/he become alienated from the community of origin but be unable to enter another legally, with a consequent loss of security as well as participation in national life? What mechanisms for equal citizenship exist?[17]
- *Asylum and change of nationality* (UDHRWR 14, 15). If a person's residence in the country of origin is made untenable by the act of changing religion, is he/she entitled to leave,[18] and is there a viable place of asylum? Will it be possible to acquire new citizenship elsewhere?
- *More inclusive interests* (UDHRWR 28). What rights of the community become the duty of the individual? Do duty to others and/or legal measures stand in the way of changing religion on behalf of a perceived larger good? What rights/duties does the family have in this respect?

MECHANISMS OF HOPE: CONTRIBUTIONS OF RELIGIOUS DIALOGUE

A religious ideal articulates an ultimate value based upon tradition, scripture, and experience. The articulation of a universal human right assumes the convergence of values as a necessity of justice. Some would say we must be resigned to a permanent clash of religious values, given the existence of multiple religions/beliefs and, therefore, would view the right to change one's religion as an impossible dream on which convergence is not possible.[19] Neither Christians nor Muslims would want to lose the right of change for those who freely wish to become a part of their communities. The way forward can be based upon compelled compliance or moral suasion.

The WCC dialogue model assumes that important results come noncoercively—from selected members of communities joining to speak religiously, bringing their own particular religious values, beliefs, and reasons for action into a listening/speaking mode that interacts with others' values and beliefs.

Christians and Muslims can contribute, through dialogue, to a discourse on human rights that can help reconcile the truly universal principles and the culturally specific claims. Such a discourse needs to be grounded in the respective religions to be genuinely inclusive and universal. (*Striving* ¶31)

The Muslims and Christians convened by the WCC (especially in Malta, 1995) have considered the mechanism of one or more ongoing forums to foster cooperative human rights work, especially when religion is misused—whether the issue be a common concern, a case of difficulty between the two communities, or an instance of members of one community seeking help from the other concerning matters internal to that community. A regional Arab Working Group on Muslim-Christian Dialogue has already been formalized by a covenant (*CD* 39:60–65).

Assuming that the support of human rights often involves bilateral concerns as well as multilateral ones, establishing an institutional base for such dialogue between Muslims and Christians in any region of the world will be complicated by the lack of symmetry between their structures and the varying agendas their organizations carry. In the United States, discussion of religious freedom would need to examine the U.S. role in global interactions—American religious organizations' service/witness efforts, actions of the U.S. government relative to international religious freedom,[20] civil liberties of Muslims residing in or visiting the United States. Important questions about scriptural interpretation, law, and theology remain within each religious tradition, as issues of religious choice are explored.

NOTES

1. The author participated in many of the dialogues and her notes have been used throughout this article.

2. See Fr. Thomas Michel "Differing Perceptions of Human Rights: Asia-Africa Interventions at the Human Rights Conference" in Mitri, 1995, p. 132, re subtle but important differences in belief at the UN human rights conference in Vienna (1993): the Holy See held that human rights "belong to the dignity bestowed on all people by the Creator" while the general Muslim view was that they "do not arise from the nature of the human person, but are rather granted to humans by the Creator." Elsewhere, An-Naim 1990, p. 22, argues that the concept of human rights "to which every human being is entitled by virtue of being human was unknown to Islamic jurisprudence or social philosophy until the last few decades and does not exist in Shari'a"; cf. Monshipouri 1998, p. 19.

3. Key attendees included general secretaries of Organization of the Islamic Conference and Islamic Call Society; senior leaders of WCC and Vatican's Council for Interreligious Dialogue, and Iran's vice president.

4. In 1948 UDHR 18 specified "freedom to change [one's] religion or belief," while a more ambiguous freedom "to have or to adopt" a religion of choice is specified in 1996 in ICCPR 18 and in 1981 in DEAFID 1.2.

5. Qur'an لَا إِكْرَاهَ فِي الدِّينِ

6. Even God does not compel humans to believe against their will, see Qur'an, 24.3–5.

7. Leaving Islam is frequently described as apostasy, a form of treason toward the community that may be punishable by death. See Talbi 1986, 182,187, for a Muslim perspective; also Mitri 1999, *CD* 33:47, for Christian comments by a Middle Eastern Orthodox: "Freedom of belief and worship— *strictu sensu,* guaranteed by law in most Muslim countries—is not in serious jeopardy. Freedom of conscience, and more particularly the right of conversion from Islam, is problematic. While most countries do not enforce, by law and practice, the prescribed capital punishment of apostasy . . . , conversion from Islam is quite often not tolerated socially. Such intolerance has taken, in a number of cases, extreme forms of violence. There have been cases where converts from Islam were not only discriminated against and harassed, but were subjected to legal sanctions on the grounds of disturbance of civil peace, social order or inter-communal harmony." Monshipouri 1998, p. 230, writes that "the most daunting challenge facing Islamic law is the international outcry against its treatment of apostasy and heresy" and quotes Donna E. Arzt in saying that international law denies the right of religious orthodoxy to punish heresy or dissension by criminal sanction or physical/ psychological intimidation, though threat to public order may justify limiting public expression of heretical views.

8. Cf. ICCPR 18.3, developed in 1966: "Freedom to manifest one's religion or beliefs may be subject only to such limitations as are prescribed by law and are necessary to protect public safety, order, health, or morals or the fundamental rights and freedoms of others."

9. For a brief review of broad Christian theological views, see Pittman et al. 1996, pp. 55–61. For WCC contributions, see *Baar Statement* 1990 and "Guidelines for Dialogue and Relations with People of Other Religions" 2002, *CD* 40:16–21.

10. On becoming a Muslim, see Dutton, 1999, pp. 151–65.

11. For different Christian understandings, see the Institute for Ecumenical and Cultural Research publication *Confessing Christian Faith* 1995, ¶ 33–43, and Bria 1980, esp. pp. 7–11, 12.

12. *Da'wah* translates as "call." See Davies and Pasha 1989, pp. 13f., 45ff.

13. See Kerr for history of Christian perspectives on proselytism.

14. See JWG 1995, ¶20, for an explicit statement encouraging such use.

15. Competition between Christians and Muslims for adherents occurs even in places where both reach out to persons of yet another religion (such as in Africa where both have conversions from African Traditional religion).

16. UDHR 18 includes the right to "manifest religion" with others but it is not included in UDHRWR, except see Article 20 for the "right of assembly."

17. A work group at the WCC 2002 consultation suggested there should be greater sharing of national experiences regarding equal citizenship, proposing that the right to citizenship should now be formally inscribed in international conventions with the cooperation of Christian and Muslim organizations as well as governments and NGOs. CD 40:33.

18. Cairo Declaration 12 states that every man, "if persecuted, is entitled to seek asylum in another country. The country of refuge shall ensure his protection until he reaches safety, unless asylum is motivated by an act which *shari'ah* regards as a crime."

19. Wisdom 2003 seems to be pessimistic in the final analysis.

20. Madeleine K. Albright 1997, then U.S. Secretary of State, cited the UDHR and emphasized the importance of religious freedom in the human rights supported by the United States around the world. "We have not hesitated to speak out when governments persecute Christians or fail to ensure the safety of any religious group. And we use all the tools available to work for change within societies and with authorities. . . . We have changed the way the State Department looks at religious questions, in order to strengthen our opposition to violations of religious freedom in our bilateral relationships and our efforts to shape the work of international organizations."

BIBLIOGRAPHY

Published by World Council of Churches (WCC), Geneva, Switzerland

Baar Statement. 1990.
Bria, Ion, ed. 1980. *Martyria/Mission: The Witness of the Orthodox Churches Today.*
Brown, Stuart. 1989. *Meeting in Faith: Twenty Years of Christian-Muslim Conversations Sponsored by the World Council of Churches.*
Current Dialogue (CD). Journal of WCC Office on Inter-Religious Relations. Report from the Consultation on "Religious Freedom, Community Rights and Individual Rights: A Christian-Muslim Perspective," held in Hartford, CT, 1999.
Issues in Christian-Muslim Relations: Ecumenical Considerations. 1992.

Joint Working Group between the WCC and the Roman Catholic Church (JWG). 1995. *The Challenge of Proselytism and the Calling to Common Witness.*

Mitri, Tarek, ed. 1995. *Religion, Law and Society: A Christian-Muslim Discussion.*

———, ed. 1996. *Religion and Human Rights: A Christian-Muslim Discussion.*

Striving Together in Dialogue: A Muslim-Christian Call to Reflection and Action. 2001.

"Towards Common Witness: A call to adopt responsible relationships in mission and to renounce proselytism." *Minutes of the Forty-eighth Meeting of the WCC Central Committee.* 1997. Document No. 2.3A.

Other Religious Documents

Christian Mission and Islamic Da'wah. 1982. Leicester: Islamic Foundation. [cited as Chambésy].

Confessing Christian Faith in a Pluralistic Society. 1995. Collegeville, MN: Institute for Ecumenical and Cultural Research.

Human Rights Documents

Islamic Conference of Foreign Ministers. 1990. The Cairo Declaration on Human Rights in Islam (CDHRI).

United Nations. 1981. Declaration on the Elimination of All Forms of Intolerance and Discrimination Based on Religion or Belief (DEAFID).

———. 1966. International Covenant for Civil and Political Rights (ICCPR).

———. 1948. Universal Declaration of Human Rights (UDHR).

Universal Declaration of Human Rights by the World's Religions (UDHRWR). 1998.

Universal Islamic Declaration of Human Rights (UIDHR). 1981. Available in Shaikh Shaukat Hussain. 1990. *Human Rights in Islam.* New Delhi: Kitab Bhavan.

Other Publications

Albright, Madeleine K. 1997. Forward to *United States Policies in Support of Religious Freedom: Focus on Christians, Report Consistent with the*

Omnibus Consolidated Appropriations Act, Fiscal Year 1997d, House Report 3610. Bureau of Democracy, Human Rights, and Labor Affairs.

An-Naim, Abdullahi Ahmed. 1990. "Human Rights in the Muslim World: Socio-Political Conditions and Scriptural Imperatives." *Harvard Human Rights Journal* 3:13–52.

Davies, Meryl Wynn, and Adnan Khalil Pasha, eds. 1989. *Beyond Frontiers: Islam and Contemporary Needs*. London and New York: Mansell.

Dutton, Yasin. 1999. "Conversion to Islam: the Qur'anic paradigm." In Christopher Lamb and M. Darrol Bryant, eds., *Religious Conversion*. London and New York: Cassell.

Educational Broadcasting Corporation. 2003. "Iraq Humanitarian Update," Episode 634, Religion and Ethics, April 25.

Horowitz, Michael. 2003. "Cry Freedom." *Christianity Today* 37:3.

Kerr, David A. 1999. "Christian Understandings of Proselytism." *International Bulletin of Missionary Research* 23:8–14.

Lochman, Jan Milič. 1977. "Human Rights from a Christian Perspective." In Allen O. Miller, ed., *Christian Declaration on Human Rights*. Grand Rapids, MI: Eerdmans.

Monshipouri, Mahmood. 1998. *Islamism, Secularism, and Human Rights in the Middle East*. Boulder and London: Lynne Rienner.

Pickthall, Mohammed Marmaduke. 1963. *The Meaning of the Glorious Koran: An Explanatory Translation*. New York: Mentor.

Pittman, Don A., Ruben L.F. Habito, Terry C. Muck, eds. 1996. *Ministry and Theology in Global Perspective: Contemporary Challenges for the Church*. Grand Rapids, MI: Eerdmans.

Refugee Reports (News Service of the Immigration and Refugee Services of America) 17:2, 29 February 1996. "Congress Looks at Persecuted Christians."

Seiple, Robert. 2002. "The USCIRF Is Only Cursing the Darkness." 16 October 2002. www.christianitytoday.com/ct/2002/140/31.0.html

Talbi, Mohammed. 1986. "Religious Liberty: A Muslim Perspective." In Leonard Swidler, ed., *Religious Liberty and Human Rights in Nations and in Religions*. Philadelphia/New York: Ecumenical Press/Hippocrene.

Wisdom, Alan. 2003. *Guidelines for Christian-Muslim Dialogue*. Washington, D.C.: Institute for Religion and Democracy.

Yusuf Ali, Abdullah. 1983. *The Holy Qur'an: Text, Translation and Commentary*. Brentwood, MD: Amana.

CHAPTER 11

Human Rights and Nonviolence

Testament of a Christian Peace Activist

JOHN DEAR

E very human being on the planet has the right to live in peace. In pursuit of this basic human right, Mahatma Gandhi concluded that the only hope for the human race was for every one of us to become nonviolent. He concluded that we were created to live nonviolently with one another. To be human, he said, is to be nonviolent; the whole world has to reject violence and adopt the wisdom and practice of active nonviolence. Nonviolence, he determined, is our only way toward a future of peace with justice. Nonviolence therefore is the first and most essential ingredient if every human being alive is to possess all their human rights.

"The basic principle on which the practice of nonviolence rests," Gandhi suggested, "is that what holds good in respect of oneself equally applies to the whole universe."[1] Given this vision of nonviolence, I would like to reflect on violence and nonviolence, the theology and practice of the Christian peace movement, the example of Christian peacemakers, my own experience, lessons from the recent U.S. war on Iraq, the right of conscientious objection, and finally how Christian nonviolence interacts with the Declaration on Human Rights.

WAR AND NUCLEAR WEAPONS, THE ULTIMATE HUMAN RIGHTS VIOLATION

As we know, we suffer a wide variety of human rights violations, from homelessness to torture to the lack of affordable medicine to hunger. But I submit that the ultimate human rights violation is war and the nuclear weapons that sustain our culture of war. With nuclear weapons, we have the potential to destroy all human life and the entire planet. Everyone's rights are violated by the mere existence of these weapons.

When the United States vaporized 130,000 people at Hiroshima on August 6, 1945, and 30,000 people three days later in Nagasaki, we violated their fundamental human rights and unleashed the threat of total annihilation upon us all. When we bombed Baghdad in 1991 and again in 2003, when we bombed Vietnam, Panama, Grenada, Libya, Nicaragua, and El Salvador, we violated the human rights of ordinary human beings. When we sell weapons for mass murder to warring nations, when we flame the violence in the thirty-five wars currently being fought, we violate the human rights of countless, nameless millions. When we use depleted uranium and poison the earth from Basra to Kosova, we violate the human rights of generations to come, who will be born with birth defects and die early from cancer. When we send radioactive materials into outer space and risk an explosive catastrophe that could spread a plague of cancer on the planet, we violate the human rights of every human being. When we explode nuclear weapons at the Nevada Test Site, build them in Los Alamos, perfect them at Lawrence Livermore Laboratories and maintain thirty thousand others in bunkers everywhere, we violate our own basic human rights to live in peace, in good health, without fear. We hold the planet hostage. We put the nuclear gun to everyone's head. We violate the human rights of every person alive.

Instead of spending billions of dollars on our weapons of mass destruction, we should spend our resources to meet the basic human rights of the world's poor, for food, housing, healthcare, jobs, education, and environmental cleanup. Instead of pursuing global domination, imperial control, corporate greed, and nuclear hegemony, we should commit ourselves to honoring the basic human rights of every human being alive, especially the rights of the poor and hungry, the right to life, the right to peace, the right to live in peace. We all have the right to live without the threat of war, the presence of nuclear weapons, the fear of being vaporized, the threat of global destruction.

ACTIVE NONVIOLENCE: THE WAY FORWARD

On the night before he was killed, Martin Luther King Jr. said, "The choice is no longer violence or nonviolence. It's nonviolence or nonexistence."[2] Unless we adopt the vision and practice of nonviolence, the prophet King announced, we are doomed. We will destroy the planet in a conflagration of violence. The loss of our human rights is only a prelude to the great catastrophe to come, unless the world rejects violence as a means of resolving conflict and commits itself to nonviolent conflict resolution.

Nonviolence is far more than a tactic or a strategy. Nonviolence is a way of life. It is the force of active love and truth that seeks justice and peace for every human being and all creation, that resists injustice, reconciles with everyone, and transforms violence into wholeness. Nonviolence understands the world's crisis as an addiction to violence. It sees every human rights abuse as an act of violence, whether toward individuals, nations, or the whole human family. It seeks to end, heal, and transform the world's violence, at every level from the personal to the international and global.

For nonviolence, the method and the goal are one. Nonviolence understands that the means are the ends, that we reap what we sow, that we cannot achieve a nonviolent world through the use of violence, that we cannot reach peace and justice by waging war and supporting systems of injustice, that we cannot attain our common human rights by any method that violates human rights. Nonviolence requires a complete inner change that becomes contagious, politically revolutionary, and globally transforming.

The wisdom of nonviolence teaches us that violence does not work, that violence in response to violence always leads to further violence. As Gandhi said, "An eye for an eye only makes the whole world blind." As Jesus said, "Those who live by the sword will die by the sword." Those who live by the bomb, the gun, the nuclear weapon, will die by bombs and guns and nuclear weapons. When we see the world through the lens of nonviolence, we realize that war can never stop terrorism because war is terrorism. War never ends wars; war only sows the seeds for future wars. War can never lead to lasting peace or true security or a better world or help us become more human or overcome evil or deepen the spiritual life or uphold human rights. Furthermore, the spirituality of nonviolence denounces the lie of the spirituality of violence and insists that war is not the will of God. War is never blessed by God. War is not endorsed by any religion. War is the ultimate mortal sin. War is demonic, evil, antihuman, antilife, and anti-God. Peaceful means are the only way to a peaceful future, the human right of peace and the God of peace.

Active nonviolence begins then with the vision of a reconciled humanity, the truth that all life is sacred, that we are all equal sisters and brothers, all children of the God of peace, already reconciled, already one, already united. Given this vision of the sanctity of human life, we can never hurt or kill another human being, much less remain silent while our country wages war, builds nuclear weapons, and allows others to starve. We have to defend everyone's human right to live in peace with justice.

But nonviolence is not passive. It is active, creative, provocative, and challenging. It is a life force that when harnessed can disarm nations and change the world. Gandhi described nonviolence as "a force more powerful than all the weapons of the world combined." "Nonviolence is the greatest and most active force in the world," Gandhi wrote. "It is mightier than the mightiest weapon of destruction devised by the ingenuity of humanity. When we tap into the spirit of nonviolence, it becomes contagious and can topple empires."[3]

The world claims there are only two options in the face of violence: we can fight back or run away. Nonviolence gives us a third option: creative, active, peaceful resistance to injustice. We stand up and resist war publicly, through creative nonviolent love, trusting in God, loving our enemies and opponents, and wearing them down until injustice is transformed into justice. But nonviolence carries with it one absolute condition. It insists that there is no cause, however noble, for which we support the killing of any human being. It claims that we cannot pursue the human rights of others while violating the human rights of anyone. Instead of killing others, we give our lives in the nonviolent struggle for justice and human rights, and are even willing to be killed in the process, but we will not retaliate with further violence, murder, or war. Instead of inflicting violence on others for the noble cause of justice or the ignoble cause of global hegemony, we accept and undergo suffering in pursuit of justice and peace, without even the desire to retaliate or seek revenge. Nonviolence calls us to lay down our lives for suffering humanity, indeed, for everyone on all sides.

Nonviolence begins in the heart where we renounce the violence within us. Then it moves out with active nonviolence to our families, local communities, cities, nation, and the world. When organized on the large scale, active nonviolence can transform nations and the world. Gandhi demonstrated this with India's revolution against Britain, Dr. King and the civil rights movement revealed it in the United States, and the People Power movement showed the results of active nonviolence in the Philippines. Archbishop Tutu, Nelson Mandela, and the struggling, heroic blacks of South Africa demonstrated this transformation as they worked against apartheid. Gandhi dreamed of a new world of nonviolence, where we fund and support unarmed international peace teams that travel to conflict zones, disarm opposing sides, and work out peaceful resolutions. He hoped every school and every religious and civic organization in the world would teach children to act and live according to the discipline of nonviolence. He taught that where nonviolence has been tried, even against Nazi Germany, it has worked.

Today, nonviolence is spreading throughout the world as never before, but it receives little attention on the evening news. Nonetheless, it remains the only way forward if we are to secure the human right of peace for every person alive.

LOVE YOUR ENEMIES, THE THEOLOGY
OF CHRISTIAN NONVIOLENCE

All the world's religions, I believe, are rooted in active nonviolence. Islam means peace. Judaism upholds the vision of shalom, where people beat swords into plowshares and study war no more. Gandhi exemplified Hinduism as the spiritual life of active nonviolence. Buddhism calls for compassion toward all living beings.

Christianity, too, requires active, creative nonviolence. Gandhi said that Jesus was the most active practitioner of nonviolence in the history of the world, yet many Christians seem unaware that Jesus was nonviolent. Jesus practiced creative, public nonviolence. He called us to love our neighbors, show compassion toward everyone, seek justice for the poor, forgive those who hurt us, put down the sword, take up the cross in the struggle for justice, and lay down our lives in love for humanity. At the climax of the Sermon on the Mount (Matthew 5–7), he spoke the most significant, revolutionary words ever uttered: "You have heard it said, 'Love your countrymen and hate your enemy,' but I say to you, love your enemies and pray for those who persecute you that you may be children of your heavenly God, for God makes the sun rise on the bad and the good, and causes rain to fall on the just and the unjust. Be compassionate as God is compassionate" (Matt. 5:43–48).

If this is the core message of Jesus, then Christians can no longer support war or nuclear weapons. Christians must renounce violence and the just war theory and practice the nonviolence of Jesus. Starting in Galilee, Jesus served the poor. Then he walked on a campaign of active nonviolence into Jerusalem's Temple, the symbol of imperial and religious oppression of the poor, the center of systemic injustice. There, in an act of nonviolent civil disobedience, he turned over the tables of the moneychangers. He said, "This is a house of prayer." He did not hurt anyone, kill anyone, or bomb anyone, but he was not passive. Jesus engaged in peaceful, dramatic, nonviolent action for justice on behalf of the victims of the empire. For this, he was immediately arrested, brutally tortured, and executed, a victim of the death penalty. His words to Peter, as the soldiers dragged him away to his death, become words to the community, to the church, and to us: "Put your sword away" (John 18:11).

Jesus died on the cross warning people of the violence to come (Luke 23:28–31). Then he forgave those who crucified him (Luke 23:34). Jesus sent his disciples into the world to love one another, even to the point of dying for one another: "My command is this: Love each other as I loved you. Greater love has no one than this, that he lay down his life for his friends" (John 15:12, 13). Christians believe that God raised Jesus from the dead, and that he then sent his disciples into the culture of violence to teach and practice the way of loving nonviolence. From now on, if we want to claim to follow this nonviolent Jesus, we Christians can no longer support war, injustice, nuclear weapons, or violence of any kind. We not only uphold human rights for all people everywhere, we love our enemies, beginning with the people of Iraq, Palestine, Afghanistan, and Colombia. Instead of bombing them and killing them, we serve them, stand with them, and defend them.

If we follow the teachings of the nonviolent Jesus, it becomes clear that war is never justified. According to the Gospel of Jesus, there is no such thing as a just war. War has nothing to do with the Gospel. The just-war theory was originally invented by Cicero, a Roman pagan, as a way for the empire to get this dynamic Christian movement involved in its brutality. Over time, St. Augustine espoused it and declared that we could love our enemies by killing them. Now nearly two thousand years later, we have long ago abandoned the Sermon on the Mount as impractical and invoke this theory of justified war to gain control of the planet and maintain our nuclear hegemony. In the process, we completely reject the nonviolent Jesus and his church of nonviolence.

Now that we stand on the brink of global destruction, however, we are beginning to realize that even if we wanted to meet the conditions of a just war, as Thomas Merton declared, we can no longer do so.[4] War has changed so much in the last century that it has become a complete disaster of total violence. The strict condition that noncombatants, civilians, will not be killed in war is now impossible to meet. With our weapons of mass destruction, dropped from 35,000 feet, we will always kill ordinary civilians in war. So the conditions for a just war can never be met again, war can never be justified again, and so war and the just-war theory must be abolished once and for all. As the late Bishop Carroll Dozier once said, "The just war theory belongs in the same drawer as the flat earth theory."[5]

THE WITNESS OF CHRISTIAN PEACEMAKERS

Though the world stands on the brink, Christians everywhere support war, nuclear weapons, and human rights violations. Yet many Christians are beginning to understand and accept Jesus' nonviolence and are starting to speak out and act for peace. Three great Christians, Martin Luther King Jr., Dorothy Day, and Philip Berrigan, exemplify the way to follow the nonviolent Jesus in these times of total violence.

Martin Luther King Jr. epitomized the modern Christian vocation of active nonviolence. He taught nonviolence around the nation through his sermons, lectures, and above all, his campaign against segregation and racism. But one year to the day before he was assassinated, on April 4, 1967, this great prophet of nonviolence broke new ground when he linked the struggle for civil rights and equality with peace and an end to the war in Vietnam. King connected all the issues in the web of life and summoned us to protect the rights of everyone, including the right of the suffering Vietnamese people to live in peace without fear of our napalm.

> "Somehow this madness must cease," he said that night in his famous speech at the Riverside church in New York City. "We must stop it now. I speak as a child of God and brother to the suffering poor of Vietnam. I speak for those whose land is being laid waste, whose homes are being destroyed, whose culture is being subverted. I speak for the poor of America who are paying the double price of smashed hopes at home and death and corruption in Vietnam. I speak as a citizen of the world, for the world as it stands aghast at the path we have taken. I speak as an American to the leaders of my own nation. The great initiative in this war is ours. The initiative to stop it must be ours. . . . America, the richest and most powerful nation in the world, can well lead the way in this revolution of values. There is nothing, except a tragic death wish, to prevent us from reordering our priorities, so that the pursuit of peace will take precedence over the pursuit of war. . . . We still have a choice: nonviolent coexistence or violent co-annihilation. . . ."[6]

On the night before he was assassinated, Dr. King said in Memphis, "In the human rights revolution, if something isn't done, and in a hurry, to bring the people of color in the world out of their long years of poverty, their long years of hurt and neglect, the whole world is doomed."[7] King called on us to link all the issues as one struggle for the nonviolent transformation of humanity. He did so as a Christian, a follower of the nonviolent Jesus.

Dorothy Day founded the Catholic Worker in 1932 with Peter Maurin to offer hospitality to the homeless and hungry, to give them their human right of housing and food. But as a Catholic Christian, her genius was to link this day-to-day practical work of mercy with concrete suffering people on the streets of New York to the global struggle to bring peace and justice to people everywhere. She announced that as a follower of Jesus she would also oppose war, nuclear weapons, and poverty. She called Christians to enact the works of mercy, justice and peace, to stand with the poor wherever they live, and to speak out for peace and justice for all the world's poor. She was arrested repeatedly for protesting war and singlehandedly gave birth to a new church of peace and nonviolence. "The greatest challenge of the day," she said, "is how to bring about a revolution of the heart, a revolution which has to start with each one of us. War and the poverty of peoples which leads to war, are the great problems of the day and the fundamental solution is the personal response which each of us makes to the message of Jesus. It is the solution which works from the bottom up rather than from the top down."[8]

Philip Berrigan, along with his brother Daniel Berrigan, gained international fame when they and their friends burned draft files with homemade napalm in Catonsville, Maryland, in May 1968 to protest the Vietnam War. They spent years in prison for their symbolic action, "for the burning of paper, instead of children," but did not stop their resistance once the war ended. On September 9, 1980, Phil, Dan, and six others hammered on a nuclear weapon nosecone at the General Electric Plant in King of Prussia, Pennsylvania, in the first of eighty "Plowshares" disarmament actions to begin symbolically the process of nuclear disarmament. They invoked the prophet Isaiah who said that some day people will "beat their swords into plowshares and study war no more" (Isa. 2:4).

Until his death on December 6, 2002, Philip Berrigan called upon North American Christians to practice nonviolent resistance to imperial America as a way of life. More than anyone else I have known, Phil embodied nonviolent resistance. For twenty years, I heard him speak about the imperative of steadfast resistance to imperial America as a moral requirement for these times, indeed as a spiritual duty of faith in the God of peace and justice. This resistance was not just a periodic fling for Phil, but hard work every day.

Phil spent over eleven years of his life in prison for protesting our country's wars and nuclear weapons. When he was not in prison, he lived in Jonah House, a community of nonviolent resistance in innercity Baltimore, where friends study the issues and the scriptures, serve the neighborhood poor, organize vigils and demonstrations, write and speak out for disarmament, and storm heaven for the coming of God's reign of nonviolence.

This might sound romantic or idealistic, but Phil made revolutionary nonviolence a day-to-day spiritual practice. He did not just dream about it, speak about it, or write about it. He lived it, suffered through it, and died resisting imperial America so that we would no longer live under the nuclear shroud, so that all might one day have the human right of peace. Christians need to learn from Phil's example, and take up that same tireless, persistent resistance.

A PERSONAL TESTIMONY TO GOSPEL NONVIOLENCE

My own journey has taken me into soup kitchens, homeless shelters, innercity community work, and death rows across the country, as well as into the war zones of El Salvador, Nicaragua, the Philippines, Guatemala, Northern Ireland, Palestine, and Iraq. For years, I have tried every legal means of working for peace and justice, from lobbying and organizing, to holding press conferences and rallies, to speaking, teaching, and preaching. But as our addiction to violence gets worse and I study the witness of these peacemakers and the challenge of Gospel nonviolence, I have decided to cross the line and risk arrest to protest war, nuclear weapons and our human rights violence. I have been arrested over seventy-five times in acts of nonviolent civil disobedience around the country, from the Pentagon and the White House to Trident submarine bases and the Nevada Test Site, the Lawrence Livermore laboratories in California and the School of the Americas at Fort Benning, Georgia, where the United States trains terrorist Latin American death squads to assassinate and murder their people.

On 7 December 1993, along with Philip Berrigan and two friends, I walked onto the Seymour Johnson Air Force Base in Goldsboro, North Carolina, right through the middle of wargames, and hammered twice on an F-15 nuclear-capable fighter bomber in a "Plowshares" disarmament action. We were immediately surrounded by armed soldiers. I said on behalf of our group, "We are unarmed, peaceful people. We mean you no harm. We're just here to dismantle this weapon of death." For that nonviolent action, I faced twenty years in prison, was found guilty of two felony counts (destruction of government property and conspiracy to commit a felony crime), and spent eight grueling months in a tiny jail cell, never to leave except for the few days we went to court. It was a terrible experience, as well as the most powerful experience of my life. From our action to our trials and imprisonment, it was a spiritual experience, a daily encounter with the God of peace.[9]

My journey on the path of active nonviolence is teaching me the difficult lesson of the abolitionists, the suffragettes, the labor and civil rights movements, and the antiwar and antinuclear movements—that positive, nonviolent social change comes about through risk and sacrifice, when good people break bad laws which legalize injustice and war and accept the consequences, when we accept suffering without retaliating as we insist on the truth of justice and peace with love. Peace and justice come about, in the end, through our participation in the paschal mystery of Jesus, through our sharing in the cross and resurrection.

While living in New York City, I began immediately to volunteer after the horrific events of 11 September 2001, and became the local Red Cross coordinator of over five hundred chaplains at the Family Assistance Center in Manhattan serving tens of thousands of grieving relatives. I personally counseled over fifteen hundred grieving relatives, escorted hundreds of them to pray at Ground Zero, and talked with hundreds of rescue workers at Ground Zero. At the same time, I marched and spoke out against the U.S. bombing of innocent civilians in Afghanistan. I was trying to defend the human rights of New Yorkers, Afghanis, and Iraqis, to practice the nonviolence of Jesus, which commands us to love our neighbors and our enemies. It has been a difficult, painful journey for me, but a great blessing because, through active nonviolence, I am learning not only what it means to be a Christian, but what it means to be a human being.

NONVIOLENCE, HUMAN RIGHTS, AND IRAQ

The human rights revolution around the world is making great strides toward protecting the rights of suffering peoples. But I suggest that the human rights movement needs to connect with the global movement for peace and use the strategies and wisdom of Christian and Gandhian nonviolence to push for the transformation of the world.

The U.S. invasion and ongoing war in Iraq shows the need for combining forces. When I led a delegation of Nobel Peace Prize winners to Baghdad in 1999, we met with United Nations, non-governmental organizations (NGOs), religious and political leaders. But it was meeting hundreds of dying children who suffered because of our economic sanctions that was most devastating. Hundreds of thousands of Iraqi children died during the 1990s because of our unjust sanctions. Now, since the U.S. invasion, bombing, and occupation of Iraq in 2003, innocent civilians continue to suffer and die.

In the name of democracy we have violated every one of the human rights. The U.S. war on Iraq remains, among other things, one massive violation of human rights. The innocent Iraqi people suffered under Saddam, then under our sanctions, then under our bombs, and now under our occupation. They did not ask to be invaded or bombed. Literally, thousands of Iraqis told me during our delegation that they wanted the sanctions lifted, that they wanted food and medicine to survive, and that they wanted nonviolent support for their own democratic movements. At that time, they believed our country had more concern for their oil than for their human rights. Today, despite democratic elections, Iraq remains an occupied territory.

If we want to pursue global human rights, we need to stand for peace and denounce war—the ultimate violation of human rights, as the catastrophe in Iraq shows. Unless we join forces and demand an end to our own arsenal of weapons of mass destruction and the Pentagon's imperial war machine, the world's poor will continue to suffer every kind of human rights abuse, and we may risk future Hiroshimas and the destruction of the planet itself.

THE DECLARATION OF HUMAN RIGHTS BY THE
WORLD'S RELIGIONS AND CHRISTIAN NONVIOLENCE

The beautiful vision of the Universal Declaration of Human Rights by the World's Religions, endorsed by religious leaders on 10 December 1998, gives us hope and strength in its call for respect for human rights and a future of peace.

In particular, the first several articles lay the foundation for a new world of peace and nonviolence. "All human beings have the right to be treated as human beings and the duty to treat everyone else as a human being," we read in Article 1. "Do unto others as you would have them do unto you," Jesus put it (Luke 6:31). We have the right to live in peace and nonviolence, I hear the religious leaders saying, which means we ourselves have to treat every human being on earth nonviolently if we are going to fulfill our human and spiritual potential.

"Everyone has the right to freedom from violence in any of its forms," we read in Article 2. "Everyone has the right to life, longevity and liveability," we read in Article 3. "No one shall be subjected to torture or cruel, inhuman or degrading treatment or punishment," we read in Article 3. "One is duty bound, when asserting one's rights, to prefer nonviolence over violence," we read in the conclusion (Article 29).

These statements summon us ultimately as people of faith to stand up against war and nuclear weapons. The Christian vision of nonviolence runs throughout the document. I would only suggest the addition of two specific points: "Everyone has the right to live in a world without nuclear weapons and the threat of nuclear destruction"; and "Everyone has the right of conscientious objection, the right to refuse when ordered to kill by their government."

The UDHRWR offers a blueprint for a nonviolent world. If every major religion began to promote these articles, we would all come to Gandhi's conclusion that we must renounce our war and violence and become individuals, communities, and nations of nonviolence. Indeed, we would find ourselves finally taking up the great commandment of Jesus not only to love one another, but to love even our enemies (Matt. 5:43–45).

CONCLUSION

The Universal Declaration of Human Rights by the World's Religions invites us to repent of violence and walk the way of nonviolence. It calls us first back to the God of peace who will disarm our hearts and send us forth as God's instruments for the disarmament of the world. It challenges us to delve deep into the roots, spirituality, and practice of peace at the heart of every religion. In particular, it challenges Christians to adhere to the nonviolence of Jesus. Everyone has the right to live in peace, we read between its lines. That means, every one of us, beginning with people of faith, has to undergo the spiritual conversion toward nonviolence; renounce our violence; denounce war, nuclear weapons, and poverty; and practice creative nonviolence for a global transformation into a new world of peace with justice.

If we dare take up the challenge of nonviolence, we will discover what it means to be human. We will receive the blessing reserved by Jesus for peacemakers, and be called "sons and daughters of the God of peace" (Matt. 5:9).

NOTES

1. John Dear, ed., *Mohandas Gandhi: Selected Writings* (Maryknoll, NY: Orbis, 2002), p. 98.
2. James Washington, ed., *A Testament of Hope: The Essential Writings of Martin Luther King, Jr.* (San Francisco: Harper and Row, 1986), p. 280.
3. John Dear, *Mohandas Gandhi*, pp. 95–96.
4. Thomas Merton, *The Nonviolent Alternative* (New York: Farrar, Straus, and Giroux, 1980), p. 90.
5. Bishop Carroll Dozier, *Peacemaking Day by Day* (Erie, PA: Pax Christi USA, 1985), p. 79.
6. James Washington, *A Testament of Hope*, pp. 238, 241, 243.
7. James Washington, *A Testament of Hope*, p. 280.
8. Dorothy Day, "The Meaning of Poverty," *Ave Maria Magazine*, Notre Dame, IN, 1966 (see also, *St. Anthony Messenger*, Jan.–Feb. 2003).
9. For a the full story of my experience in prison for antiwar action, see *Peace Behind Bars: A Peacemaking Priest's Journal from Jail* (Chicago: Sheed and Ward, 1998).

BIBLIOGRAPHY

Dear, John. *Jesus the Rebel*. Chicago: Sheed and Ward, 1999.
———. *Living Peace*. New York: Doubleday, 2001.
———, ed. *Mohandas Gandhi: Selected Writings*. New York: Orbis, 2002.
———. *Peace Behind Bars: A Peacemaking Priest's Journal from Jail*. Chicago: Sheed and Ward, 1998.

Dozier, Bishop Carroll. *Peacemaking Day by Day*. Erie, PA: Pax Christi USA, 1985.

Ellsberg, Robert, ed. *By Little and By Little: The Selected Writings of Dorothy Day*. New York: Knopf, 1983.

Merton, Thomas. *The Nonviolent Alternative*. New York: Farrar, Straus, and Giroux, 1980.

Washington, James, ed. *A Testament of Hope: The Essential Writings of Martin Luther King, Jr*. San Francisco: Harper and Row, 1986.

CHAPTER 12

Christian Views in Dialogue with the UDHRWR

ARVIND SHARMA AND FRANCES S. ADENEY

This concluding chapter will attempt to analyze the implications of the interface between Christian and human rights discourse—to which the preceding chapters of this book have been devoted—for the formulation of a Universal Declaration of Human Rights by the World's Religions.

The United Nation's Universal Declaration of Human Rights was not meant to be a static document but was intended to spawn a movement. We can see the Universal Declaration of Human Rights by the World's Religions and conversations around it as part of that movement. The tensions among religious bodies around the world today increase the importance of such conversations. The UN Declaration was a statement of ideals, intended to move the consciences of people around the world to work together for humanitarian values. The UDHRWR responds to that goal of the UDHR. Although people are located within inherited traditions, values must be sorted out in each generation. Contrasting viewpoints can be found, not only between but also within religions. People of religious faith can affirm the values of the UDHR as they dialogue with it from different points of view. Both philosophical and religious circles will benefit from that dialogue.

TWO STREAMS OF DISCOURSE REGARDING CHRISTIANITY AND HUMAN RIGHTS

There are two main streams of discourse in relation to Christianity and human rights. According to one stream the concept of human rights is to be

197

traced back, in *nuce*, to Christianity itself. The fact that a human being is made in the image of God imbues the human person with a unique dignity, and it is from this inherent moral worth of the human being that the moral entitlements known as human rights are to be derived. The individual worth of human beings flows from such a religious imagination, which then finds its full expression in the secular concept of individual rights.

It could be argued that, at least on the face of it, this bifurcation into the sacred and the secular and the assigning of the emergence of rights to the secular realm indicates that only secularity and not Christianity could prove capable of being midwife to the concept of individual human rights. But this might also amount to a somewhat superficial reading of the situation, because the Christian injunction of rendering unto Caesar what is Caesar's and unto God what is God's might be interpreted as providing a Christian basis for the emergence of the secular realm. Some would argue that this is particularly true of Protestant Christianity. After the Reformation, the secular and sacred realms gradually undid their Constantinian juxtaposition, bringing about a separation that Christianity itself was privy to, once the secular world had emerged. The principle of religious tolerance, so crucial to modern democratic societies, may be traced to the Christian view that God would only truly accept the uncoerced individual faith decision of the believer as authentic. That conviction provided the opening for the flourishing of all kinds of freedoms, once religious freedom on Christian religious grounds became widely accepted. In this way, and perhaps in an even more detailed way, it would then become possible to argue that Christianity is not only consistent with human rights discourse but, in a sense, its progenitor and protector.

The other stream of discourse argues the opposite. It sees human worth, implied in human beings as made in the image of God, fatally compromised in the lapsarian period. Moreover, the actual expansion of Christianity in secular history represents the denial of rights to others—first to the Jews, then to the Romans who were forced to convert to Christianity, and then to the other forms of religiosity in Europe. In more modern times the same story of the denial of the most fundamental rights is repeated in the expansion of Catholic Christianity into the Americas under the Spanish empire and then of Christianity in general to Africa and Asia under the European empires that followed it. The emergence of human rights discourse in Europe itself is then seen as a movement which, like the kite, rises against and not with the Christian wind. From such a perspective human rights discourse expanded as Christianity gradually contracted in terms of its influence over various areas of secular life. By the time the Universal Declaration of Human Rights was developed by the United Nations, the theistic coloration of proposed references to the divine was clearly unacceptable for a universal ethic of human rights. Thus the UDHR emerged as a secular document.

It might be possible to align these two contrasting perspectives in some measure with models of church-state relations that have emerged in the modern world and thus demonstrate the power of both these "models" as it were. The United States maintains a strong wall of separation between church and state but the separation is not hostile to the practice of Christianity in particular or religion in general. The United States of America is well known for statistical reports of the highest level of church attendance among the industrialized countries of the world. By contrast, the separation of church and state in France tends to be hostile to religion, although both the United States and France view themselves as champions of human rights in the most general terms.

There is thus variation within the first stream itself of how religion in the secular realm is to be handled, and many possible patterns of relationship between church and state per se can also be identified. A similar variation is also possible to identify within the second stream, when Christianity includes the secular realm within its orbit. Here again Christianity may display variable patterns, some more hospitable to human rights than others.

While it is true that the overall orientation of the first stream will have to be judged as favorable to human rights, and that of the second stream unfavorable to them, this need not necessarily be so. The differences between the two streams lies in whether Christianity *on its own* frees up a secular realm or insists on trying to control it. As Christians support freedom of religious expression or humanitarian values, they support human rights. But when Christians insist that the secular realm respond to their particular religious views, their insistence may mitigate against human rights norms.

For example, a Christian emphasis on its exclusivism may compromise religious freedom—yet it does not follow that this must be the case uniformly. The influence of Catholic Christian thought on the formulation of socioeconomic rights has been well documented. The emergence of liberation theologies points in the same direction, using political means to gain human freedom. Christian voices can affirm not only Christian values but human values as well.

CHRISTIANITY AND THE UDHRWR

Both these viewpoints have their own implications for how Christianity might be brought into relationship with the proposed UDHRWR. By following the first route, Christianity would be seen as paradoxically providing a *secular* platform on which all the religions of the world could stand together. From such a perspective the great contribution of Christianity would consist in the recognition of the UDHRWR as a secular document, which the various religions of the world are willing to endorse. Religion can be seen as a private affair between humans and God; in public, religion does not play a specific role but its values reinforce the aspirations that nations have articulated in the Universal Declaration of Human Rights adopted by the UNO. The UDHRWR is an extension and enlargement of the process.

From the second point of view, the contribution of Christianity to the UDHRWR will have to be seen in a different light. From this perspective each religion brings something special to the table and this then constitutes its contribution to human rights. In this view, there is a role for *public theology*. One could argue, for instance, that the right to asylum from persecution would be one such right that finds a firm place in the UDHRWR on account of the history of persecution Christianity suffered under the Roman Empire, until, by a marvelous reversal of fortune, Christianity itself became the religion of the Roman Empire, and so on.

A VOICE FOR RELIGIONS IN HUMAN RIGHTS DISCOURSE

On a more wholistic level, the UDHRWR is framed by the relationship of each religion to the divine. Religious concerns were present from the beginning of the development of the concept of human rights. As understanding among the world's religions increases, it is no longer necessary for Christians to limit religious aspirations for human rights to theistic language—language which implies that the divine is a transcendent being or force. Instead, Christians can affirm the UDHRWR which, by its affirmation of the relevance of religious thought to human rights, says something more about sources of human rights than the UN Declaration was able to say, because its context and audience required the exclusion of religious language.

The tolerance expressed during the negotiations of the Third Committee in preparing the UDHR demonstrated that persons of all faiths or none could work together for the human rights of all. This tolerance was appropriate to the setting, the crafting of a universal declaration to be appropriated by nation states.

The UDHRWR demonstrates another kind of tolerance. The tolerance expressed among those of many faiths is a tolerance of other religious beliefs that may differ from one's own but that one holds in respect. This tolerance encouraged by Christians at the founding of the United States is appropriate to another setting, the augmenting of a secular statement on human rights with the voices of religious leaders. The UDHRWR shows that religions can find commonality in a spiritually expansive framing of human rights. That is something that a secular statement cannot do; nor is it meant to. The UDHRWR brings into voice the religious convictions of people of faith—convictions that source both understandings and actions with regard to the rights of all of the human family.

Rather than a redundant or superfluous statement, the UDHRWR deepens and expands the UDHR by clearly demonstrating the interest and convictions of people of faith with regards to human rights.

MINIMALIST AND MAXIMALIST CHRISTIAN CONTRIBUTIONS TO THE UDHRWR

Christianity can contribute to that project in two ways. Both the secular and public theology streams of Christianity can serve to irrigate human rights discourse in a fertile way. This can be illustrated by the way they impinge on the concept of religious freedom. Chrisianity contains both these thrusts within itself: that one must turn toward God in a purely voluntary act, and that Christianity has been imbued by the same God with a sense of mission, being called upon to baptize the nations. It is the secularization of the first of these that has led to the formulation of the right to change one's religion as a fundamental human right. For if one must *choose* Christianity of one's own free will to be a true believer, it follows that everyone has the right to exercise his or her own free will in relation to any religion. Hence freedom to change one's religion becomes an integral part of one's freedom. How different and how Christian such a contribution is may be judged from the fact that according to the Saudi Arabian government "our view is that freedom of religion (which is a basic issue in the Universal Declaration of Human Rights) has double edges: (a) the freedom of *any country* to adhere to, to protect and preserve its religion; and (b) the respect and tolerance towards religious minorities of the country's citizens as long as they respect the constitutional tenets of their country."[1]

The second stream, which upholds a more open participation of Christianity in public life, makes its contribution to another dimension of religious freedom—namely the right to manifest one's religion *in public*. This dimension of the right to freedom of religion is quite prominent an element in its formulation of Article 18 of the Universal Declaration of Human Rights, which reads as follows:

> Everyone has the right to freedom of thought, conscience and religion; this right includes freedom to change his religion or belief, and freedom either alone or in community with others and in

public or private, to manifest his religion or belief in teaching, practice, worship and observance.[2]

It is clear that both a minimalist and a maximalist perspective on the relation of Christianity in relation to the public realm make key contributions to the concept of religious freedom. Indeed one way of exploring the subtlety involved here might be to distinguish between the terms "conversion" and "proselytization." Such a distinction is not usually drawn and the two are sometimes used interchangeably. But if we identify conversion as an act undertaken by an individual and proselytization as an act performed upon the individual to get him or her to convert, then the point becomes clear. Christianity embraces both these phenomena, but the one of conversion, as distinguished above from proselytization, ties more naturally into what we described as the first stream, and proselytization into the second.[3]

This distinction highlights the fact that even when the role of Christianity in the context of a contribution to human rights discourse is contested, it should not blind us to the fact that it may have contributed to this discourse in the very process of this contestation and may similarly contribute to the UDHRWR despite such contestation. Such contestation may be said to characterize not just Christianity but religion per se in relation to human rights. It has been said for instance that:

> No topic generates more controversy—or indeed more complex ideas—than relationships between (1) institutionalization of religion in the state or religious belief or practice and (2) human rights norms. From one perspective, religious beliefs and human rights are complementary expressions of similar ideas, even though religious texts invoke the language of duties rather than rights. Important aspects of the major religious traditions—canonical text, scholarly exegesis, ministries—provide the foundation for, or reinforce, many basic human rights. Evident examples include rights to bodily security, or to economic and social provision for the needy. From another perspective, religious traditions may impinge on human rights, and religious leaders may assert the primacy of those traditions over rights. The banner of cultural relativism may here be held high. If notions of state sovereignty represent one powerful concept and a force that challenges and seeks to limit the reach of the international human rights movement, religion can then represent another.[4]

The point this book helps us make is that, despite such anxious ambiguity in the relationship between the two, the case of Christianity illustrates that creative contact can emerge between religious discourse and human rights discourse, just as a marriage might involve constant tension and yet produce worthy citizens of the next generation.

The Declaration of Human Rights by the World's Religions presents just such an opportunity by bringing those discourses into relationship. Those conversations will pose different issues depending on their historical location and social/economic contexts. A stress on duties over rights, for example, may be an appropriate reminder for those holding positions of power in society. On the other hand, those with little power may need to stress rights over duties in their struggle to gain access to basic human rights. Whatever the context, discussions of human rights around the UDHRWR allow the religious sources of human rights, which were muted in the UDHR, to come to the fore. Conversations around the two documents put the sources of human rights in law, philosophy, and religious theologies into conversation, a conversation that can enrich understandings and strengthen the will to uphold human rights throughout the world.

NOTES

1. Henry J. Steiner and Philip Ashton, *International Human Rights in Context: Law, Politics, Morals* (New York: Oxford University Press, 2000), p. 454.

2. Ian Brownlie, *Basic Documents on Human Rights* (third edition) (Oxford: Clarendon, 1992), p. 25.

3. For some of the complexities involved see Ted Stahnke, "Proselytism and the Freedom to Change Religion in International Human Rights Law," *Brigham Young University Law Review* (1999): 251–350.

4. Henry J. Steiner and Philip Ashton, op. cit., p. 445.

Universal Declaration of Human Rights by the World's Religions

The following Universal Declaration is a collaborative project of the Forum. The initial declaration was composed at McGill University. Professor Arvind Sharma, a member of the Forum's International Board of Consultants, then directed a revision of the declaration in consultation with numerous scholars and religious leaders. Two of the venues for these revisions were the April 1999 Forum-sponsored conference on "Human Rights and Responsibilities in the World Religions" at Chapman University and the March 2000 Forum-sponsored conference on "Ethics and Religion for a Global Twenty-First Century" at Chapman and Loyola Marymount universities. An earlier version of the declaration has been published in the *Journal of Religious Ethics* 27, 3 (1999). The most up-to-date version of the declaration appears in *Human Rights and Responsibilites in the World Religions*, volume 4 of "The Library of Global Ethics and Religion" (Oneworld Publications, Oxford, England) in 2003.

Whereas human beings are led to affirm that there is more to life than life itself by inspiration human and divine;

Whereas the Universal Declaration of Human Rights, as adopted by the General Assembly of the United Nations on December 10, 1948, bases itself on the former;

Whereas any exclusion of the world's religions as positive resources for human rights is obnoxious to the evidence of daily life;

Whereas the various communities constituting the peoples of the world must exchange not only ideas but also ideals;

Whereas religions ideally urge human beings to live in a just society and not just in any society;

Whereas one must not idealize the actual but strive to realize the ideal;

Whereas not to compensate victims of imperialism, racism, casteism, and sexism is itself imperialist, racist, casteist, and sexist;

Whereas rights are independent of duties in their protection but integrally related to them in conception and execution;

Whereas human rights are intended to secure peace, freedom, equality, and justice—and to mitigate departures therefrom—when these come in conflict or the rights themselves;

Now, therefore, on the fiftieth anniversary of the Universal Declaration of Human Rights and the fiftieth anniversary of the founding of the Faculty of Religious Studies at McGill University, Montreal, Quebec, Canada.

The signatories to this Universal Declaration of Human Rights by the World's Religions, as legatees of the religious heritage of humanity do hereby propose the following as the common standard of achievement for the followers of all religions or none, on the tenth day of December, 1998, as all people are brothers and sisters on the face of the earth.

ARTICLE 1

All human beings have the right to be treated as human beings and have the duty to treat everyone as a human being.

ARTICLE 2

Everyone has the right to freedom from violence, in any of its forms, individual or collective; whether based on race, religion, gender, caste or class, or arising from any other cause.

ARTICLE 3

(1) Everyone has the right to food.
(2) Everyone has the right to life, longevity, and liveability and the right to food, clothing, and shelter to sustain them.
(3) Everyone has the duty to support and sustain life, longevity, and liveability of all.

ARTICLE 4

(1) No one shall be subjected to slavery or servitude, forced labor, bonded labor, or child labor. Slavery and the slave trade shall be prohibited in all its forms.
(2) No one shall subject anyone to slavery or servitude in any of its forms.

ARTICLE 5

(1) No one shall be subjected to torture or to cruel, inhuman, or degrading treatment or punishment, inflicted either physically or mentally, whether on secular or religious grounds, inside the home or outside it.
(2) No one shall subject anybody to such treatment.

ARTICLE 6

(1) Everyone has a right to recognition everywhere as a person before law; and by everyone everywhere as a human being deserving humane treatment, even when law and order has broken down.
(2) Everyone has the duty to treat everyone else as a human being both in the eyes of law and one's own.

ARTICLE 7

All are equal before law and entitled to equal protection before law without any discrimination on grounds of race, religion, caste, class, sex, and sexual orientation. It is the right of everyone to be so treated and the duty of everyone to so treat others.

ARTICLE 8

Everybody has the duty to prevent the perpetuation of historical, social, economic, cultural, and other wrongs.

ARTICLE 9

(1) No one shall be subjected to arbitrary arrest, detention, or exile by the state or by anyone else. The attempt to proselytize against the will of the person shall amount to arbitrary detention, so also the detention, against their will, of teenage children by the parents, and among spouses.
(2) It is the duty of everyone to secure everyone's liberty.

ARTICLE 10

Everybody has the right to public trial in the face of criminal charges and it is the duty of the state to ensure it. Everyone who cannot afford a lawyer must be provided one by the state.

ARTICLE 11

Everyone charged with a penal offense has the right to be considered innocent until proven guilty.

ARTICLE 12

(1) Everyone has the right to privacy. This right includes the right not to be subjected to arbitrary interference with one's privacy; of one's own, or of one's family, home, or correspondence.
(2) Everyone has the right to one's good name.
(3) It is the duty of everyone to protect the privacy and reputation of everyone else.
(4) Everyone has the right not to have one's religion denigrated in the media or the academia.
(5) It is the duty of the follower of every religion to ensure that no religion is denigrated in the media or the academia.

ARTICLE 13

(1) Everyone has the right to freedom of movement and residence anywhere in the world.
(2) Everyone has the duty to abide by the laws and regulations applicable in that part of the world.

ARTICLE 14

Everyone has the right to seek and secure asylum in any country from any form of persecution, religious or otherwise, and the right not to be deported. It is the duty of every country to provide such asylum.

ARTICLE 15

(1) Everyone has the right to a nationality;
(2) No one shall be arbitrarily deprived of one's nationality nor denied the right to change one's nationality.
(3) Everyone has the duty to promote the emergence of a global constitutional order.

ARTICLE 16

(1) Everyone has the right to marriage.
(2) Members of a family have the right to retain and practice their own religion or beliefs.
(3) Everyone has the right to raise a family.
(4) Everybody has the right to renounce the world and join a monastery, provided that one shall do so after making adequate arrangement for one's dependents.
(5) Marriage and monasticism are two of the most successful institutional innovations of humanity and are entitled to protection by the society and the state.
(6) Motherhood and childhood are entitled to special care and assistance. It is the duty of everyone to extend special consideration to mothers and children.
(7) Everyone shall promote the outlook that the entire world constitutes an extended family.

ARTICLE 17

(1) Everybody has the right to own property, alone as well as in association with others. An association also has a similar right to own property.
(2) Everyone has a right not to be deprived of property arbitrarily. It is the duty of everyone not to deprive others of their property arbitrarily. Property shall be understood to mean material as well as intellectual, aesthetic, and spiritual property.
(3) Everyone has the duty not to deprive anyone of their property or appropriate it in an unauthorized manner.

ARTICLE 18

(1) There shall be no compulsion in religion. It is a matter of choice.
(2) Everyone has the right to retain one's religion and to change one's religion.
(3) Everyone has the duty to promote peace and tolerance among different religions and ideologies.

ARTICLE 19

(1) Everyone has the right to freedom of opinion and expression, where the term "expression" includes the language one speaks, the food one eats, the clothes one wears, the religion one practices and professes, provided that one conforms generally to the accustomed rules of decorum recognized in the neighborhood.
(2) It is the duty of everyone to ensure that everyone enjoys such freedom.
(3) Children have the right to express themselves freely in all matters affecting the child, to which it is the duty of their caretakers to give due weight in accordance with the age and maturity of the child.

ARTICLE 20

(1) Everyone has the right to freedom of assembly and association, and the duty to do so peacefully.
(2) No one may be compelled to belong to an association, or to leave one without due process.

ARTICLE 21

(1) Everybody over the age of eighteen has the right to vote, to elect or be elected, and thus to take part in the government or governance of the country, directly or indirectly.
(2) Everyone has the right of equal access to public service in one's country and the duty to provide such access.
(3) It is the duty of everyone to participate in the political process.

ARTICLE 22

Everyone, as a member of society, has a right to social security and a duty to contribute to it.

ARTICLE 23

(1) Everyone has the right to same pay for same work and a duty to offer same pay for same work.
(2) Everyone has the right for just remuneration for one's work and the duty to justly recompense for work done.
(3) Everyone has the right to form and to join trade unions for the protection of one's interests.
(4) Everyone has the right not to join a trade union.

ARTICLE 24

(1) Everyone has the right to work and to rest, including the right to support while seeking work and the right to periodic holidays with pay.
(2) The right to rest extends to the earth.

ARTICLE 25

(1) Everyone has the right to health and to universal medical insurance. It is the duty of the state or society to provide it.
(2) Every child has the right to a childhood free from violence and it is the duty of the parents to provide it.

ARTICLE 26

Everyone has the right to free education and the right to equality of opportunity for any form of education involving restricted enrollment.

ARTICLE 27

(1) Everyone has the right to freely participate in the cultural life of the community and the right to freely contribute to it.
(2) Everyone has the right to share scientific advances and its benefits and the duty to disseminate them, and wherever possible to contribute to such advances.
(3) Everyone has the right to the protection of their cultural heritage. It is the duty of everyone to protect and enrich everyone's heritage, including one's own.

ARTICLE 28

Everyone has the right to socioeconomic and political order at a global, national, regional, and local level, which enables the realization of social, political, economic, racial, and gender justice and the duty to give precedence to universal, national, regional, and local interests in that order.

ARTICLE 29

(1) One is duty bound, when asserting one's rights, to take the rights of other human beings; of past, present, and future generations, the rights of humanity, and the rights of nature and the earth into account.
(2) One is duty bound, when asserting one's rights, to prefer nonviolence over violence.

ARTICLE 30

(1) Everyone has the right to require the formation of a supervisory committee within one's community, defined religiously or otherwise, to monitor the implementation of the articles of this Declaration; and to serve on it and present one's case before such a committee.
(2) It is everyone's duty to ensure that such a committee satisfactorily supervises the implementation of these articles.

APPENDIX 2

Christian Theological Sources
for Human Rights in Relation to
the UDHR and the UDHRWR

FRANCES S. ADENEY

1. PERSON: IMAGE OF GOD

UDHR: "Whereas human rights are intended to secure all three—freedom, equality and justice . . ."

Characteristics

- Human Dignity
- Worth of each individual created in God's image

Justice Ethic

- Freedom to choose
- Freedom from harm
- Equality of all persons
- Protection of life
- Individual rights
- Responsibility to the poor and weak

Examples

Catholic Church
- Right to life
- Right to one's own parents
- A favorable moral environment

213

- Right to seek and know truth
- Right to work and provide for self and family
- Right to raise a family

Protestant Christian Feminists in Indonesia
  - Image of God major construct for partnership with men
  - Rights of women to choice and leadership in the church

UDHRWR: Articles 1, 4, 9.2, 11, 12, 16, 18, 19, 23

---

2. WORLD: ORDER OF CREATION

UDHR: *"Whereas . . . rights and duties are correlative: sub-human creatures may have rights without corresponding duties and in exceptional cases, persons . . . duties without corresponding rights."*

Characteristics

- Creation ordered by God
- Humans as stewards appointed to do God's will as caretakers.
- Rights and responsibilities ordered by domains: social order, protection of weak, value of earth

Care Ethic

- Management of all domains under God's will
- Understanding and value of creation

Examples

- Calvinism and Reformed Protestant Church, e.g. Presbyterians

UDHRWR: Article 9.2, 15, 17, 23.2, 28, 29.1

---

3. SOCIAL ORDER: HUMAN COMMUNITY

UDHR: *"Whereas the various communities constituting the peoples of the world must exchange not only ideas but also ideals;"*

Characteristics

- Covenant with God for good of community
- Dialogue
- Respecting difference

Responsibility Ethic

- People in relationships
- Responding to one another for the good of the whole
- Emphasis on understanding others
- Advocacy for human rights for all

Examples

- World Council of Churches
- National Council of Christian Churches, U.S.A.
- United Church of Canada
- Ecumenical groups

UDHRWR: Article 6, 10, 13.2, 14, 15, 16, 18.3, 19, 20, 21, 22, 25, 26, 27, 30

---

4. SIN: HUMAN FAILURE, STRUCTURAL EVIL

UDHR: "Whereas not to compensate victims of imperialism, racism, casteism, and sexism is itself imperialist, racist, casteist, and sexist;"

Characteristics

- Human failure
- Wrong intentions
- Structural evil

Evaluative Ethic

- Need for self-examination and revision of practices
- Work of resistance and responsible action
- Vigilance in protecting human rights

Examples

- Christian feminists and other liberation movements
- Focus on power dynamics in seeking justice

Catholic Church
- Makes qualifications to human rights because of the danger of self-interest that destroys justice
- Therefore, obedience to truth and respect for rights of others

Reformed Church
- Emphasis on responsibilities rather than rights
- Therefore, dependence on God, God's will, and God's grace

UDHRWR: Article 2, 4, 5, 7, 8, 9, 12.4, 14, 29.2

Contributors

FRANCES S. ADENEY, Benfield Professor of Mission at Louisville Presbyterian Theological Seminary in Louisville, Kentucky, earned her Ph.D. at the Graduate Theological Union in Berkeley, California, and has taught comparative religious ethics as Distinguished Brooks Professor of Religion at the University of Southern California (1997–1999), associate professor of ethics at Satya Wancana Christian University in Indonesia (1991–1997), and Visiting Scholar at the Von Heugel Institute, Cambridge University (1989–1990). Her recent contributions to interreligious dialogue, human rights, and gender equality are published in *Ethics and World Religions* (Orbis, 1999), *Gospel Bearers: Gender Barriers* (Orbis, 2001), *Christians Talk about Buddhist Meditation: Buddhists Talk about Christian Prayer* (Continuum, 2003), and her book *Christian Women in Indonesia: A Narrative Study of Gender and Religion* (Syracuse University Press, 2003). Forthcoming books include *Christians Engage the World's Religions* (Baker, 2007) and *Beyond the Great Divide: Liberals and Conservatives Reexamine Christian Mission* (Baker, 2008).

JOHN DEAR is a Jesuit priest, pastor, and peace activist. He is the author/editor of twenty books on peace and nonviolence, including *Living Peace; Disarming the Heart; The God of Peace; Peace Behind Bars;* and *Jesus the Rebel.* He served as the executive director of the Fellowship of Reconciliation, the nation's oldest and largest interfaith peace organization; as Red Cross coordinator of chaplains in the New York Family Assistance Center after 9/11; spent time in prison for nonviolent action against war; and currently lives in the desert of New Mexico. For more information, see: www.fatherjohndear.org.

217

JEAN BETHKE ELSHTAIN is a political philosopher whose work shows the connections between our political and our ethical convictions. She is the Laura Spelman Rockefeller Professor of Social and Political Ethics at the University of Chicago, a position she has held since 1995. Prior to that, she taught at the University of Massachusetts and at Vanderbilt University where she was the first woman to hold an endowed professorship in the history of that institution. She has also been a Visiting Professor at Harvard and Yale. Professor Elshtain holds nine honorary degrees, and in 1996 she was elected a Fellow of the American Academy of Arts and Sciences. She has authored and/or edited twenty books and written some five hundred essays. Her books include: *Democracy on Trial, Who Are We? Critical Reflections and Hopeful Possibilities, Politics and Ethical Discourse,* and *Just War against Terror.* Professor Elshtain was born in the high plains of Northern Colorado, where she grew up among people who were hard working, forthright, and dedicated to their families, friends, and community.

DAVID LITTLE joined the Faculty of Divinity at Harvard University in 1999. Before that, he was senior scholar in religion, ethics, and human rights at the United States Institute of Peace in Washington, D.C., where he directed the Working Group on Religion, Ideology, and Peace, which conducted a study of religion, nationalism, and intolerance in reference to the United Nations Declaration on the Elimination of Intolerance and Discrimination. From 1996 to 1998, he was on the State Department Advisory Committee on Religious Freedom Abroad. He writes in the areas of moral philosophy, moral theology, history of ethics, and the sociology of religion, with an interest in comparative ethics, human rights, religious liberty, and ethics and international affairs. He is author with Scott W. Hibbard of *Islamic Activism and U.S. Foreign Policy,* and author of two volumes in the USIP series on religion, nationalism, and intolerance.

TERRY C. MUCK joined Asbury's E. Stanley Jones School of World Mission and Evangelism in the fall of 2000 after teaching ten years at Austin Presbyterian Theological Seminary. During the decade of the eighties, Dr. Muck held various positions at Christianity Today, including executive editor of *Christianity Today Magazine* and editor of *Leadership Journal.* He has also taught at Wheaton College, Northwestern University, and Bethel College. Dr. Muck has authored nine books, including *A Pocket Guide to American Religion* (Doubleday, forthcoming), *Buddhists Talk about Jesus, Christians Talk about the Buddha* (Continuum, 2000), and *Ministry and Theology in Global Perspective: Contemporary Challenges for the Church* (Eerdmans, 1996). His articles have appeared in various theological dictionaries and encyclopedias and in such periodicals as *Missiology, Books and Culture, Journal of the*

Evangelical Theological Society, Buddhist-Christian Studies, Evangelical Missions Quarterly, and *The Washington Post*. He co-edited the Buddhist Christian Studies Journal from 1995 to 2005 and is the general editor of the NIV Application Commentary, a nineteen-volme New Testament commentary and twenty-three-volume Old Testament commentary. Dr. Muck also took over as Editor of *Missiology: An International Review* in 2002. Dr. Muck, an ordained minister in the Presbyterian Church (U.S.A.), is a popular speaker and member of numerous denominational and ecumenical commissions and committees. He is married to Frances S. Adeney, professor of mission at Louisville Presbyterian Theological Seminary.

KAM WENG NG, Research Director and Resident Scholar at Kairos Research Centre since 1993, earned his Ph.D. at the University of Cambridge, in the United Kingdom. He was Lecturer and then Dean of the Graduate School, Malaysia Bible Seminary from 1889 to 1992. He has edited *Doing the Right Thing* (Kairos, 2004), a practical manual on issues of law and religion in the Malaysian context; *From Christ to Social Practice: Christological Foundations for Social Practice in the Theologies of Albrecht Ritschl, Karl Barth and Jürgen Moltmann* (Hong Kong, Alliance BS, 1996); *Modernity in Malaysia: Christian Perspectives* (Kairos, 1998); and *A Well-Founded Faith: Tools for Effective Intellectual Witness* (Kairos, 1996). *Christianity and Altered Consciousness Spiritualities* is his forthcoming book. His ongoing research projects include public theology and civil society, spirituality and self-fulfillment, comparative studies between Christianity and Buddhism, and inter-religious dialog in an Islamic context.

STEPHEN G. RAY JR. is Associate Professor of African American Studies at the Lutheran Theological Seminary at Philadelphia and director of the seminary's Urban Theological Institute. From 1999 to 2005 he was Associate Professor of Theology and Philosophy at Louisville Presbyterian Theological Seminary. Previously, he was a lecturer at Yale Divinity School and Hartford Seminary. He is the author of several articles on African American Christian history, theology, and race, and of the book *Do No Harm: Social Sin and Christian Responsibility*.

ARVIND SHARMA was born in Varanasi (Banaras) in India in 1940. He had his early education in Delhi and Allahabad. After a spell in the Indian Administrative Service (1962–1968), he resumed his academic career in the United States, where he obtained an M.A. in Economics from Syracuse University, an M.T.S. from the Harvard Divinity School, and a Ph.D. in Sanskrit and Indian Studies from Harvard University. He taught in Australia for ten years before moving to McGill University, Montreal, in 1987, where he is currently the Birks Professor of Comparative Religion. He has published extensively in the fields of Hinduism and Comparative Religion and also in the field of Religion and Human Rights. He is currently engaged in promoting the adoption of a Universal Declaration of Human Rights and Duties by the World's Religions.

MAX L. STACKHOUSE is the Stephen Colwell Professor of Christian Ethics at Princeton Theological Seminary. He has spent much time teaching and studying in India, China, and Eastern Europe and shorter periods in Africa and Latin America. He is the author or editor of more than a dozen books, including *Creeds, Society and Human Rights* and *On Moral Business: Classical and Contemporary Resources for Ethics in Economic Life.* He is currently working on the fourth and final volume of *God and Globalization,* which surveys the religious and socioeconomic forces that are shaping globalization—the economic, technological, legal, familial, and political trends that are both disrupting traditional life and faith, and providing the possible bases for a new transnational civilization and transcultural value systems. He argues that those forces are both a chief locus of new religious developments and the primary challenge for society, theology, and ethics in this new century.

MARGARET O. THOMAS was formerly the Coordinator for Interfaith Relations of the Presbyterian Church (U.S.A.) and a member of the advisory committee on interreligious relations of the World Council of Churches, participating in international interactions between Muslims and Christians. She also acted as chair of the interfaith commission of the National Council of Churches of Christ in the United States and has served on the boards of interfaith organizations working for peace, justice, and dialogue. As well as traveling throughout the Middle East, she has lived for a significant period of time in Iran, where she worked as an educator and related to the Evangelical Church of Iran. A Presbyterian minister, she currently lives in New York City, where she is a parish associate at the West End Presbyterian Church. Her theological education was at San Francisco Theological Seminary in California.

SUMNER B. TWISS (Ph.D. in Religious Studies, Yale University) is the Distinguished Professor of Human Rights, Ethics, and Religion at Florida State University. He is also Professor Emeritus of Religious Studies at Brown University, and co-editor of the *Journal of Religious Ethics* (Blackwell), having completed a five-year term as co-editor of the *Annual of the Society of Christian Ethics* (Georgetown University Press) as well as an eight-year term as Book Discussion Editor of the *Journal of Religious Ethics.* He was Co-Chair of the Religion and Human Rights Consultation of the American Academy of Religion, and currently serves on the Editorial Advisory Board of Religious Studies Review. He is co-author or co-editor of six books: *Comparative Religious Ethics: A New Method* (Harper and Row, 1978); *Genetic Counseling: Facts, Values and Norms* (Alan R. Liss, 1979); *Experience of the Sacred: Readings in the Phenomenology of Religion* (Brown University/University Press of New England, 1992); *Religion and Human Rights* (Project of Religion and Human Rights, 1994); *Religious Diversity and American Religious History: Studies in Traditions and Cultures* (University of Georgia Press, 1997); *Explorations in Global Ethics: Comparative Religious Ethics and Interreligious Dialogue* (Westview, 2000). He has published numerous articles in major journals and anthologies on comparative ethics, philosophy of religion, biomedical ethics, and intercultural human rights. His current writing projects include articles on Confucianism and human rights, method and theory in comparative ethics, intercultural influences on the shaping of human rights conventions, as well as a co-authored book on religion and human rights in the contemporary world.

Index

abortion, 140, 143

activism (activist), 163; Asian, 152–53, 161; Christian peace, 18, 183; human rights, viii, 2, 154, 158; social, 152, 163

Adeney, Frances S., 1–2, 19–39, 197–203, 213–15, 217

African-American Church, 23, 27–28

agapé, 9, 119, 173. *See also* love

Al Qaeda, 152

American Declaration of the Rights and Duties of Man, 57

Anabaptist traditions: Amish, 25; Plymouth Brethren, 25, 35n38; Quakers, 23, 28, 33n23, 86

animism, 61, 69

anthropology, 134, 142–43; minimalist, 148

anti-human rights, 25–26

apartheid, 133, 186

Aristotle, 131

Articles of Religion, Anglican, 171

"Asian Values," 3, 11, 44, 151–65; assumptions of, 151–52; debate of, 30; limitations of, 13; major components of, 11–12; what is, 159

atheism (atheist), 48, 61, 170

Augustine, 20, 188

authority: Asian respect for, 156; of church, 25–26, 85; of God, 85; hierarchical, 26; moral, 60, 152; necessity of, 34n28; orders of, 1; policy-making, 111; of state, 26, 27, 49, 81, 86; spheres of,

21–22; theology of women's symbolic, 139

Bangkok Governmental Declaration, 152, 154

Baptists, 28, 34n32, 86

Bellah, Robert, 34n32

Berrigan, Daniel, 24, 190

Berrigan, Philip, 189–90, 191

Bill of Rights, 138n12, 144. *See also* United States Constitution

bodies, 10, 139; objectification of, 128–29; significance of, 126–29, 131–37; well-being of, 117–18

Buddhism (buddhist), 59, 69, 88, 151; core principles of, 157; non-violence of, 187; record of human rights, 104–5, universalism of, 157

Cairo Declaration on Human Rights in Islam, 170, 179n18

Calvin, John, 6–7; category of pride, 137n2; influence on Protestant Reformed Church, 22, 25, 77, 92, 137n2. *See also* Calvinism

Calvinism, 130, 214; ambiguity of, 79–86; in contemporary human rights, 86–88; history of, 77–79; liberal tendencies of, 82–86, 91–93; misrepresentations of, 96n20; reactionary tendencies of, 80–82; social thought of, 95n18; theological conviction of, 92–93

223

caste, 51n2, 105, 206, 207, 215

Catholic, 213, 215; articles of peace, 25, 34n31; Christian thought, 199; church, 20, 25; doctrine on moral duty, 170; expansion of, 198; Latin American heritage of, 66–67; peace movement of, 29; "rights talk" of, 143; social encyclicals of, 143; social teachings of, 22, 24, 33n21, 141–42, 144, 147; social tradition of, 57; social thought of, 148; societies, 139; understanding of rights, 139–48; using image of God, 20

Choice: freedom of, 213–14; problem of, 144; religious, 14, 105–6, 168, 169, 177, 178n4, 210; reproductive choice, 128

Christianity, 27, 59; Asian, 161; contribution to human rights, 202; contribution to UDHRWR, 197–203; history of, 104, 111; identification as oppressor, 14, 174; major constructs of, 27; non-violence of, 187; political authority of, 49–50, 105–6; Protestant, 77; Reformed, 79, 89–90; relationship with human rights, vii–ix, 2, 168; self-advocacy of, 105; traditions as source of human rights, 30–31, 59

church: denunciation of, 171; expectation of, 22; formation of, 49–50; leadership of, 24; non-violence of, 188–89; of Korea, 12, 163–64; relationship with Islam, 174–75; role in human rights, 12, 24–27, separation from state, 29, 78, 85, 87, 91, 105–6, 199; social philosophy of, 163–64; understanding of gender, 21, 81, 146, 164–65. *See also* Roman Catholic Church

Cicero, 188

Civil Rights Movement, 23, 121, 134–37, 186, 191

civilization, Western, 57, 104, 160–61

Clinton, Bill, 151

Cold War, 14, 153, 158

colonialism, 12, 13, 163

communism, 8, 42, 140, 147–48; anticommunism, 140

communitarian, 4, 12, 30, 44, 47, 65, 68–69; Confucianism, 66; Roman Catholic Church is, 57; social philosophy of, 157

community (communal), 27–29, 206; Asian sense of, 155–56; church as, 1, 48, 164; concept of, 143; duties to, 57, 61, 65; in balance with individual rights, 11–12, 102–3, 111, 154, 155–58; manifesting religion in, 175; membership of the, 9; right to, 212; staying within, 14, 170–72

Confucianism, 59, 62, 69, 151–52, 157; communitarianism of, 66

conscience, 175; freedom of, 22, 25, 34n32, 61, 63, 81, 84, 87, 91, 178n7, 202; sovereignty of, 7, 81– 83, 85, 87–88, 91–93

covenant (covenantal), 36n45, 46, 49, 177; concept of, 27–28, 163; of human rights, viii; of Israel, 27; of UNDHR, 41, 43; with God, 214

Creation, order of, 21–22, 214

Creator, 120, 177; endowed by, 9, 119, 124, 130; moral obligations to, 61, 119, 120, 177n2; relationship with man, 60

Cromwell, Oliver, 83–84

Cultural Specificity Principle, 7–8, 100–1, 109, 112

culture: American, 9, 126, 128–31; Asian, 160–61; changes in, 175–76; common experience among, 30; communal/individual, 105; contamination of, 135–36; contemporary, 143–45; diversity of, 30, 57, 69, 109–10, 161, 175; human, 135–36; of human rights, 11, 141–42, 148, 154–55; importance of, 112; plurality of, 151; rights of, 8; subversion of, 189; of war, 184; world's, vii, 6, 43–45, 73, 100, 112. *See also* cultural specificity principle

da'wah, 13, 172–174, 178n12

Day, Dorothy, 189–90

Dear, John, 14–15, 183–95, 217

Decalogue, 46, 82, 91
Declaration of Independence, 9, 138n12;
    Christian alternative to, 132; preamble
    as basis of human rights theory, 117,
    119, 121–26; self-evident truths of, 130,
    132, 138n12; violability of, 126
democracy, 42, 192; constitutional, 84, 91;
    pluralistic, 49, 160; representative, 78
depravity, 9, 118–19
diakonía, 173, 174
dialogue: intrareligious, 169, 173;
    Muslim/Christian, 13–14, 168–69,
    176–77, World Council of Churches
    model, 176–77. *See also* interreligious
    dialogue
Dignitatis Humanae, 20, 54, 141, 144, 145,
    170
dignity, 135–37, 139, 141, 144–47, 164,
    213; inherent in man, 60; moral, 148
diversity: ideological, 57; of Christian the-
    ologies, viii; 29, 61; of local cultures,
    161, 175; of religions, 44, 59, 61, 175
divine, 60, 82; as human rights origin, 55,
    61; inspiration for UDHRWR, 5, 69;
    law, 34n31; manifestations of, 56; refer-
    ence to in UDHRWR, 5, 69–70, 200,
    205; in UDHR, 60, 199
Dred Scott Decision, 9, 123, 124
dualism: East-West, 157
duty, 142, 169, 175–76, 193, 206; Asian
    sense of, 155; Catholic doctrine on
    moral, 170; of Christians, 28; individ-
    ual, 21, 84; moral, 170; religious, 46,
    169, 190; rights over, 203; sense of,
    141–42; social, 56; in UDHRWR, 55,
    70, 74, 193, 206–12

Elshtain, Jean Bethke, 10–11, 139–49,
    218
Enlightenment, 2, 22, 43, 45, 53, 86–87
equality, 23, 28, 30, 56, 61, 77; gender,
    20–21, 91; before God, 58; inherent,
    122; before law, 84, 207; in marriage,
    85, moral, 148; right to, 212
essentialism, 142

euthanasia, 148
exclusivism, 171, 199

facism (fascist), 8, 89
feminism: central tenant of, 20–21; Chris-
    tian: 215; in Indonesia, 21, 214
First Amendment, 54n15, 144
freedom: to choose, 20; civic, 144; defini-
    tion of religious, 170; of expression,
    210; from harm, 20, 213; of movement,
    209; orientation towards, 142; of reli-
    gion, 20, 24, 48, 58, 59, 62, 144, 145,
    169, 198 201–2; of speech, 160; from
    violence, 193, 206, 211
French Revolution, 54n16, 96n35

Gandhi, Mahatma, 14, 41, 185–87, 193;
    practice of non-violence, 183
gender, 47, 84–85, 124, 141, 146; equality
    of, 20–21, 91; in UNDHRWR, 206, 212
genocide, 14, 36n45, 89–90
globalization, 3, 42, 50; deglobalizing con-
    flicts of, 171–72; forces of, 163; global
    actors, 156
God: authority of, 21; image of, 19–21;
    48–49, 56, 58, 146, 148, 198, 213–14;
    of peace, 185; as source of human
    rights, 56, 58; sovereignty of, 77
Golden Rule, 148
Gothard, Bill, 26
government: Asian, 153–54, 158, 160;
    authoritarian, 161, 164; criticism of
    western, 153–54; participation in, 211;
    Western style of, 159

happiness, pursuit of, 9, 119–20, 130–32.
    See also U.S. Declaration of Indepen-
    dence
Heksinki Final Act of 1974, 49
Helsinki Accords of 1975, 41
Hinduism (Hindu), 59, 69, 88, 104; active
    non-violence of, 187; record of human
    rights, 105
Hiroshima, 184, 192
Hitler, Adolf, 106

human rights: abuse of by Asian governments, 151; to change religion, 13,
167–81, 210; Christian perspectives of,
19–29; civil/political, 12, 156; communal, 111; definition of, 100–2; discourse
of Christianity, 198–99; individual, 111,
198, 213; in Islam, 177n2; to privacy,
208; social/economic, 12, 158, 160; theological basis for understanding, 146;
theological justifications, 61; understanding of, 19; universality of, 29–30,
42, 59, 119, 154–55, 159–61; Western
concept of, 156, 158
hunger, 183

imperialism, 3, 13, 64; cultural, 44; victims of, 206, 215; Western, 64, 159
individualism, 11, 47, 143, 156–57; Western, 155
Inquisition, Catholic, 81
interreligious dialogue, 8, 99–112; Christ-
ian/Muslim, 171–73; Christian views of,
31; compromise within, 110; contributions of, 109–11; definition of, 102–4;
importance of, ix, x; as means of promoting human rights, 100
intolerance, religious, 59, 64, 178n7
Iraq, 188, 192; humanitarian relief for,
167; support of UDHR, 63; U.S. war
on, 183
Islam (Muslim), 59, 88, 104, 110–11, 151,
168; law, 63; leaving of, 178n7; record
of human rights, religious belief of, 63;
104–5; society of Southeast Asia, 12,
161–63; 178n7; teaching about compulsion, 170
Israel, covenant of, 27

Jehovah's Witnesses, 24, 110
Jesus, 46, 91, 193; core message of,
187–88; incarnation of, 147; paschal
mystery of, 191; as practitioner of nonviolence, 185, 187–90, 192, 194
John Paul II (pope), 141, 144–47
Judaism (Jewish, Jew), 44, 50, 52, 88, 133,
198; formation of, 52n6; history of, 86;

Holocaust, 88; subjugation of Jews, 27;
vision of shalom, 187
justification, universal, 8, 107, 109

Kant, 53n10, 92
King, Martin Luther, Jr., 6, 14–15, 23,
117–18, 132–37; concern with body,
10; non-violence of, 184–89
Koran (Qur'an), 63, 81, 111, 170
Kuyper, Abraham, 25

language, 10; freedom of, 210; hate
speech, 71; of choice and change, 14,
169; of communitarian implication, 68;
of duties, 67, 202; of human rights,
vii–viii, 26, 87–88, 119–26, 130, 139,
141; of religious texts, 170–71; of solidarity, 67; theistic, 200; in UDHR, 58,
67–68; in UDHRWR, 5, 167
Las Madres, 139
law, 161, 175; biblical, 26; equal before,
207; finding of, 46; natural, 52n8, 122,
142–43, 145; recognition as person
under, 207; universal moral, 83, 87–88,
90, 92
Leo XIII (pope), 20
Levellers, the, 84–85
Locke, John, 87
love, 106, 145, 185, 191; of enemies,
187–88, 192, 193; God's, 27,170; of
God, 21, 27, 48; of neighbor, 27–28, 43,
57, 118, 140; sacrificial, 36n46, 27. *See
also* agapé
Luther, Martin, 20, 78

man (men): conceptual meaning of,
124–25; historical meaning of, 124–25,
130
Mandala, Nelson, 186
marriage, 172; arranged, 47; equality in,
85, right to, 209
Marxism, 3, 41, 51, 59
maximalism, 201–3
minimalism, 201–3
mission, 13, Christian, 168, 201; concept
of, 53n10, 164n1; Islamic, 151; mission-

aries, 104–5, 176; missionary abuses,
63–64; modernity, 152–53, 161, 164;
responsible relationships in, 174–75;
witness of, 172–73
Moltmann, Jürgen, 22, 24
Mothers of the Plaza, 11, 139
Muck, Terry C., 7–8, 99–113, 218–19
Murray, John Courtney, 25, 35n31

Nationalism, 12, 43, 162–63; ethnic, 162,
ultranationalism, 89, 90
Native Americans, 86, 125
Nazism, 56, 90, 133, 186
Negro, 129, 132–34
Ng, Kam Weng, 11–12, 151–66, 219
Nineteenth Amendment, 33n24. See also
United States Constitution
nominalism, 142, 143, 147
nonviolence, 24, 212, active, 14–15,
183–95; spirituality of, 185–86. See also
Christianity; Gandhi; Jesus; Martin
Luther King, Jr.
nuclear weapons, 14, 190; anti-nuclear
groups, 23–24, 191; disarmament, 14,
190; proliferation of, 29; war and,
183–85, 187–89, 193–94

Orientalism, 155

Parks, Rosa, 10, 134
Patriot Act of 2002, 126
Paul, Apostle, 27, 89, 135
peace movement, 29, 183
People Power Movement, 186
Plowshares, 24, 187, 190–91
pluralism, x, 28, 42, 43–50
Pol Pot, 106
politics (political): power, 105–6
poverty, 170, 173, 189, 190, 194
predestination, 77, 86, 130–31
Presbyterian Church (U.S.A), 22, 25,
work of, 24, 28
Presbyterianism: history of, 78–79
prison, 190, 191; North Korean, 140–41
proselytism, 48, 55, 64, 202, 208; against
the will, 71; ethic of witness, 172–73, as

evil, 64; judgments upon, 173–74; limitations on, 68; methods of, 171. See also
self-advocacy
Protestantism, conciliar, 24
Puritans, 78

Qur'an (Koran), 63, 81, 111, 170

race (racism), 129, 141, 156, 206
rape, 47, 128–29
Rawls, John, 29
Ray, Stephen G., Jr., 8–10, 117–38, 219
Reformation, the: 35n32, 198
relativism: cultural, 8, 45, 88; universal,
44
religions: exclusion of, 205; record of
human rights, 105–6; role in Asian
societies, 161–64; rooted in nonviolence, 187; understanding of the transcendent, 108–9
Rerum Novarum, 20
resources, moral, 153, 161
Roosevelt, Eleanor, 67

secularism, 43, 148
self-advocacy: religious, 105–6. See also
proselytism
September 11, 2001, 11, 152, 171, 191
Sermon on the Mount, 187–88
Servetus, Michael, 80–81
sexism, 206, 215
Sharma, Arvind, 1–15, 31, 197–203, 205,
219–20
sin, 136, 215; contemporary, 142; response
to, 22–26; theology of, 24
slavery, 28, 36n45, 47, 79, 131, 207; anti-
slavery movements, 23, 33n23, 131;
chattel, 129, 130
socialism, 57, 59, 89
solidarity, 11, 143 156, 164, 171, 175; language of, 66–68
somebodiness, 118, 132–34, 137
sovereignty, national, 12, 45, 67, 154,
158–59
Stackhouse, Max L., 3–4, 41–54, 220
Stalin, 106

state: duties of, 69–70, 148, 208, 211; expectations of, 164; regulation of religious activity, 64–65
Sung, Kim Il, 140
Supreme Court, United States, 124

Ten Commandments, 26, 47, 57, 58, 109
terrorism, 43, 185
theology (theological), 56, 67, 172, 177; Christian, 20, 69, 117; moral, 3, 44, 218; public, 200, 201; of sin, 24–25, 26
third basket, 41
Third Committee, 74; debate of, 4, 55–71; 200; shorthand for, 72n3
Thomas, Margaret O., 13–14, 167–181, 220
tolerance: for human rights, 12; pluralistic, 63–64; 200; principle of, 5; religious, 4, 57, 60, 62, 69–71, 82, 86, 105, 198, 200–1, 210
totalitarianism, 8, 107, 109, 165n14
transcendent, the, 8, 112; universal demands of, 106–9
Tutu, Archbishop, 186
Twiss, Sumner B., 4–6, 55–75, 220–21

union, trade, 154, 211
United States Constitution, 54n15, 125, 138n12, 144; First Amendment of, 54n15; Nineteenth Amendment of, 33n24
Universal Declaration of Human Rights (UDHR), 14, 41, 100, 104, 105, 159, 167, 169, 197; Article 1, 57, 58–62, 66; Article 2, 88; Article 18, 57, 58, 60, 62–65; Article 29, 57, 64–68; complaints against, 55, 68–69; 102, 147; covenants of, 43; erosion of, 43; historical account of, 55–71; 201–2; as secular document, 198–99; supporters of, 25

Universal Declaration of Human Rights by the World's Religions (UDHRWR), viii, ix–xi, 1, 15, 55, 174; Christianity's contribution to, 197–203; language of, 4–6, 167; shortcomings of, 69–71; text of, 205–12; vision of, 193
Universal Islamic Declaration of Human Rights, 170
Universality Principle, 7, 101

values, 197; collision of, 167; humanitarian, 199; most valued by East Asians, 156; religious, 176; western, 151, 156
Vatican II, 20, 25, 34n30
Vienna Declaration on Human Rights, 152

war, 14–15, 28–29, 62; against Al Qaeda, 152; Christianity and, 187–90; Civil War, 79; Cold War, 153, 158; dirty, 139; on Iraq, 183, 192; just-war theory, 188; nuclear, 183–84; protest of, 191–92, 194; religion and, 183–87; times of, 125; Vietnam, 189, 190; World War II, 24
Weber, Max, 79, 83, 95
Wesley, John: works of, 33n20
Williams, Roger, 34n32, 85–86, 92, 93
woman (women), 23; abuse of, 148; equality of, 21, 124–25; objectification of, 128–29; personhood of, 145–47; rights of, viii, 21, 42, 107, 121, 145; role of, 79, 85, 139; view of, 148
World Council of Churches, 215; bilateral Christian-Muslim consultations of, 13, 167–70; dialogue model of, 176–77; work of, 24, 28, 99
World Reformed Alliance of Churches, 25, 28